HENRY VIII
AND
CHARLES V

To Deborah for the help and encouragement that has made this book
possible and to our children and grandchildren for
their interest and support – with much love.

HENRY VIII AND CHARLES V

RIVAL MONARCHS, UNEASY ALLIES

RICHARD HEATH

PEN & SWORD
HISTORY

AN IMPRINT OF PEN & SWORD BOOKS LTD.
YORKSHIRE - PHILADELPHIA

First published in Great Britain in 2023 by
PEN AND SWORD HISTORY
An imprint of
Pen & Sword Books Ltd
Yorkshire – Philadelphia

ISBN 978 1 39908 457 4

Typeset in Times New Roman 11/13.5 by
SJmagic DESIGN SERVICES, India.
Printed and bound in the UK by CPI Group (UK) Ltd.

Pen & Sword Books Limited incorporates the imprints of Atlas, Archaeology,
Aviation, Discovery, Family History, Fiction, History, Maritime, Military, Military
Classics, Politics, Select, Transport, True Crime, Air World, Frontline Publishing,
Leo Cooper, Remember When, Seaforth Publishing, The Praetorian Press,
Wharncliffe Local History, Wharncliffe Transport, Wharncliffe True Crime and
White Owl.

For a complete list of Pen & Sword titles please contact
PEN & SWORD BOOKS LIMITED
47 Church Street, Barnsley, South Yorkshire, S70 2AS, England
E-mail: enquiries@pen-and-sword.co.uk
Website: www.pen-and-sword.co.uk

Or
PEN AND SWORD BOOKS
1950 Lawrence Rd, Havertown, PA 19083, USA
E-mail: Uspen-and-sword@casematepublishers.com
Website: www.penandswordbooks.com

Contents

Preface

The focus of this book is the relationship between two leading figures of the first half of the sixteenth century, Henry VIII and Charles V, and their sometimes complex and often duplicitous foreign policies. It is rare for unanimous conclusions to be reached about such rulers either by their contemporaries or by historians – so much depends on the point of view of those making the judgement. But when the actions of individuals had consequences for centuries to come, they are even more likely to be the subject of lively debate.

Henry VIII and Charles V were two such characters. Henry did more to influence the future history of England than almost any other monarch. His forceful personality stands out, for good or bad, in his dominance of the Royal Council, his marriages, his ruthless removal of those he distrusted, his leadership of the national church and his commissioning of grand palaces. But should he be seen as a builder of the nation or a destructive tyrant, a king who established England as a leading power in Europe or one who wasted its resources on wars that gained little?

In England Charles V does not receive the attention given to Henry and the Tudors. His Habsburg family name is familiar but it is usually associated with inbreeding and, later, a failure to move with the times. Yet for thirty-five years Charles V controlled more territory in Europe than any ruler since the days of the Romans. However, as a Holy Roman Emperor born in the Low Countries who also became the ruler of Spain and its growing empire, he has rarely been recognised as having a central role in the history of any particular nation. He has been characterised at various times as an aggressive religious bigot, an ineffective seeker of reconciliation, and a ruler who struggled, with some success, to deal with the multitude of problems that he faced.

Henry and Charles did not have a close personal relationship. They met on only four occasions, just once for any length of time, and not after 1522. Nevertheless, relations between them were of great importance. They were always rivals but they also had interests in common. At times they were brothers in arms, yet within a few years would be exchanging vitriolic insults. Each took a keen interest in the shifting policies of the other and often had to adapt their own plans accordingly, at times distracting them from their long-term foreign policy objectives. Of course, they were not the only rulers who mattered in Europe at the time. The actions of two others, Francis I, King of France, and Sultan Suleiman of the Ottoman Empire, played a significant role in determining the foreign policies of both England and Spain.

It is important to have some contextual understanding of the period in which they lived and of the circumstances in which they ruled in order to make sense of their decisions. Their upbringing and education shaped how they viewed the world and their place in it. Major issues at home interacted with their foreign policies, sometimes in the background, but at other times as vital factors. Their limited resources often constrained what they were able to achieve, but Henry VIII and Charles V could rarely be ignored, either during their lifetime or by subsequent historians.

A note on names and currency

I have generally used the established English versions of the names of individuals and places where these exist – thus Francis I, Maximilian I, Aachen, Mechelen. The notable exceptions are Francis I's son and successor as King of France, who I have referred to as Henri II to avoid any chance of confusion with Henry VIII, and the names of Charles V's Spanish family, his mother Juana, uncle Juan and daughters Maria and Juana, for whom I have retained their Spanish names. Where there are several individuals with the same name, particularly Mary (a sister and a daughter of Henry VIII and a sister of Charles V) and Margaret (Henry's sister, Charles's aunt and Charles's natural daughter), it is usually clear from the context or from an additional name – 'of Hungary', 'of Austria' – who is being referred to. Where named individuals have been mentioned in quotations, I have not altered the original spelling. The term 'the Low Countries' is used throughout to refer to those lands now in the Netherlands, Belgium, Luxembourg and those parts of France that were controlled by Charles V in his role as Duke of Burgundy.

Various currencies were in use in the sixteenth century. The following may be used as an approximate guide to their relative value in about 1525.

Money of Account: the English pound sterling was worth 10 French *livre tournois (Lt)*. The pound was divided into 20 shillings, with each shilling being worth 12 pence (as it was until decimalisation in 1971). Thus, one *livre tournois* was worth 2 shillings.

Coins: there were approximately 5 English gold crowns to the pound. A crown was therefore worth 4 shillings. This was close to the value of the *ecus d'or au soleil*, the main French gold coin. The *florin* was also in use, with approximately 6 florins to a pound. The *ducat* was a trade coin originally of a similar value to the *florin*.

Family Trees

Family Tree of Emperor Charles V – showing his relationship with the royal houses of Spain, Burgundy and Austria (Habsburg)

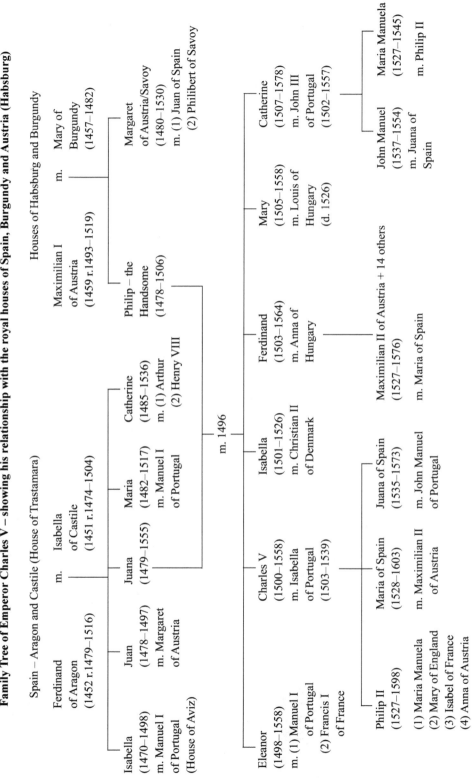

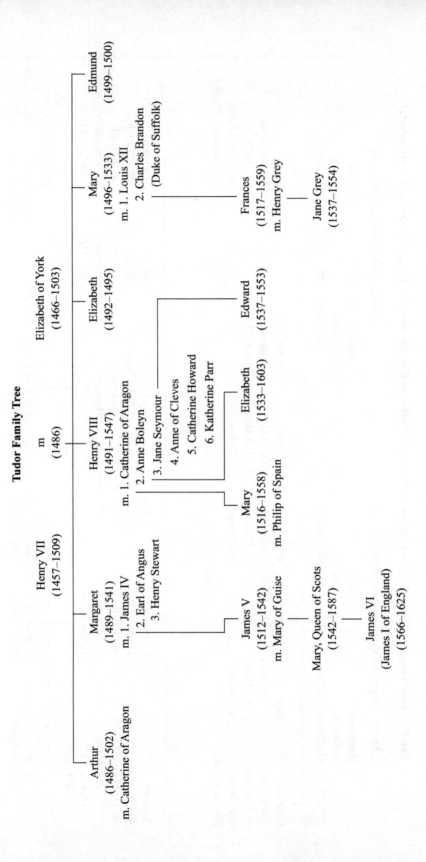

Tudor Family Tree

Henry VII
(1457–1509)

m
(1486)

Elizabeth of York
(1466–1503)

Arthur
(1486–1502)
m. Catherine of Aragon

Margaret
(1489–1541)
m. 1. James IV
2. Earl of Angus
3. Henry Stewart

Henry VIII
(1491–1547)
m. 1. Catherine of Aragon
2. Anne Boleyn
3. Jane Seymour
4. Anne of Cleves
5. Catherine Howard
6. Katherine Parr

Elizabeth
(1492–1495)

Mary
(1496–1533)
m. 1. Louis XII
2. Charles Brandon
(Duke of Suffolk)

Edmund
(1499–1500)

James V
(1512–1542)
m. Mary of Guise

Mary
(1516–1558)
m. Philip of Spain

Edward
(1537–1553)

Elizabeth
(1533–1603)

Frances
(1517–1559)
m. Henry Grey

Mary, Queen of Scots
(1542–1587)

James VI
(James I of England)
(1566–1625)

Jane Grey
(1537–1554)

Chapter One

Dynastic Marriages and the Anglo-Spanish Alliance

The marriage in 1501 of Catherine of Aragon to Prince Arthur was central to the alliance between England and Spain. It had been planned for many years, arranged in 1489 as part of the Treaty of Medina del Campo. This promised 'true friendship' between King Henry VII and the 'Catholic Monarchs', Queen Isabella of Castile and Ferdinand II, King of Aragon, Naples and Sicily, by assisting 'in defending their present and future dominions against any enemy', particularly France, and in denying refuge to each other's internal enemies.[1] It also encouraged trade between the two countries by reducing tariffs. The union of the youngest daughter of the Spanish monarchs and the heir to the English throne was intended to ensure the longevity of the alliance. As the princess and prince were only 3 and 2 years old when the original treaty was signed, it would be many years until the marriage vows could be celebrated. While such marriage alliances were frequently made by the ruling dynasties of Europe, they were often renounced before the couple came of age. Not in this case.

Henry VII had wanted Catherine to be sent to England as soon as possible, but Catherine's parents delayed her departure. It was not until May 1501 that she left the Alhambra Palace in Granada and travelled north through Spain. The journey was slow in the summer heat, delayed by cities that wished to honour her and by a detour to the shrine at Santiago de Compostela. Setting sail in September, her ship was at first driven back by severe weather in the Bay of Biscay but on the second attempt, after a five-day voyage and more terrible storms in the Channel, she landed at Plymouth on 2 October. She was never to return to her homeland. Her journey across England continued at a leisurely pace, taking thirty-three days to reach Dogmersfield, near Fleet, in northern Hampshire. Unable to restrain himself any longer, Henry VII took Prince Arthur to meet her there, breaking the Spanish custom of not meeting a husband-to-be before the marriage ceremony.[2] The language barrier meant that their conversation was restricted and took place in Latin.

As early as June 1500, de Puebla, the Spanish ambassador, had mentioned the 'great preparations' being made for Catherine's arrival and how 'the whole nation desire to see her'. Henry VII might have had a reputation for avarice but he understood the importance of putting on a show to impress both London's citizens and the numerous foreign dignitaries present. His main aims since he had won the throne at the Battle of Bosworth Field in 1485 had been to defeat Yorkist claimants and pretenders to his crown, and to be accepted by other European monarchs as the unchallenged king of England. He had secured his throne by the execution of Edward Plantagenet and Perkin Warbeck in 1499, and now the marriage of his eldest son into a leading royal family was not only a recognition of his international acceptance but also secured a vital alliance with Spain against their mutual enemy, France.

For Catherine's ceremonial entry into the capital on 12 November, the streets along the route from London Bridge to St Paul's Cathedral had been cleaned and decorated with silk, gold and silver cloth hangings.[3] People of all classes turned out in their finery to welcome their future queen and enjoy the celebrations. Riding alongside Catherine as the procession made its way through the City was the 10-year-old Prince Henry, Duke of York, Arthur's younger brother. This was one of his first major appearances on the public stage and although it was Catherine who the crowds had turned out to see, all accounts suggest that he carried it off with style.

It seems likely that the young Henry was somewhat in awe of the 15-year-old princess. She made a very favourable impression on all who saw her. They admired her clothes and the small hat that allowed her beautiful hair to flow down her back. Thomas More was not alone when he wrote that no words could convey her beauty and charm and 'everywhere she receives the highest of praises; but even that is most inadequate'. Not so her companions. Ferdinand and Isabella had been asked by Henry VII and his wife, Elizabeth of York, to ensure that the ladies in Catherine's company be 'of gentle birth and beautiful, or at least that none of them should be ugly'.[4] This, however, was obviously not how More viewed them. He wrote to a friend that most of them were laughable, poorly dressed, and unpleasant to look at, like 'refugees from hell'. This can perhaps be explained by the Spanish custom of the ladies-in-waiting, unlike those in England, wearing black clothes and long headdresses so as not to draw attention away from their princess.

Two days later, it was again Prince Henry who escorted the bride to the cathedral door and along the raised walkway inside; after the service he led her out through the west doors of St Paul's to the adjacent palace of the Bishop of London.[5] There followed a magnificent wedding feast and

2

then, between 7 and 8 o'clock, Catherine was escorted to the bedchamber where she was soon joined by Arthur. What happened there, and later when the couple moved to Ludlow Castle, has been a much-discussed topic for over 500 years. Testimonies given at the time and afterwards are at variance and, since so much depended on them twenty years later, it is doubtful if any can be trusted. The different English and Spanish accounts of their first night together cannot be reconciled. Did Arthur appear calling for a drink of beer because he had 'been in the midst of Spain' which had a hot climate and the journey had made him dry, or were Catherine's attendants so quiet and downcast because Arthur had left early and it had all been a great disappointment?

Whatever did or didn't occur in the bedchamber only became important because Arthur died five months later at Ludlow. The grief of Henry VII and his wife was genuine. Perhaps less so was that of Isabella and Ferdinand in Spain who naturally offered their condolences, but at the same time were instructing their ambassador in England to let the king know of their confidence that he would honour his responsibilities to Catherine and give her the estates due to her. This almost certainly meant that they had little faith that he would! Nevertheless, they were keen to maintain the English alliance. Their powerful neighbour France was still a threat to Spanish interests in Italy and very little time elapsed before it was proposed that the young widow should marry the new Prince of Wales, Henry. To encourage English acceptance, it was suggested that the alternative was for Catherine to return to Spain and marry into another royal dynasty.

Having delayed matters for months, the death of Henry VII's wife, Elizabeth, less than a year after that of his eldest son, jolted Henry into action. After briefly considering that he could marry Catherine himself, much to the horror of her parents, he summoned his remaining son and informed him that agreement had been reached – Prince Henry should marry Catherine. In June 1503 the deal was signed and a marriage 'per verba de praesenti' took place. This was when the two parties gave their consent, often by proxy, but without any formal solemnisation of the marriage. Usually, these vows were renewed when the participants reached the age of consent, in this case when Henry reached his fourteenth birthday, at which time the agreement would become binding.

Why then did the marriage not take place for six years? It certainly could not happen immediately. A papal dispensation was required because Catherine would be marrying Arthur's brother. The original request stated that the marriage had been consummated. but two months later, Ferdinand was declaring to the papal ambassador that it had not been. He wished to remove any doubts there might be about the legitimacy of the children that Henry and Catherine might have. Pope Julius II sidestepped the issue. When the dispensation eventually arrived in England, the wording was that 'perhaps' the marriage had been consummated.

The main reason for the long delay was the ever-changing international political situation. Henry VII, in common with all sixteenth-century monarchs, was engaged in diplomatic manoeuvres to achieve security and favourable alliances. The most powerful rulers in Christian Europe in 1503 were the king of France (Louis XII of the Valois dynasty), the Holy Roman Emperor (the Habsburg, Maximilian I), and the rulers of Spain (Ferdinand and Isabella). They often had conflicting ambitions so they would look for an alliance with one of their rivals against the other, as well as with other rulers. The most significant of these were the king of England (Henry VII), the papacy (Pope Julius II) and the Duke of Burgundy (Duke Philip, son of Emperor Maximilian by his marriage to Mary of Burgundy). Duke Philip ruled most of the provinces in the Low Countries, but Burgundy itself, further south, had been lost to France in the late fifteenth century. Italy was divided into numerous states and had increasingly become a battleground for the major powers as they fought for control of Naples and Milan. The expanding Ottoman Empire to the east was to become a major threat to Christian Europe in the reign of Sultan Suleiman (1520–1566). Europe was inherently unstable and a change of policy or the death of an individual monarch could result in a complete reconfiguration of alliances.

The death of Queen Isabella of Castile, Catherine of Aragon's mother, in 1504 meant that Juana, her eldest surviving daughter, became queen. Juana was married to Duke Philip of Burgundy. He intended to travel to Spain with Juana to take power rather than allow her father to act as regent. This would seriously weaken Ferdinand's position and strengthen that of the Habsburg family, headed by Philip's father, Emperor Maximilian (Plate 1). An alliance with Ferdinand now looked less favourable for Henry VII than developing closer links with Duke Philip. In June 1505 Prince Henry was given a statement to read out privately in front of his father and a small group of royal councillors just before his fourteenth birthday. It declared that as his marriage to Catherine had been arranged in his youth, he had decided not to ratify the agreement and that it was now null and void.[6] Not for the first time, a marriage contract had been repudiated.

Henry VII's position was improved further when, during Philip and Juana's voyage to Spain from the Low Countries, a violent storm in the Channel broke up their fleet and drove them ashore on the Dorset coast. Not one to miss such an opportunity, the king insisted that Philip be entertained as his guest. Prince Henry was sent to greet him at Winchester, where he proudly showed Philip the famous Round Table and then escorted him to Windsor. The prince was greatly impressed by his guest, renowned for his looks, his sporting prowess, his bravery and skill at the joust. Furthermore, he had been brought up in the Burgundian court in the Low Countries, famed for its chivalric values. He was the epitome of a Renaissance prince. He was the man the young Henry wished to emulate, rather than his dour father, and he talked about his meeting with Philip for years afterwards. While at Windsor the reluctant Philip was subjected to a charm offensive, with Henry VII putting on a show to match any in Europe – receptions, banquets, dances and hunting. Philip was invested with the Order of the Garter in St George's Chapel and then he, in turn, created Prince Henry a member of the Order of the Golden Fleece, the highest honour in the gift of the Burgundian ruler. Philip's wife Juana arrived later to meet her sister Catherine, who was distressed by Juana's state of mind and the brevity of her stay.

Although treated well, Philip knew that he would not be able to leave England until he had heard and probably agreed to Henry's demands. The outcome was the Treaty of Windsor. This included a trade deal between England and the Low Countries, giving English merchants considerable advantages, a mutual defence alliance, and an agreement to hand over Edmund de la Pole, Duke of Suffolk, a nephew of Edward IV and a potential claimant to the English throne, who was living in exile in Philip's lands. The Burgundians later claimed that there was an understanding that Suffolk would be treated with respect, but he spent the next seven years in the Tower of London before being executed in 1513.

Matrimonial affairs were not ignored. Henry VII was still looking for a new bride. Philip's sister Margaret, widowed for the second time in 1504, seemed a strong candidate. Henry even had a flattering portrait of himself sent to Margaret. Philip and his father Emperor Maximilian, being conscious of the wealth supposedly amassed by Henry VII, showed interest but it soon became clear that Margaret had no intention of re-marrying. Usually known as Margaret of Austria (because of her Habsburg father), though sometimes referred to as Margaret of Savoy (after her second husband), she was to play a significant role in the upbringing of her nephew, Charles, who was also the nephew of Catherine of Aragon (see family trees).

Born in 1500, Charles, Duke Philip and Juana's eldest son, became the focus of another possible Tudor-Habsburg/Spanish marriage which was discussed at Windsor. Henry VII's youngest daughter, the 9-year-old Mary, attractive, lively, talented and confident, had taken centre stage at an entertainment put on for Philip. Would she not be the ideal match for Charles? Henry VII certainly knew that it would be a major coup for the Tudor dynasty. Charles's marriage had been a talking point since his birth. As early as June 1500, during a brief meeting between Henry VII and Duke Philip just outside Calais, this possible match had been mentioned, along with that of Henry, then Duke of York, to Charles's sister, Eleanor.[7] Nothing, though, was decided. Charles had then been more formally linked with Claude, the daughter of Louis XII of France, but this arrangement was dropped in 1505 when Claude was betrothed to Louis' heir, Francis of Angoulême, who, as King Francis I, was to play such an important part in determining the policies of both Henry VIII and Emperor Charles V. On his birth in Ghent, Charles was the heir to the Duchy of Burgundy but deaths in his mother Juana's Spanish family meant that he might eventually inherit all its Spanish dominions. He was also the grandson of the Habsburg Emperor Maximilian. Charles was destined to become a powerful, if not the most powerful, ruler in Christendom, but given that his parents were still in their twenties this might not happen for decades. However, just a few months after the signing of the Treaty of Windsor, events brought that eventuality much closer.

Having arrived in Castile and established himself as ruler through a deal with Ferdinand, overriding Juana's rights as queen, Philip, now King Philip I of Castile, died in Burgos in September 1506. Relations between Philip and Juana had been strained for some time. Upset by his frequent affairs, many real, some imagined, and his intention to exclude her from power once she came into her inheritance, there were reports of Juana demonstrating erratic behaviour, of the couple shouting at each other and even of Philip confining her to her apartments. He deprived her of independent funds and let it be known that she was too unstable to rule. Her actions after his death were perhaps proof that this may have been the case. She refused to leave his body, taking it with her as she travelled around Castile, hence becoming known as Juana 'la loca' ('the mad'). Ferdinand reasserted his influence in Castile as 'governor', though the day-to-day running of the country was left to Cardinal Cisneros (Ximenes), the Archbishop of Toledo. With Juana again shut out of power, this time by her father, she was eventually confined in a convent in Tordesillas 'for her own safety'. Henry VII had been attracted to Juana during her short stay at Windsor and he later seriously considered the possibility of marrying her when it became known that Margaret of Austria was not interested. He had not been convinced by Philip's claims about her insanity and he was perhaps encouraged by Catherine, who would have welcomed her older sister joining her in England. Ferdinand, whose value as an ally was now restored, responded that Henry was the preferred choice from amongst many suitors. In fact, he had no intention of marrying off Juana and, by doing so, opening up a challenge to his control of Castile.

The Holy Roman Emperor, Maximilian, meanwhile, was keen to further the plans for his grandson Charles's marriage to Princess Mary. Signed in December 1507, Henry VII's treaty with Maximilian confirmed the mutual defence alliance agreed at Windsor and arranged for the formal betrothal of Charles and Mary to take place at Easter in 1508. After Philip's death and Juana's isolation in Spain, Maximilian had made his daughter Margaret of Austria responsible for the upbringing of Charles and his three sisters, Eleanor, Isabella and Mary. They were now being raised at her court in Mechelen. The emperor was open about his motives. He explained to Margaret that he expected to get a considerable amount of money out of Henry VII. The king for his part believed that although the initial cost might be high, what with the loans that the impecunious Maximilian was bound to request on top of the dowry, the young Charles's status made it well worth it. Even though there were delays, when the betrothal ceremony took place just before Christmas 1508 it was another splendid, and costly, affair. After the final details were agreed at Greenwich, the whole English court, along with the Burgundian diplomats, moved to Richmond where Mary, aged 12, took her vows in perfect French. This was followed by three days of jousting. Presumably the 8-year-old Duke Charles was informed that he was now committed to marrying the English princess.

But still the marriage of Henry VII's remaining son to Catherine, Charles's aunt, did not take place, even though it suited both monarchs to keep her in England. Henry did not wish to return the dowry he received when she married Arthur. He complained about Ferdinand's failure to send the outstanding dowry money, argued about the means of payment (cash or jewellery and gold) and whose control it should be under. He also used Ferdinand's reluctance to ratify the marriage of his grandson, Duke Charles, to Mary, in order to delay the final settlement. He wished to extract as many concessions from Ferdinand as he could and to keep alternative options open for as long as possible. It suited Ferdinand to have Catherine in England so that she could not threaten his control of Castile and to keep pressure on Henry VII. In 1507 he formally accredited her as an ambassador to work alongside his long-standing representative in England, Roderigo de Puebla.

Relations between the two kings deteriorated. Catherine herself believed that de Puebla was not forceful enough in pushing Henry VII to agree to her marriage to his son. However, his replacement in 1508, the aristocratic former soldier Gutier Gomez de Fuensalida, whose diplomatic skills consisted of bluster and attempted bullying, made matters worse. He was no match for the experience of men such as Richard Foxe, Bishop of Winchester; Nicholas West, later Bishop of Ely; and Charles Somerset, later Earl of Worcester, who negotiated for the English king. By April 1509, even though Ferdinand still wished the marriage to take place, he was clearly exasperated.

He produced a lengthy document for another ambassador who was to be sent to England with the clear instruction to 'as speedily as possible arrange the difficulties concerning the marriage of the Princess Katharine with the Prince of Wales.'[8] In the document, Ferdinand gave his account of the obstacles that King Henry VII had placed in its way and outlined the concessions that he was willing to make, but also authorised the ambassador to tell Catherine that she must prepare to leave England if Henry still refused to come to an agreement. Ferdinand was very critical of the king stating that 'he [Henry VII] thinks he can do and ask what he likes because he holds the Princess Katharine in his power', and that he only 'pretended' feelings of 'love and true friendship' towards him.

What Ferdinand did not know for another two weeks was that Henry VII had died on 21 April. It frequently took that long to deliver even urgent dispatches between Spain and England and it was not uncommon for duplicate messages to be sent in case one was delayed or went missing. On receipt of the news that the new king had 'peacefully ascended the throne', Ferdinand and his secretary fired off a series of letters and instructions[9] to Ambassador Fuensalida, to Catherine, and to the new king, Henry VIII. To Henry, he expressed his 'great sorrow' at the loss of his father and wrote that he had 'gained a son by losing a father', promising him any military assistance that he might require if there was opposition to his taking the throne (already knowing that this would not be required). To Catherine, he explained that he had refused to give in to the old king's demands because he was 'neither his nor her friend' but assured her that he was now doing everything possible to remove 'all impediments to her marriage' out of his love for her. Her marriage, together with the union of Duke Charles and Princess Mary, he wrote, were of great importance in securing an alliance between himself, the Emperor Maximilian, Duke Charles and the king of England. He told her that Fuensalida, about whom she had complained, was at fault and would be replaced, despite telling the ambassador that he retained his full confidence.

To Fuensalida, he made clear that while the old king 'had been a bad friend and ally … he [Ferdinand] was now willing to concede to him [the new king, Henry VIII] what he had denied to his father' as long as the marriage was 'immediately consummated'. The remaining money for the dowry would be forthcoming, though in the form of bills of exchange rather than cash because of the risk of the cash arriving too late if it went by sea and 'if sent by land it would be exposed to the danger of being taken by the French.' He would also give his approval, if absolutely necessary, to the marriage of Charles and Mary 'even before the Princess Catherine is married to the King of England'. Ferdinand urged the ambassador to inform the king of these concessions 'in the kindest and sweetest manner possible' and to treat the affair 'with the greatest delicacy and caution', suggesting that he knew that this was not the ambassador's usual negotiating tactic! He was to convince the young king that such a marriage was 'perfectly lawful as the pope had given a dispensation for it' and that they would enjoy great happiness and have many children. Indeed, it would be a sin to break his engagement to Catherine. The ambassador was also to point out that any delay would give the French, as well as others, time to 'enter into all kinds of intrigues to prevent the marriage'. Furthermore 'should he think it expedient to corrupt some of the most influential councillors of the king, he may offer them money.'[10]

There is plenty of evidence to suggest that Henry did not require much persuading to marry Catherine. He had been impressed, perhaps infatuated, by her appearance and dignity when, as a youth, he had escorted her as she entered London. His 'objection' to the betrothal in 1505 had been his father's, not his. In 1506 he referred to Catherine formally as 'the princess my wife' in a letter to Duke Philip in Castile and had later written affectionate letters to her. He claimed that it was his father's dying wish he should marry Catherine to honour the alliance with Spain, although others reported that his father had actually said that he could marry whomsoever he wished. It is likely that Henry had already told Catherine that he would marry her, even before all those dispatches were written in Spain.

Their marriage took place at Greenwich on 11 June 1509, less than two months after his father's death, but seven years after Arthur's. At last, Catherine was queen of England, as she had expected to be from a young age. It was not the grand state occasion at St Paul's that her first marriage had been. There were few guests and little record of the details of the service, but it will have conformed to all the rites of the Church, including a mention of the papal dispensation given years before.

The major spectacle came two weeks later at their coronation. It might be expected that Henry would want this to be his day and, of course, in many ways it was, but it could now be shared with his new bride. There was a magnificent procession through the capital with Henry dressed in velvet and gold cloth, covered in jewels, while Catherine was in pure white, her long hair beautiful to behold.[11] On the next morning, 24 June, the couple walked to Westminster Abbey where the coronation ceremony was conducted by William Warham, Archbishop of Canterbury. The king was enthusiastically acclaimed by the onlookers. As he wrote to his 'most beloved father' Ferdinand, 'the multitude of the people who assisted was immense, and their joy and applause most enthusiastic.'[12] There followed a sumptuous feast in Westminster Hall. The tone was set for the new era that England was entering.

Soon after the wedding and coronation, Henry VIII wrote to Margaret of Austria, Duke Charles's guardian and regent of the Low Countries, informing her of his marriage. He emphasised that he had been happy to fulfil his part of his father's agreement with Ferdinand and Isabella. He also wrote favourably about the alliance between the Emperor Maximilian, the House of Burgundy and Spain, to which England would be linked through the marriage of his sister Mary to Charles, who Henry referred to as the 'Prince of Spain'. Hopes of joining an anti-French alliance were already at the forefront of Henry's thinking.

But just how secure were these international agreements, even if backed by a royal marriage? At that time an alliance lasted for an average of three years,[13] a king's wife often had very little influence on foreign policy[14] and a betrothal was no guarantee that a marriage would be completed. Margaret of Austria (Plate 2) knew this better than most. At the age of 3, she had been betrothed to King Charles VIII of France and lived in France for eight years before the king reneged on the agreement so that he could marry Anne, Duchess of Brittany. Anne was already betrothed to Maximilian, soon to become emperor, but Charles VIII took the opportunity to win Brittany for the French crown and prevent a union which would threaten France. The fact that Anne was an unwilling bride and is said to have taken two beds to her wedding, indicating that she had no desire to share the French king's, made no difference. It is hardly surprising that both Maximilian and his daughter Margaret were not well disposed towards the French.

Henry VII's foreign policy had essentially been about seeking security – for the Tudor dynasty and the nation. International treaties provided credibility and recognition both abroad and at home. He had been prepared to threaten war, as he did to the Scots in 1496 and, if necessary, to lead troops into action, as when he besieged Boulogne in 1492. That conflict had been ended by the Treaty of Étaples, under which Henry received a healthy annual pension from the French king and a promise not to assist Yorkist rebels. But war was always expensive. Henry VII wanted alliances without too great a financial commitment. His alliance with Spain was important to him, but he also wanted to avoid war with France. He was in many ways fortunate that the European powers at the time were focused on protecting or increasing their lands and influence in Italy. They were no immediate threat to England.

In 1509 Henry VIII inherited a country free from the fear of invasion in which his father had built up considerable wealth, even though his fortune was less than many believed. But the new king wished for more than survival, he wanted honour and glory. France was England's traditional enemy and it was in France where his reputation could be enhanced. For centuries English kings had held extensive territories there, especially in Normandy and Aquitaine, as vassals of the French king. This status caused much conflict. The extent of English lands varied, but much had been lost as the French slowly expanded and consolidated their lands and power. The conflict had been given new impetus in the fourteenth century when Edward III, to make good his claim to the French throne, began what became known as the Hundred Years War.

Although ultimately unsuccessful, the Battles of Crecy and Poitiers in Edward's reign and Agincourt in Henry V's provided the English with victories that were long celebrated. Henry VIII admired the achievements of his namesake which motivated him to renew claims to the French throne that had lain dormant since the defeats of nearly seventy years before. He wished to be a great player on the European stage, respected and perhaps even feared by his fellow monarchs. This called for alliances, and his relationship with Duke Charles of Burgundy, soon to become king of Spain and then Holy Roman Emperor, his nephew by marriage to Catherine of Aragon and recently betrothed to his sister Mary, was therefore central to his ambitions.

Chapter Two

The Education of Princes

No-one could doubt the success of the marriage between Henry VII and Elizabeth of York. It brought together the rival houses of the Wars of the Roses (known at the time as the Cousins' War), the Lancastrian victor of Bosworth Field and the eldest daughter of the Yorkist king, Edward IV. It had also been rapidly blessed with children. After Arthur and Margaret, a second son, Henry, was born at Greenwich (Plate 3), his mother's favourite palace, on 28 June 1491. The Palace of Placentia, as it was often called, had been built by Humphrey, Duke of Gloucester, the younger brother of Henry V, and extensively remodelled by Henry VII. The christening in the nearby church of the Friars Observant, decorated with tapestries for the occasion, was performed by the Bishop of Exeter and Lord Privy Seal, Richard Foxe. Though not without appropriate pageantry, it was a quiet affair in comparison to that held nearly five years previously for Arthur. The fact that Henry was the second son was to be an important factor in determining the nature of his upbringing.

By then, Arthur, the Prince of Wales, already had his own household that was soon to move to Ludlow Castle on the Welsh border. Henry's nursery, on the other hand, was combined with that of his sister, Margaret, only eighteen months older, and then joined by a newborn sister, Elizabeth, in July 1492. Initially at Greenwich, the household moved to Eltham, where Edward IV had constructed a great hall, less than 5 miles from Greenwich and within easy reach of London. In infancy Henry was in the care of a wet nurse, Anne Uxbridge, who was later invited to his coronation, but he remained close to his mother, both physically and emotionally.

In the autumn of 1494, it was from Eltham that Prince Henry travelled for his inauguration as the Duke of York, his first major public appearance. Henry VII had taken the decision to give him that title in order to counter the numerous ceremonies that had taken place in the Low Countries, where the 'pretender' Perkin Warbeck had been feted as Richard, Duke of York, son of Edward IV and the younger of the 'princes in the tower'. Warbeck's claims to be the true king of England had been encouraged by the Dowager Duchess of Burgundy, Margaret of York, the sister of Edward IV and Richard III.

This needed to be challenged and a well-publicised and impressive event was organised. Henry, only 3 years old, rode unaided through London to Westminster. He then undertook the rituals associated with becoming a Knight of the Bath – serving on the king at table, ceremonial bathing (physical cleansing), church service (spiritual cleansing), sleep and rising as a knight.[1] The following day, in a magnificent ceremony attended by most of the nobility of England, he was created Duke of York in the Parliament Chamber. Three days of jousting in his honour took place a week later, with his sister Margaret presenting the prizes. Henry would have enjoyed being the centre of attention.

With Arthur in the Welsh Marches and his father kept busy by the pressures of government, Henry's early upbringing was one in which he was surrounded by women and girls – his nurses, his sisters, his mother, her ladies-in-waiting, one of whom, Elizabeth Denton, was in charge of the nursery at Eltham, and his formidable grandmother Lady Margaret Beaufort. He hardly knew his older brother, only meeting him at major state occasions and religious festivals. Whereas Arthur is said to have taken after their father, Henry increasingly resembled his mother's father, Edward IV, tall, with pale skin, auburn hair, a broad face with close-set eyes, and in later life, bloated and overweight. This was his Yorkist heritage. Unlike Arthur, Henry had regular contact with his mother. When her husband campaigned in France in the autumn of 1492, she lived at Eltham and later she probably taught Henry and his sisters to read and write.[2] In June 1497 it was his mother who took him from Eltham into the City and then to the Tower of London to ensure his safety from the Cornish rebels who had advanced as far as Blackheath, between Greenwich and Eltham, before being defeated by Henry VII's forces.

Henry's formal education from the age of 4 or 5 was at first under the guidance of John Skelton. He might well have been separated from his sisters, as Arthur had, but Skelton taught them together. Although Elizabeth died, aged 3, in 1495, Mary, born in March 1496, joined Henry and Margaret. We know this because of an account of a visit to Eltham three years later. William Blount, Lord Mountjoy, thirteen years Henry's senior, had been educated at Cambridge and Paris, and studied under Erasmus who was soon to become the most famous scholar in Europe. Mountjoy had been appointed Henry's 'companion of studies', not a full-time teacher but someone who could guide his learning. In 1499 he invited Erasmus to come to England and they stayed for a time at Mountjoy's country house at Sayes Court. Mountjoy's friend Thomas More joined them and together they visited Eltham, a few miles away. Erasmus described how they met

Henry, his sisters and their infant brother, Edmund, born earlier in the year (and who died a few months later). More presented Henry with a number of poems and the 8-year-old prince was confident enough to ask Erasmus to produce some verse especially for him as well. Later, between 1510 and 1515 in the early years of Henry VIII's reign, Erasmus was based at Queens' College, Cambridge, teaching theology at the university, though he refused a permanent post – he thought the living conditions poor and disliked the weather and English ale, much preferring wine that he believed was good for his gallstones.

Skelton, best known as a poet, was expected to develop his students' English grammar and teach them Latin, in which he was well qualified. He had wide-ranging interests and probably introduced the royal children to other areas of study – astronomy, mathematics, history and certainly poetry. He had a high opinion of himself and, in later years, claimed that he not only taught the future king spelling, grammar and a mastery of Latin but also provided advice on his future conduct. In *Speculum Principis* (The Mirror of a Prince), a guide to 'proper princely behaviour' written by Skelton in 1501, he suggested that a prince should exceed everybody in virtue and learning, these being more important than wealth or nobility. He believed that councillors could not be trusted because they had their own interests at heart, and that a ruler should trust his own judgement, although he should first hear all sides of an argument. He argued that the best way to learn statecraft was by reading chronicles and history. He also urged his readers not to be mean and to avoid gluttony. We must make our own judgement as to how successful he was in influencing Henry's later behaviour.

Soon after publication of the guide, Skelton was replaced by John Holt and then, after Holt's premature death in 1504, William Hone. Holt, an experienced professional educator, had taught at Magdalen College School, Oxford, and then in the household of Cardinal Morton, Archbishop of Canterbury, where he met Thomas More. On Morton's death he taught at Chichester Cathedral School and was then appointed royal tutor on the advice of Mountjoy and More. Holt and Hone were assisted by Giles Duwes who taught French and music, the same subjects he had earlier schooled Prince Arthur in, and later, Henry's daughter, Mary. With Skelton's initial work developed by his new teachers, Henry, now without his sisters, made excellent progress, so much so that Erasmus once refused to believe that a letter he received from the prince was Henry's own work.

Henry developed a respect for scholars and a love of books. He studied English, French and Latin, he read classical texts, especially histories, and, of course, the scriptures. If thought about at all by people in continental

Europe, the English were regarded as pious, religiously orthodox and loyal to the papacy. Like his parents, Henry comfortably fitted this stereotype. He was taken on a pilgrimage to Walsingham by his mother in 1497, something he repeated when king, and he fervently believed in the power of prayer and in the sanctity of relics. By the time of his accession, he was possibly the best educated king of England for many hundred years. He was much praised for his intelligence, his ability in languages and music, and his knowledge of philosophy, theology and history. As Mountjoy wrote to Erasmus in a surfeit of enthusiasm, Henry 'does not desire gold or silver, but virtue, glory and immortality.' The final two, of course, can be achieved in various ways, not all virtuous.

It was not only in the schoolroom that Henry excelled. He became a fine horseman, loved playing tennis (or 'real tennis', as it would now be known) and enjoyed dancing. But jousting became his real passion, his enthusiasm having been encouraged by Duke Philip of Burgundy. In these activities Mountjoy was a major influence. Though well educated, interested in the new learning of the Renaissance and a patron of the arts, he was primarily a nobleman with a family background at court and on the battlefield. He later became the Master of the Mint, the governor of Tournai when under English occupation, and attended Henry's meetings with King Francis at the Field of Cloth of Gold in 1520, and with Emperor Charles V at Greenwich in 1522.

However, the events that had the greatest impact on the young Henry were personal. Two deaths were to change his life. On 2 April 1502, Arthur, married for less than six months, died. In an instant Henry's future was altered irrevocably. He was no longer the 'spare' but now the heir. Although his parents had always taken great interest in his progress, his very survival was now critical to the dynasty. Plans were soon being discussed for his marriage to his brother's widow. Although, as Elizabeth reassured her husband, they were still young enough to have more children, nothing was certain. Elizabeth did become pregnant, but, in February 1503, after the premature birth of her daughter Katherine, she died, the day after her new baby. Prince Henry had lost his mother and soon came under the much closer gaze of his father's watchful eyes.

On 23 February 1504 he was created Prince of Wales and by his thirteenth birthday in June, his separate household had been disbanded and he had joined his father's court. His sister Margaret had left for Scotland in 1503 having married King James IV, leaving the 7-year-old Mary as the only remaining child at Eltham. Whereas Arthur had been sent to the Welsh Marches with his own carefully selected officials to learn about the business of government, Henry VII decided that he would supervise the prince. Henry was to live in the company of his father.

This would mean attending ceremonial occasions in the public eye, but as Henry VII's health deteriorated, his wish to be on show diminished. He preferred to be at his palaces at Greenwich and Richmond, travelling between the two by river, or in his more private estates at Hanworth (near Richmond) and Wanstead (across the river from Greenwich).[3] Traditionally the royal court had two sections, that of the Household, under the Lord Steward, dealing with practical issues like food, heating and transport, and the Chamber, under the Lord Chamberlain, where the king met his council, ambassadors and petitioners. The Lord Chamberlain was also responsible for organising ceremonial events and royal progresses.[4] Henry VII added a privy chamber, access to which was much more restricted, under the guidance of Hugh Denys. There the king could work with those completely of his own choosing, not necessarily the privileged noblemen who dominated the Chamber. In his reign Henry VIII made considerable use of the privy chamber and an appointment there was an important route to influence. However, under Henry VII, it was associated with the meanness and avarice of his later years. Dubious legal practices were used to extract substantial sums from the nobility and wealthy merchants, enforced by the Council Learned in the Law. The money was paid over to the 'privy purse' controlled by Denys on behalf of the king.

How did the young Henry fare in this set-up? Very badly, according to the new Spanish ambassador who, in 1508, wrote that the prince's movements were controlled by his father, he often ate alone and his only contacts were with those appointed by the king. The Henry we know would have hated it but Fuensalida's report is not supported by other evidence. Mountjoy was still at court, seeing the prince on a regular, almost daily, basis. He encouraged his education but also helped to keep him in touch with the other world that existed at court – that of the courtiers well versed in the chivalric code of knightly behaviour. Henry was certainly open to the excitement and risks that the code demanded, especially if it provided an escape from the restricted life around his father. At the heart of this group was Sir Thomas Brandon, master of the horse, but there were plenty of younger men, a few years older than Henry, such as Sir Thomas's nephew Charles Brandon, Thomas Knyvet and Edward Howard, second son of the Earl of Surrey. Henry became close to several of them. He must have had the opportunity to develop his skills since, by 1508, he was taking part in tournaments but initially only 'running the ring', where the rider uses his skill to catch a small wooden ring with his lance, and not in the more dangerous jousts (Plate 8).[5]

Henry was at his father's deathbed at Richmond in April 1509, though as custom demanded he was not involved in the funeral. News of the death was withheld from the public for three days until Henry VIII was proclaimed king on 24 April, and, on the same day, he moved to the Tower of London. Any accession could be a dangerous time, with the risk of plots to usurp the crown and the inevitable jockeying for position amongst the former king's councillors. There seemed to have been little danger of the former, and Henry VII's councillors initially remained in control. It suited them and the young king that his accession should be seen as a new beginning. What better way of doing this, and deflecting any blame from themselves, than to remove those most closely associated with Henry VII's unpopular financial impositions? Within days Edmund Dudley and Richard Empson of the Council Learned in the Law were arrested. They were executed the following year, on fabricated charges of plotting against the king. In fact, they had merely been the instruments of Henry VII's policy, enriching themselves in the process.[6] Outstanding fines and penalties that they had imposed were cancelled by a general pardon.

Though arranged by the council, who were anxious to regain the power they had lost to the privy chamber, the changes were widely held to be the work of the new king. London rejoiced and although Henry VII's funeral was carried out with appropriate dignity, there was no doubt in most people's minds that better times were on the way. Thomas More was especially enthusiastic, writing flattering poems for the new king. Mountjoy persuaded Erasmus to come to England to take advantage of the new opportunities now that 'Heaven smiles, earth rejoices; all is milk and honey and nectar.' Erasmus wrote that Henry VIII's was the only court that 'he would consider being a part of.' They saw Henry as a Renaissance prince brought up to believe in the ideals of the new learning, while his obvious enthusiasm for sporting and martial activities, and his apparent bravery and self-confidence, appealed to people throughout the country.

His power was for a while circumscribed by the Royal Council. Although he was quick to hand out positions and honours to those whom he had come to know and trust in his youth, the council used the formal procedures to delay their confirmation. His instructions were vetted and his letters counter-signed. Nevertheless, Henry gradually asserted his will in a number of respects. The restraining hand of his grandmother, Lady Margaret Beaufort, was removed by her death just days after his coronation. He restored some of his Yorkist family, who had been excluded by his father, to royal service. He started to participate in the jousts that he so much enjoyed and saw as part of his persona. He revelled in the activities that he had only limited opportunities to indulge in when controlled by his father – dressing up, appearing in disguise at public events, jesting, entertaining, drinking and dancing.

He was never going to be his father's kind of ruler, one who wished to control every detail. By the end of 1509, he was still only 18 and, despite the years with his father, he had not gained much experience of the nitty-gritty of government or decision-making. He had chosen to marry Catherine and wished to enjoy all that life had to offer a young monarch. He could be charming and had the natural ability to make people feel that they were of particular importance. He was self-indulgent, a show-off and desired popularity. As is sometimes the case, the appearance of confidence can be misleading. The bravado disguised a certain insecurity. It has often been remarked that he rarely looked people in the eye when he spoke to them, especially when giving bad news. Later in life, he left others to communicate death sentences. Decision-making did not come easily, but once he had made up his mind, he usually became convinced that he was right, rarely willing to revisit difficult questions. Concentration for long periods was not his strength, and he was not one for writing lengthy letters or policy documents. He would need trusted ministers and was often happy for them to get on with the work. However, he would listen to the sometimes-conflicting advice that his council provided and was well able to understand the issues involved. Policy might be suggested and then carried out by others, but his sharp eye for significant detail meant that little was done without his knowledge. His approval of the execution of Dudley and Empson revealed a ruthless streak that was to become a feature of his reign. Ultimate power rested with the king.

***

Charles was nine years younger than Henry. His birth on 24 February 1500 was greeted with the customary celebrations by his family, followed by a magnificent christening ceremony. The citizens of Ghent were unlikely to witness anything like it again. He was a first son, not a second like Henry. A raised walkway of 700 metres was constructed from the Prinsenhof Palace to St John's Church. It was decorated with gateways representing Justice, Peace and Wisdom, covered with coats of arms and lit by thousands of torches. Large crowds turned out to watch the evening procession of magistrates, councillors and knights of the Order of the Golden Fleece. They were followed by the family, led by Margaret of Austria and the Dowager Duchess Margaret of York who, as the senior female member of the family, held the infant. The boy, named after the duchess' deceased husband Charles the Bold, Duke of Burgundy, was known at various times in his youth as Charles of Ghent, Charles of Luxembourg, Duke Charles of Burgundy, Archduke Charles (as heir to the Habsburg lands in Austria), and Prince Charles (as heir to the Spanish thrones).

The marriage of his parents, Philip and Juana, was the result of the policy of 'matrimonial imperialism'[7] pursued by his grandfathers, Ferdinand of Aragon and Emperor Maximilian – marriage alliances intended to achieve greater security against the increasing threat of France. Theirs was an international dynastic marriage, not one focused on internal unity as that of Henry's parents had been. It brought together three powerful ruling families (see family tree). Philip had inherited Burgundy from his mother, the daughter of Charles the Bold, while his father was the Habsburg Emperor Maximilian. Juana was from the Spanish Trastamara dynasty, daughter of the Catholic monarchs, Ferdinand and Isabella, and an older sister of Catherine of Aragon. There was no doubting Charles's lineage. If he survived, he was destined to become a major figure in Europe, but at the time of his birth no-one knew quite how much he would inherit. Early death, the consequence of ill health and limited medical knowledge was common even in the most powerful of families, and such deaths had a significant impact on international affairs in the early sixteenth century.

Charles saw little of his parents. This was not unusual in royal families at the time. Traditionally the eldest son was brought up in a separate establishment, presided over by a trusted senior nobleman. Duke Philip, accompanied by Juana, was expected to travel widely through his lands, to be seen by his subjects and to carry out the duties required of a ruler. However, events in Spain resulted in longer periods of separation than was usual. The deaths of both Juana's older brother Juan (in 1497) and eldest sister Isabella (in 1498) had left Isabella's infant son, Miguel, as the heir to the throne of Castile. His death in July 1500, before his second birthday, meant that Juana would now inherit Castile on her mother's death.

The ambitious Philip could now add the title of Prince of Castile to that of Duke of Burgundy and Archduke of Austria. Juana and Philip travelled to Spain in October 1501 so that they could be acknowledged as heirs. They left their young family, Charles, older sister Eleanor and younger sister Isabella, in the Low Countries. They were to return separately, Philip in 1503 and Juana the following year, having given birth to a second son, Ferdinand, who remained in Spain under the guardianship of her parents. Queen Isabella died in November 1504. Philip and Juana were then expected to go back to Spain, but had to wait until Juana gave birth to another daughter,

Mary, in September 1505. It was not until January 1506 that they set sail from Arnemuiden, near Middleburg, and it was on that voyage that they were driven ashore on the south coast of England, much to Henry VII's advantage. They were never to return to the Low Countries.

Although Ferdinand and Isabella had wished Juana and Philip to take their eldest son to Spain, Philip had refused. He regarded the Low Countries as his homeland and insisted that Charles be brought up at the Burgundian court. The Spanish monarchs had to make do with glowing reports of Charles's progress by their ambassador, Fuensalida, who later became their representative in England. Whether he was merely telling them what they wanted to hear or whether his descriptions of Charles as being advanced for his age[8] were accurate is impossible to judge. Like Henry, Charles had a wet nurse with whom he developed a close bond, remaining in contact for the rest of her life, but unlike Henry he never had the chance to become close to his mother. On their first visit to Spain, Philip and Juana left Charles and his sisters in the household of the Dowager Duchess Margaret of York at Mechelen (often referred to by its French name of Malines at that time), between Brussels and Antwerp, where Philip himself had spent much of his youth. It was a name that would have been familiar to Prince Henry as a safe haven for Yorkist rebels whose purpose had been to prevent him from becoming king.

The city had been part of Margaret's dower settlement on her marriage to Duke Charles the Bold. It was regarded by Philip and his father Maximilian as more loyal to the ruling family than the more populous Ghent or Bruges, whose citizens had shown a strongly independent streak in previous decades. Mechelen had become the judicial centre for the Low Countries, had sound defences, was relatively prosperous and was supposed to be healthier than other towns because of its numerous paved streets, constructed after a major fire in the fourteenth century. Margaret of York had purchased a substantial property there and by 1500, with rebuilding and extensions, it had fine reception rooms, a council chamber, gardens, a tennis court and baths. It was of a similar size to Eltham, but not on the scale of the palaces at Greenwich or Richmond. This became the centre of a household of nearly 100, headed by the ageing Margaret, which provided for the needs of the children.

Even though Margaret of York died in November 1503, Charles and his sisters remained in Mechelen under the supervision of one of Juana's ladies-in-waiting, Anna de Beaumont. On their parents' return from Spain, Philip had them taken to Brussels for a time but it is reported that while he took a considerable interest in their upbringing, Juana seemed to get little pleasure from their company. It was Philip who commissioned illuminated picture books and first reading books for them, although Charles did not make rapid progress with his writing. He was still struggling at the age of 8 and his handwriting was never good, as his sister Mary complained many years later. After Philip's death in Spain, his sister Margaret of Austria returned to the Low Countries as regent and guardian of the children. They stayed in their existing quarters while Margaret established her court nearby. To an existing Gothic structure she added a new gatehouse, one of the first Renaissance-style buildings in northern Europe. It was Margaret who came closest to being a mother-figure for Charles and she was to remain important to him for most of the first thirty years of his life.

While continuing his education with tutors alongside his sisters, it was here in the 'Court of Savoy', as it became known, that Charles was first introduced to the world of government. The buildings were not on the scale of a large palace. Both administrative and living quarters were based around a small courtyard (Plate 4). There was a staff of about 150 but few lived in. Margaret's Chancellor, Mercurio Gattinara, who, in the 1520s, was to become a leading adviser to Charles, headed the Privy Council. With Margaret's role as regent of the Low Countries, the court was often crowded with representatives from the various cities and provinces, as well as many petitioners pressing for favourable judicial decisions or financial favours.

Margaret followed the tradition of the Burgundian court as a centre of culture, epitomised by Philip 'the Good', duke between 1419 and 1467. Patronage of the arts had attracted painters, such as Jan van Eyck and Rogier van der Weyden, and Margaret continued this custom, collecting works by Hans Memling, Hieronymus Bosch and Bernard van Orley. In the 'Chambre de Madame', her private quarters, she put together a fine collection of portraits, miniatures, tapestries and dining services, along with an extensive collection of books by classical and Renaissance humanist writers. In 1520, the artist Albrecht Dürer, in the Low Countries seeking to renew the pension granted to him by Emperor Maximilian, wrote that on his visit 'Lady Margaret showed me all her beautiful things, and amongst them I saw forty small pictures in oils, the like of which for cleanliness and excellence I have never seen ... Then I saw many other costly things and a fine library.'[9] Many of the best thinkers and artists of the day were made welcome.

The Burgundian court was also renowned for its refinement, taste, comfort and, of course, chivalry and courtly love, something other courts, such as that of England under Edward IV and his wife Elizabeth Woodville, wished to emulate. The children of noble families from across Europe were sent to Mechelen. For the daughters, as ladies-in-waiting, it was where they could mix with Europe's future rulers and gain the knowledge of poetry, music, art and courtly behaviour that would be expected of them. It was here that the as-yet-little-known Anne Boleyn, daughter of Sir Thomas Boleyn, was sent in 1513, spending a year at Margaret's court, and surely coming across Charles, before moving on to Paris, a decade before her charms gained the attention of Henry VIII. The sons became pages of honour and would imbue the qualities of the medieval knight and learn the skills of riding, hunting, fencing and jousting. This was still a world in which rulers and the nobility were expected to show bravery and gain honour on the battlefield. Charles pleased his family with his enjoyment of these activities. He was 9 years old when Margaret, in one of her regular letters to Maximilian informing him of Charles's progress, wrote 'our son Charles takes such pleasure hunting.' The emperor replied that this was to be expected 'because otherwise people might think he was a bastard.'

In his youth Charles was surrounded by the young men at court, Henry of Nassau, Frederick Count Palatine and Charles de Lannoy, ten or fifteen years older than him, who excelled in horsemanship and jousting. These men would later become the advisers and commanders of his early years in power. He was greatly influenced by the writing of Olivier de la Marche who had written about the importance of the splendour and rituals of a ruler's household in impressing others, using the court of Charles the Bold as an exemplar. In *Le Chavalier delibere* (The Resolute Knight), the traditional chivalric virtues of bravery, honour and loyalty are extolled. The book inspired Charles. Years later he used these ideas when offering advice to his son and he kept a copy with him in his final years. It is little wonder that his membership and later leadership of the Order of the Golden Fleece was of such importance to him. The order existed to uphold the ideals of the medieval knight and to encourage the need for Christian unity to fight the infidel.

Maximilian and Margaret were particularly pleased about Charles's enthusiasm for such activities and ideas because he did not have the typical appearance of the heroic knight. Whereas his father is sometimes referred to as Philip 'the handsome', Charles did not cut an obviously striking figure. Despite Ambassador Fuensalida's reports that he was tall and strong at 5 months old, and that a year later he was very strong for his age, it is generally accepted that in his youth Charles had a pale complexion and was considered delicate. His earlier guardians, and then Margaret of Austria, were very protective of him; they certainly had experience of how fragile a young life could be. He rarely left Mechelen because they feared travelling might damage his health and that his safety might be threatened. While spending a short time in Brussels, he was not allowed back to Mechelen for a while because of an outbreak of smallpox there. Sensible precautions, but even so he was not spared and suffered from the disease for over a month.[10] He also developed the large lower jaw, now associated with the Habsburgs, making it difficult for him to close his mouth completely. Self-consciousness about this might explain why he was said to be shy, with a preference for eating alone. Some people at the time considered that he appeared dull and apathetic. However, those that knew him better recognised that this was misleading. He might not have had the reputed good looks of the youthful Henry VIII, but he developed a well-proportioned body and was more than able to take a lively part in the physical activities of court life and became almost obsessed with hunting.

Charles's introduction to affairs of state started early. He was encouraged to sign letters to his parents when they were in Spain and he made his first public speech to the representative assembly of Louvain (Leuven) at the age of 7. This would have been in French, his first language. He also became fluent in Flemish, was taught some Latin and later in life was able to communicate in Spanish, German and Italian with varying degrees of fluency. It has been said that he spoke French to his friends, Spanish to his confessors, Italian to his women and German to his horses, which he loved the most. Witty but wide of the mark – it was the Latin and German that he never really mastered.

At court Charles came into contact with some of the best minds of the age. Maximilian and Margaret both recognised the importance of a good education and ensured that his tutors were men of high calibre. In his early years there was the Spaniard Luis Cabeza de Vaca, later Bishop of the Canary Islands, Salamanca and then Palencia, who taught Charles and his sisters. Charles's first confessor was Michel de Pavie, the former rector of Paris University. The best known and perhaps the most influential, however, was Adrian Florensz Boeyens – Adrian of Utrecht. The son of a carpenter, Adrian studied at Zwolle and entered the University of Louvain in 1476, supported by a scholarship granted by the Duchess of Burgundy, Margaret of York. After studying and then teaching theology and philosophy, he became vice-chancellor of the university by 1493. Influenced by his time with the Brethren of the Common Life, and like many humanist scholars of the age, he was concerned about the abuses and great wealth of some in the church hierarchy, and believed in the need to lead a simple religious life, though he opposed any doctrinal changes. In 1507 he was appointed Charles's tutor and remained in his service as adviser, ambassador and later regent in Spain for the next fifteen years.

Charles was also influenced by the writings of Erasmus of Rotterdam (Plate 5), perhaps the most famous humanist philosopher. Though never his teacher, Erasmus dedicated his book *The Education of a Christian Prince* (Institutio principis Christiani), published in 1516, to Charles. A special edition was also sent to Henry VIII the following year. In it, Erasmus argued that the sovereign must not forget that 'a large part of authority depends on the consent of the people.' In common with other humanists, he believed in the virtues of peace. This clashed with the chivalric emphasis on achieving honour through war, but most rulers managed to justify their actions by claiming that they were acting to secure the peace against an aggressor. Erasmus also advised kings to 'conduct your own rule as if you were striving to ensure that no successor could be your equal, but at the same time prepare your children for their future as if to ensure that a better man would indeed succeed you.'

Scholars at the time often took posts and accepted commissions in various countries, tempted by the patronage of the wealthy. Erasmus was no exception. As we have seen, he had been invited to England in 1499 by Lord Mountjoy and visited the young Henry at Eltham Palace.[11] The international nature of scholarship meant that Henry and Charles were both introduced to the new ideas generated by the Renaissance.

Like Henry, Charles developed sincere, orthodox religious beliefs. He gained a good knowledge of the scriptures, attended Mass frequently and believed in divine intervention. Victory and defeat were both God's will, to be accepted. Later, his generals were sometimes alarmed by the risks that he took, putting his unshakeable faith in God, but more often than not it paid off, confirming his belief. Although, in retirement, he enjoyed reading history and philosophy as well as discussing theological issues raised in sermons and Bible readings, he was not someone who would challenge the doctrines of the Catholic Church. The influence of his humanist teachers is revealed in his recognition of the need for some reform of the clergy and the removal of obvious abuses of power. Even though he had frequent clashes with the papacy on political issues and, at times, considered that the Popes were untrustworthy and deceitful, he was not going to question their spiritual authority. He believed, as Erasmus had written to him, that 'Caesar is not the doctor of the scriptures, he is their champion.'

In his political education, the most influential person in his formative years, besides Margaret of Austria, was Guillaume de Croy, Lord of Chièvres. A leading figure in Duke Philip's court and respected by both Philip and Maximilian, he was left in charge of the Low Countries when Philip and Juana travelled to Spain in 1506. Three years later he was appointed Charles's governor and Grand Chamberlain. He was constantly with Charles guiding his ideas and beliefs. Like Margaret, he wished to ensure that the young man was capable of coping with the life that he was going to lead. 'I do not want him to be incapable because he has not understood affairs nor been trained to work.'[12] Most observers at the time, and since, have concluded that he was successful. Although a more subdued character than Henry VIII, Charles could, and did, enjoy the pleasures of life and despite his somewhat unprepossessing appearance, most would agree with the papal ambassador when, in 1521, he reported that 'this prince is gifted with good sense and prudence far beyond his years and indeed has, I believe, much more in his head than appears on his face' (Plate 6).

While Margaret and Chièvres both had Charles's best interests at heart, their priorities were different. Whereas Margaret saw Charles as the future head of the Habsburg dynasty, with responsibilities throughout Europe, Chièvres, as the leading regional nobleman, wished to use his influence to pursue narrower, Burgundian interests. Chièvres spoke French and, like most of the Burgundian nobility, had much in common with France and its culture. They did not particularly relish the idea of conflict with their powerful neighbour. Margaret had more pro-English leanings. Her Habsburg background meant that France was often seen as a rival for influence in northern Italy, and although she realised that war with France was potentially damaging for the Low Countries, she also recognised the importance of the trading links with England.[13] It was this conflict of interest that eventually brought forward Charles's coming of age and official assumption of power in the Low Countries.

***

Although there are obvious differences in their early experiences, such as in their relations with their parents, and the fact that Henry only became heir to the throne at the age of 10, the upbringing of the two princes had many features in common. This was only to be expected as the sons of leading royal houses of Europe. A Renaissance humanist education was linked to a late medieval chivalric code. This education focused on grammar, rhetoric, history and moral philosophy to prepare the sons, and occasionally daughters, of the elite and wealthy to be able to engage fully in civic life. For royalty it emphasised the virtues generally considered to be necessary for a monarch's honour, such as devotion to the Christian faith, the fair dispensation of justice, prudence, generosity as a patron of courtiers, academics and artists and, of course, bravery, both on the battlefield and in adversity.[14]

Such ideas played a vital part in the concept of monarchy with which both Henry and Charles identified. Winning the loyalty of their subjects and the respect of their fellow monarchs was only possible by gaining honour and reputation, which was essentially a personal matter. In their youth they were both strongly influenced by the dashing knights at court and were keen to show their courage while hunting and, later, in jousting, thus learning and demonstrating their strength and skills in horsemanship, all regarded as excellent preparation for future battlefield action. These activities were enjoyed by both monarchs for as long as they were able to take part. The chivalric orders of the Garter, founded by Edward III in 1348, and the Golden Fleece, established by Duke Philip 'the Good' in 1430, of which they became leaders were of great significance to them. Charles was rarely portrayed without his chain of office.

But honour was not simply a matter of physical bravery. If honour was to be achieved through war, it had to be a just war. This meant following a shared set of rules, such as not only declaring war but also declaring the causes of the war. Thus, Henry and Charles would often use similar explanations as to why they were going to war. Defence of the Catholic faith, the recovery of lands taken from them and the defence of their kingdoms were the three most widely claimed justifications, but it was rare for either monarch to risk conflict without a careful consideration of the chances of victory, and, if not victory, then a good negotiating position and potential gain. Honour and prestige could also be achieved through a peace settlement, especially if a monarch could be seen as the peacemaker and at the same time achieve his diplomatic objectives.

Henry and Charles, then, had numerous shared values and beliefs. But what of their characters, their approach to work, their attitudes towards the responsibilities that they had as monarchs, and their personal lives – if a monarch of the sixteenth century can be said to have one? Some differences had already emerged by the time they came of age. Others became apparent during the thirty years which they shared as two of the most important figures in Europe.

Chapter Three

Overseas Adventures

Henry VIII's was the first undisputed accession in England for over half a century. During that time, besides four changes of ruling family, two kings, several princes and innumerable noblemen had lost their lives. Henry was not only unchallenged but well received by all sections of the population, who did not wish for a return to the uncertainty and instability of civil war. As he did not have to defend his position at home, an active foreign policy that would provide the chance to enhance the new king's status was possible. If this meant war then the obvious opponent was France. However, it was not something that he could rush into. His senior councillors remained those of his father, in particular Richard Foxe, now Bishop of Winchester; William Warham, Archbishop of Canterbury; and Thomas Howard, Earl of Surrey. They were all experienced but aging in 1509 (even though they survived a good many years – Warham was the last to die in 1532).

At first, Henry's warlike tendencies were restricted to a keen interest in new weaponry and building up the navy. In Europe the League of Cambrai had been signed in December 1508. Put together by Pope Julius II against Venice, the papacy had been joined by Ferdinand of Aragon, Emperor Maximilian and Louis XII. Ostensibly about the Venetian challenge to papal authority over church appointments in its territories, all participants were eager to take land and cities held by Venice in northern Italy. France already ruled Milan and Spain controlled Naples. England, with no real interests at stake in Italy, was not a member of the League but supported its aims. Venice suffered several defeats so, in February 1510, the republic came to terms with the Pope. This did not prevent French and Imperial armies renewing their attacks in an effort to seize more territory.

At this point Pope Julius began to fear a French domination of Italy and initiated talks for an anti-French alliance. For Henry this was ideal. He had already sent Christopher Bainbridge, Archbishop of York, to Rome in late 1509 in order to influence Julius against France. Bainbridge had obviously succeeded in winning the Pope's trust as, in March 1511, he was created a cardinal. In response to Julius's hostility, Louis XII summoned a church council to meet at Pisa with the threat that it might vote to remove the Pope.

The Pope's response was not what Louis had hoped. Rather than back off, Julius accelerated negotiations and, in October 1511, the Holy League was signed by the Pope, Ferdinand, Maximilian and various Italian states with the explicit purpose of driving the French out of Italy. The following month Bainbridge, having received the approval of the king, signed for England. Henry could now have his war against France and he could justify it as being in defence of the Church.

Although many of his senior councillors, such as Foxe and Warham, generally favoured the continuation of the policy of peace and Surrey was less keen for war than is sometimes thought, they put up little serious resistance to Henry's plans.[1] There were plenty of younger courtiers, Edward Howard, Thomas Knyvet, Henry Guildford and Charles Brandon, who shared Henry's enthusiasm. Henry was also encouraged by his father-in-law Ferdinand to reclaim former English lands in France and thus win the acclaim of his people and fellow rulers. As well as joining the Holy League, Henry agreed with Ferdinand in the Treaty of Westminster (November 1511) that there should be a joint Anglo-Spanish invasion of Gascony in south-west France the following year. Preparations were made and an army raised. In March 1512 the Pope, to encourage Henry, confidentially recognised his claim to the throne of France. Thomas Wall, the Lancaster Herald, was sent to France and in an audience with the French king at Blois issued the formal declaration of war on 3 May.

Henry was to provide 6,000 infantry (in fact, over 7,000 were sent) and Ferdinand, 4,000 foot soldiers and 2,000 cavalry.[2] The troops would be transported by requisitioned merchant ships and some vessels hired from Spain and the Low Countries. Once they had disembarked, provisions were to be supplied by Ferdinand. The army was commanded by Thomas Grey, Marquess of Dorset. Henry also had a plan to send more troops to Normandy but this was abandoned by mid-summer. English naval vessels commanded by Edward Howard were to guard the Channel and, as it turned out, he was largely unopposed. He regularly attacked French vessels and went on to carry out several raids in Brittany with the aim of stirring up opposition to French rule by demonstrating their inability to protect its inhabitants.[3] It was only in August 1512 that a French fleet sailed from Brest, but even then, most of its ships returned to the safety of the harbour without giving battle. However, in a limited engagement, known as the Battle of Saint-Mathieu, the French vessel *Cordelière* and the largest English ship, *Regent*, grappled together and were both destroyed by an explosion of the French ship's magazine. Over 1,000 perished, including the *Regent*'s captain Sir Thomas Knyvet. Howard, angered by the death of his friend, continued his attacks until the end of October. The following year he renewed his raids, now as Lord High Admiral, but on 25 April he was killed in an attack on the French fleet in Brest harbour.[4]

In Gascony the military campaign was a disaster. Having disembarked in June and moved on to Fuenterrabia close to the French border ready to advance against Bayonne, the army received no supplies or means of transport for its equipment. Soldiers started to plunder nearby villages for food. The weather was unseasonably wet and the troops had insufficient shelter. Disease spread and there was an outbreak of dysentery. In July a mutiny was only put down with difficulty and there was no improvement in the soldiers' conditions. Meanwhile Ferdinand, rather than sending his troops to join them, informed Dorset that he intended to occupy neighbouring Navarre, whose ruler was a potential ally of France. He did so successfully, but the level of mistrust and suspicion between Ferdinand and the English commanders became such that little more could be achieved. There were some English raids across the French border, causing death and destruction in St Jean-de-Luz and a number of villages, but the armies never joined forces. Although some commanders, such as Thomas Howard, wished to remain, ships were hired and the army left for England in late October having achieved nothing.

The finger of blame for this fiasco has usually been pointed at Ferdinand – his failure to provide supplies and his change of strategy. The Spanish, it is argued, used English troops to distract the French so that they could take Navarre which had been their aim all along. There is some truth in this but it is not the entire story. Ferdinand was probably correct when he argued that if they controlled Navarre then the invasion of Gascony could be achieved more easily, with less risk of being attacked from the rear. Later Henry and his council agreed with this analysis. His confidence in his ally was not undermined – yet. There can also be little doubt that Dorset failed to provide the effective leadership that the campaign required. He was indecisive, unwilling to take decisions without consulting Henry and, given the slow communications between London and Spain, this simply would not work. By the time a dispatch from Henry instructing Dorset to accept Ferdinand's strategy arrived in Spain, if it ever did, plans for the army's departure were already well under way. In any case it was unlikely that the soldiers would have agreed to stay, having declared earlier that they had no intention of remaining over the winter.

This was not the glorious campaign that Henry had imagined. Rather than achieving honour it had been an embarrassment. He needed a change of fortune if his reputation was not to be damaged. Plans were immediately prepared for another expedition against France, but this time it would be from Calais, England's only remaining foothold in France. This would remove many of the problems connected with provisions and extended lines of communication. Henry decided that he would lead the campaign, with Charles Brandon as his second-in-command. In an agreement reached at Mechelen in April 1513, Henry would launch an invasion from Calais, and Emperor Maximilian would join him from the Low Countries. Hard up as usual, Maximilian would be well paid for his services. Louis XII was in a difficult position. His forces were already under attack in northern Italy and he feared that the Spanish would give him more problems by advancing into southern France. Ferdinand, however, decided that having occupied Navarre the previous year there was little more to be gained and signed a temporary truce with Louis, much to Henry's annoyance. Anglo-Spanish relations were deteriorating.

Henry knew before his departure for France that the renewed Franco-Scottish alliance of 1512 might well result in a Scottish attack on northern England. King James IV's relations with England had generally been good. He had signed a Treaty of Perpetual Peace with Henry VII in 1502 and married Henry's oldest daughter, Margaret, the next year. When Henry VIII declared war on France, James made the fateful decision to support France. The Earl of Surrey, whose main military experience had been on the Scottish borders but who had hoped to go on the French campaign, was left behind to deal with any Scottish incursion. Another precaution that Henry took before leaving England was to order the execution of Edmund de la Pole, Duke of Suffolk, a prisoner in the Tower of London since being handed over by Duke Philip in 1506. His brother Richard had entered into the service of Louis XII, who had made it clear that he supported de la Pole's claim to the English throne, thus effectively signing Suffolk's death warrant.

Leaving Queen Catherine as regent, Henry crossed to Calais on 30 June to join the rest of his army. Another lesson gained from the Gascony campaign had been that an army of non-professional soldiers, most of whom were tenants, servants or retainers of nobles and landowners who recruited them for military service for a fixed period, could be greatly strengthened if it was supplemented by professional mercenaries. Thus in 1513, Henry's army of approximately 30,000 men contained several thousand mercenaries, mainly from Germany and the Low Countries. The cost of the campaign was therefore increased further, though to Henry, at this stage, the cost was nothing compared to the need for a victory. Assembling, equipping and supplying such an army was a complex business and much of the credit for its organisation went to Bishop Foxe's protégé, Thomas Wolsey, whose influence was rising rapidly in the king's councils. Both Foxe and Wolsey accompanied Henry to France.

By late July the army had marched 30 miles south-east of Calais and besieged the small but well-fortified town of Therouanne. Henry was joined there by Maximilian. On 16 August a French relief force of perhaps 7,000 was sent, some to divert the besieging troops and others to deliver supplies to the town. They were driven off in what became known as the second Battle of Guinegate (named after the location of Henry's camp) or, more popularly in England, as the 'Battle of the Spurs' in reference to the speed at which the French cavalry left the battlefield. The town surrendered a week later and much of it was destroyed. As the Milanese ambassador who was travelling with the emperor reported to Duke Maximilian Sforza on 4 September: 'the emperor and the king have continued up to today the work of demolishing the walls of Therouanne … [after which] the town will be burned.' Little was left except the cathedral and a few surrounding houses.[5]

After this success there was a difference of opinion as to the next move for the invading army. Henry favoured marching to Boulogne and taking the city, a plan that would be relatively risk free and, if successful, expand the territory under English control. Maximilian argued that if Henry really wanted to 'win glory and the crown of France' then he ought to not to waste time in this way.[6] It was decided that the army would move east to besiege Tournai, a French enclave in the Burgundian lands of the Low Countries. The city was 'very populous and rich', larger than nearly all English cities except London, and its bishop controlled a diocese that covered much of Flanders, including Ghent and Bruges.[7]

Henry visited Lille on 10 September and was greeted by 'All the noble lords and ladies and the merchants of Flanders, Holland and Brabant' who 'received his Majesty in very great triumph.'[8] He 'was lodged in the palace of the prince, where Madame [Margaret of Austria] also is staying. She went to meet him on the palace staircase and made him a deep reverence, while he bowed to the ground to her'.[9] Henry's four rooms were 'adorned with Madame's tapestries, worked with gold.' The victory was celebrated with a banquet and Henry was in a relaxed mood as he 'danced … from the time the banquet finished until nearly day, in his shirt and without shoes.'[10]

Henry then rejoined his army outside Tournai and it was here that he received the first news of the English victory over the Scots on 9 September at the Battle of Flodden. On 16 September Henry wrote to the Duke of Milan that James IV 'who took part with France unmindful of ties of blood and of a formal treaty' had been defeated and, in a postscript, added that he had 'received sure intelligence that the King of Scots himself perished in the battle.' It had been a shattering defeat for the Scots. James had given one month's notice of his intention to invade, in keeping with the medieval chivalric code. This gave Catherine, as regent, and Surrey, as the commander on the ground, time to prepare. It was a hard-fought engagement with orders given that no prisoners should be taken. Surrey had dispatched details of the battle to Catherine who had sent them on to Henry. According to Brian Tuke, Clerk of the Signet, who wrote from Tournai to Richard Pace, Cardinal Bainbridge's secretary in Rome, Henry was told that besides the king, 'eleven earls, fifteen barons, an archbishop, two bishops ... and a great many other nobles' had been killed. The 'rent surcoat of the King of Scots, stained with blood' had been sent to Tournai, and it is said that Catherine had to be dissuaded from sending his whole body.

Everything continued to go Henry's way. Tuke explains why this was so in his letter to Richard Pace. The weather had been mild, the army had been free of dissentions despite having men from many nations, there had been no epidemic, plenty of provisions had been supplied and the emperor had given his support as agreed – all proof of divine assistance. Days after the start of the siege, the defenders of Tournai negotiated terms of surrender agreeing to pay an indemnity towards Henry's expenses. The emperor accepted that the city should remain under English control and renounced all claims to it. Henry entered in triumph, received homage from its citizens and remained for over two weeks.

Margaret of Austria, accompanied by the 13-year-old Duke Charles, travelled to Tournai and was welcomed by the king. The Milanese ambassador described the tournament held in the rapidly erected list-yard on 11 October. Henry had a pavilion of brocade on one side of the tilting ground where he could rest between jousts. Over his armour he wore a multi-coloured vest of velvet embroidered with stripes of gold and had a white veil hanging behind his helmet. Watched by Margaret and Charles, Henry was the overall victor and 'was taken round the circle of the lists, without his helmet, in most honourable fashion' appearing vivacious and pleasant, showing no sign of exertion. Afterwards he took supper with Margaret and Charles.

On 13 October they all travelled to Lille where the king was now Margaret's guest. Henry had cut a fine figure at the jousts and dances but now, after experiencing the sophistication of the Burgundian court, he and his companions wished to replicate it back in England. Many of the splendours and refinements associated with Henry's court had their origins in these festivities. At the celebrations in Tournai and Lille, the first meeting between Henry and Charles took place. In his youth Henry's meeting with

Duke Philip, Charles's father, had a lasting impact on him. He was now keen to meet Philip's son who was betrothed to Mary, Henry's much-loved younger sister, an arrangement that the king wished to push forward. Although Charles was described as reserved in manner, Henry and his court were pleased by his quiet dignity.[11]

Charles, in turn, was impressed by the victorious and seemingly confident Henry, just as the king would have wished. Charles mentions their first formal meeting at Lille in the opening paragraph of his memoirs written over thirty-five years later. He writes that 'he had his first interview with the king, and ... amongst other things, his emancipation was discussed and resolved upon.'[12] This refers to discussions about Charles's future and were part of an attempt by Margaret to weaken the influence of Chièvres and the Burgundian nobility. By the Ordinance of Lille, it was arranged that Henry, Maximilian and Ferdinand would each nominate a representative to be Charles's governor[13] and that they would decide, and perhaps delay, when Charles should 'come of age' and start his active role as Duke of Burgundy. Although this was a victory for Margaret, some observers at the time recognised that once Charles began his personal rule it would be Chièvres who would become the most influential figure.

There was talk of the English army remaining in France over the winter, but Henry decided against this and in late October he made a triumphant return to England. He travelled to Richmond to show the keys of the captured towns to Catherine. He had led his troops to victory, gaining the honour that he so desired. In doing so he had shown that England could make its mark in continental affairs, thereby raising his own prestige and influence. These considerations were very important to Henry and he must have considered the whole expedition a success. Many of its participants were rewarded with knighthoods. Early the following year Thomas Howard, Earl of Surrey was created Duke of Norfolk, Charles Brandon made Duke of Suffolk and Thomas Wolsey was appointed Bishop of Lincoln.

However, in material terms, what had been gained and at what cost? Two towns had been taken, though one had been virtually destroyed and the other required a costly garrison and had fortifications that needed expensive improvements. Thomas Cromwell in Parliament famously referred to the towns as 'graceless dog-holes'. Tournai in English hands rather than French, and at English expense, suited Maximilian very well. Wolsey was appointed as Bishop of Tournai but was unable to collect the revenues that were due to him. This was not much to show for an expensive campaign. There had been the costs of the soldiers, their transport, provisions and munitions, the additional costs of the mercenaries and then the substantial subsidies to

Maximilian. In less than five years on the throne, Henry had managed to spend on war most of the fortune that his father had built up over the previous two decades. Nevertheless, most of Europe still considered him to be rich.[14]

Henry had reasons to doubt whether all was quite as positive as the public displays suggested. Some of those around him complained about the failure of the Spanish to join in the attacks on France. Henry himself commented that he 'had been left alone against France', even though he was acting in the interests of others as well as himself. He recognised that the cost of the expedition was very great. Before he left for home, he had talked up his wish to continue the fight against France. However, by the time he had been back in England for a few weeks he was reported by an Italian diplomat as saying that he had no wish to spend any more on war unless the marriage of Duke Charles and Princess Mary was completed quickly. Even before Henry had set out for France, Pope Julius II had died and, in March 1513, Giovanni de' Medici had been elected as Pope Leo X. He claimed to have no knowledge of the confidential promise made by his predecessor to support Henry's claim to the French throne and to remove the title of 'Most Christian King' from Louis XII and award it to Henry instead. Though wishing to have no dominant foreign power in Italy he was more inclined to peace than his predecessor. The Holy League against France was showing signs of breaking up. The diplomatic manoeuvring that took place over the first half of 1514 provides an excellent example of how quickly relations can change in international politics.

After recovering from smallpox early in the year, Henry was still planning a renewed war against France in 1514, expecting Ferdinand and Maximilian to fulfil their promises to support him. Preparations were in full swing and, as early as March, foreign ambassadors were reporting that they anticipated an invasion in the summer. However, in the same month, Henry heard that the truce between King Ferdinand and Louis XII originally made the previous year had been extended. He was furious, believing that he had been betrayed by his father-in-law just when France was at his mercy.[15] To make matters worse it became clear that Emperor Maximilian had also agreed to this peace and had committed himself to persuading Henry to accept it. Both Ferdinand and Maximilian had gained from their alliance with England. Even though Henry had achieved his aims of making a mark and raising England's status, the strategy in the campaigns of 1512 and 1513 had suited their purposes. They had little to gain from further conflict, certainly not by supporting Henry's unrealistic claim to the French throne or major territorial gains in south-west France and Normandy. If he wanted to continue the war against France then he would have to do so alone. Henry wrote to Margaret of Austria bitterly complaining that he had not been consulted and that he could not honourably take part in such an agreement[16].

At the same time the marriage of Charles and Mary, whose betrothal had taken place five years earlier and was supposed to be finalised before 15 May 1514, was now in doubt. Margaret of Austria was concerned when she wrote to her father, Emperor Maximilian, emphasising that Henry had made great preparations for war against France and urging him to come to the Low Countries from Austria to speed things up. His delaying tactics, she argued, were 'making enemies of his friends.'[17] Henry still supported the marriage and proposed that it could take place in Calais. But Maximilian found reasons not to travel, complaining that Henry had yet to come up with the 30,000 crowns that he had promised to lend him, claiming that he had kept all his promises and assuring the king that he would never make peace without Henry's consent.

In an insightful analysis of the situation, William Knight, the English ambassador to the court of Margaret, wrote from Mechelen to Wolsey on 2 May suggesting a change of policy. The emperor, he wrote, was not to be trusted, had never intended to keep his promise and had misled Henry until he and Ferdinand had come to terms with France, believing that Henry was so keen on the marriage that he would fall in with their plans. They had thus thoroughly dishonoured him. He pointed out that many in the Low Countries were opposed to the marriage and would seek to cause problems between Charles and Mary. His conclusion was that it would be better to make peace with France in order to counteract the agreement between Ferdinand and Maximilian.

Henry and Wolsey were not slow to act. Henry's frustration with his allies led to a rapid reversal of policy. Rumours of a possible peace between England and France were mentioned by the Venetian ambassador in France as early as 3 May and Pope Leo was also using diplomatic channels to encourage such a move.[18] Negotiations were opened with Louis d'Orleans, Duke of Longueville, who had been given powers to represent Louis XII. Longueville had been captured at the Battle of the Spurs and taken to England as a hostage, though he retained considerable freedom, having an affair with Jane Popincourt, a French lady-in-waiting of Catherine of Aragon, who it is claimed also had a brief affair with Henry VIII. Talks centred on how much France would pay Henry as an annual pension in lieu of his 'inheritance', French demands for the return of Tournai and a new marriage plan – that of Princess Mary to the French king.

As news of the negotiations started to surface Henry began justifying this change of direction. While accepting that Margaret of Austria was committed to the original marriage plan, Henry informed her that much had changed. The date for the marriage had now passed, the emperor had not kept his promises to help pay for the garrison at Tournai and therefore Henry was not going to lend him the 30,000 crowns. Margaret continued to send urgent letters to Maximilian to persuade him to change his attitude, also mentioning that the young Duke Charles had accidentally killed a man with his cross-bow while out hunting on Whit-Monday. Her representative in England attempted to reassure Henry by giving reasons for the delay and informing him that Charles, who had been taken ill, was now recovering (which the king already knew from his ambassadors), but to no avail.

Wolsey, Foxe and the Duke of Norfolk were commissioned to finalise the terms with France and they succeeded in gaining several concessions. Louis wished for peace having suffered a major defeat at Novara in June 1513 resulting in the loss of Milan and being driven out of Italy. He intended to regain these territories in the future so did not want to have to defend France from another English invasion. He even had hopes that Henry would support him in his Italian ambitions but this was unrealistic. The terms, signed on 7 August, took the form of an extended truce. Henry's French pensions were increased in return for his agreement to withhold his claim to the French throne, and Tournai remained in English hands despite Louis' original wish for it to be returned.[19] The agreement was to be cemented by the marriage of Henry's sister Mary, now aged 18, to the 52-year-old Louis XII of France. He had been recently widowed on the death of Anne of Brittany who he had married after the death of her first husband, the previous French king. Mary's betrothal to Charles was repudiated.

Mary wrote to the French king saying that she would 'love him as cordially as she can' and signed it 'de la main de votre humble compagne, Marie' ('from the hand of your humble companion, Mary'). A marriage by proxy took place less than a week later on 13 August at Greenwich in the presence of Henry, Catherine, the Archbishop of Canterbury and the assembled bishops and nobility of England. It was noted that neither the representative of the emperor nor that of King Ferdinand were invited. The Duke of Longueville stood in for King Louis. Both he and Mary read the words of espousal in French before Longueville placed a gold ring on the princess' fourth finger.[20] After the assembly of an expensive wardrobe, a considerable entourage led by the Duke of Norfolk travelled with Mary to France in early October. She was met at Abbeville by Louis and the final marriage ceremonies were performed. Mary was doing her duty but unsurprisingly she was not particularly happy with the situation. By 12 October she was complaining in letters to both Henry and Wolsey that her chamberlain and nearly all of her trusted servants had been discharged and that she was dissatisfied with the duke as he had done little to prevent it. Norfolk's inaction was probably because most of them had been selected by Wolsey.

Reactions to the marriage varied greatly. Sir Richard Wingfield wrote to Henry that there was 'great dissatisfaction in all the Prince's [Charles's] countries' and 'even Chièvres pretends to be displeased and sneers at the fidelity of England.' Margaret at first doubted the reports and ordered her representative at Henry's court to find out whether it was true, and if it was to tell Henry that she could not believe that he had rejected so suitable a marriage for Mary as Charles 'would be one of the greatest princes of Christendom' and to 'remonstrate against the breach of faith.'[21] By October she had to accept that her hopes for Charles's marriage to Mary had been ended. On the other hand, the marriage was generally popular in France as it decisively broke up the anti-French alliance. From Spain, King Ferdinand instructed his ambassador in England to subtly undermine the new relationship between England and France. He was to suggest to Henry that the marriage would not end the French efforts to regain Tournai, just as the marriage of Henry's other sister to James IV of Scotland had not prevented an attack on England; to remind him of the 'ancient and natural enmity between French and English'; and to put the blame for Ferdinand's truce with Louis squarely on the shoulders of Maximilian. On a more personal level Peter Martyr, an Italian working for Ferdinand in Spain, believed that the young bride 'will be his [Louis'] death' questioning why the ailing French king should make such a match 'with a handsome girl of 18'.[22]

Henry's relations with both Ferdinand and Maximilian had reached a low ebb. The emperor, disregarding his own share of the responsibility for the breakdown, accused Henry of inexcusable behaviour, claiming that Henry's successes the previous year could only have been achieved with his assistance and that in doing so he had even placed his own lands in danger. If Ferdinand's failure to act against France in 1513 had disappointed Henry, his actions in 1514 destroyed any remaining trust that he might have had. The reversal of policy is sometimes seen as the first major example of Wolsey dominating the foreign policy of Henry VIII during the 1510s and 1520s. Various interpretations have been suggested as to Wolsey's motives. It has been argued that he influenced policy in the interests of the papacy as he wished to receive a cardinal's hat and had ambitions for the papal tiara itself.[23] Alternatively the case has been made that the influence of humanists inclined Wolsey towards a peace policy.[24] To some extent these arguments are irrelevant – Wolsey might have guided Henry but he never controlled him.

What is more likely is that Wolsey was seeking to raise the status of Henry VIII on the European stage and to do so by whatever means were available at the time – an opportunistic approach that was flexible in the face of an ever-changing international situation. In 1514 there was very little else that could be done other than make peace with France. England's allies had already withdrawn their support and were now distrusted despite their protestations of friendship, and there was little, if any, money left in the coffers for another costly campaign against France. Wolsey put a positive spin on the peace with France – after all Henry had largely got what he wanted in the short term and peace could be made to look victorious.

Wolsey received his reward. Later in 1514 he was elevated to the Archbishopric of York, his predecessor Bainbridge having been murdered in Rome and, in 1515, he was made a cardinal by Pope Leo. By December 1515 he had become Chancellor of England, in practice Henry's chief minister. His relatively humble origins and rapid rise to power, though not uncommon, inevitably aroused the jealousy of the elite nobility who considered it to be their role to advise the king. Along with others they also found it difficult to accept the increasingly opulent lifestyle of the cardinal. While this was expected of those in power, it being a symbol of their success, Wolsey very obviously enjoyed the wealth and luxury that he was able to indulge in. However, Henry recognised that Wolsey's hard work and undoubted ability would serve him well. There was no real competition. The ministers of Henry VII, such as Warham and Foxe, were ageing, happy to step back and focus on their roles in the Church. Of the nobility Henry's close friend Charles Brandon, now Duke of Suffolk, had no real political ambitions or ability, Edward Stafford, Duke of Buckingham, was never going to put in the work required, while Thomas Howard, Duke of Norfolk, by now entering his seventies, was dour and cautious, not well suited to serve the young king. His son, another Thomas, who succeeded him on his death in 1524, was at this stage regarded more as a military man, though he was appointed Lord Treasurer in 1522 and became a leading opponent of both Wolsey and later, Thomas Cromwell.

The shift in international alliances brought about by the peace with France had repercussions in Henry's personal life. Ever since his marriage Henry had valued his wife's advice. Catherine had always supported the Anglo-Spanish alliance but now Henry's anger with Ferdinand was such that his trust in her views was seriously damaged. Another problem also existed – there was still no heir to the throne. Catherine had suffered a miscarriage in January 1510. A son, Henry, was born on 1 January 1511 but had died before the end of February. There had then been a stillbirth in

September 1513 shortly before Henry's return from France. Although by August 1514 Catherine was pregnant again, the child was lost in December. In Spain this was put down to her grief over the anger that Henry directed towards her because of his difficulties with her father. It was perhaps no coincidence that at about this time Henry started to have serious flirtations and affairs. Jane Popincourt has already been mentioned and it was in 1514 that the young Elizabeth Blount joined the court as maid of honour to Catherine. Henry was soon to begin a lengthy affair with her.

What impact did all these events have on Duke Charles? From the age of 8 he had been betrothed to an English princess in line with the policies of his grandfathers, Ferdinand and Maximilian. This had not been his choice, but Margaret of Austria, his aunt and guardian, was in favour of the match and Mary was reputed to be intelligent, attractive and vivacious. Such were his expectations when he reached the age of 14, though he must have been aware that things could change. Nine months later, by the autumn of 1514, his prospective bride was married in France and his grandfathers were in dispute with Henry VIII. The rejection of their young hereditary ruler by the king of England and the failure of Margaret of Austria's pro-English policy had undermined her position in the Low Countries.

Chapter Four

New Rivalries

Events in January 1515 brought to the fore the two figures with whom Henry VIII would have to compete over the next thirty years if he wished to play a major role in European politics. Both were to control lands that had far greater human and financial resources than England. One made an immediate impact on the international scene. The other, younger, was yet to come into his full inheritance but it was recognised that when he did, few rulers would be able to act without some consideration of his possible reaction.

As it turned out Peter Martyr's words of October 1514 were prophetic. On 1 January 1515, after less than three months of marriage to Mary, Louis XII died, though probably because of severe gout rather than over-exertion in the bedchamber, though no-one doubted his efforts there. It is often claimed that Henry had promised his sister the chance to marry someone of her own choice when Louis died. Nevertheless, he would have wanted it to be a match that would bring political advantage. Another French marriage was suggested but Charles Brandon, newly created Duke of Suffolk, was sent to escort Mary back to England. It is likely that she was already in love with Brandon and the couple took the risk of marrying in France without Henry's permission before returning to England. At first Henry was furious, though he eventually came to accept the marriage between his favourite sister and his close friend, partly through the subtle advocacy of Wolsey to whom Suffolk had appealed for support.

Louis XII was succeeded by his much younger cousin and son-in-law, Francis of Angoulême, who became King Francis I (Plate 10). Here was another young monarch who saw himself as a model of courtly and chivalric behaviour, well-educated, a patron of the arts, courageous and charming, who would seek glory and honour. At his birth in 1494 it was unlikely that he would one day become one of France's most renowned monarchs. King Charles VIII, his third cousin, was only 24 years old, though as yet childless. On his early death in 1498, however, the crown passed to the older Louis XII, Francis's deceased father's cousin. Francis became heir presumptive and was married to Louis' daughter, Claude, in

1514. He had numerous affairs and it has been suggested that on Mary's arrival in France, he paid considerable attention to Louis' new wife. Mary rejected his advances even though they were probably more welcome than those of Louis. In any case Francis was apparently reminded by a friend and then more forcefully by his mother, Louise of Savoy, that if Mary were to become pregnant, he might remain a mere duke rather than become a king.[1] She did not and Louis' death brought the 20-year-old Francis to the throne. He encouraged the marriage of Mary and Charles Brandon, perhaps to stir up trouble and deprive Henry of the valuable possibility of another dynastic marriage for his sister. Three years younger than Henry VIII, Francis was now a rival with a similar glowing reputation and considerable ambitions.

Only a few days later on 5 January, the coming-of-age ceremony of Duke Charles of Burgundy was held in the Great Hall of the Coudenburg Palace in Brussels shortly before his fifteenth birthday. The influence of Maximilian and Margaret of Austria in the Low Countries had been weakened by the increasing antagonism of the Burgundian nobility, led by Chièvres. Maximilian had used the marriage of Charles's sisters in an attempt to strengthen his international position. In 1514 Mary, born in 1505, was sent to live in Vienna in preparation for a future marriage to Louis Jagiellon, the heir to the Hungarian throne, while Isabella, born in 1501, was married by proxy to King Christian II of Denmark and she was to move to Denmark the following year. The Burgundian nobility rightly believed that Maximilian was acting purely in the interests of his dynasty rather than for the benefit of the Low Countries. This belief was strengthened when Charles's marriage to Princess Mary fell through, partly, they believed because Maximilian had been secretly negotiating another match for him.

Whether this was true or not scarcely mattered. It was sufficient to further undermine any faith that the nobility had left in him or in his daughter Margaret. She reported to Maximilian that the States-General (the representative body of the provinces of the Low Countries) had refused to agree to the taxes she had requested because they claimed that Charles's minority was soon to end. The States-General then pressed Maximilian to bring forward Charles's coming of age and offered him 140,000 florins to agree. Much to Margaret's annoyance he did not consult her over his decision to accept. It was unlikely that he believed Charles was ready to rule, so his motives were almost certainly that he hoped to influence Charles's future decisions and, most importantly, he needed the money. Maximilian was known to be brave and caring towards his family, but he was an unreliable ally and always short of funds. As Wilhelm Wem, an Augsburg merchant, wrote of him: 'He was pious, not of great wit, and always poor. In his lands he had mortgaged many cities, castles, rents and rights.'

The ceremony in Brussels involved Frederick, Count Palatine, in place of the absent Maximilian, reading a formal declaration that Charles had come of age. The documents that gave Margaret her powers were torn up and their seals smashed, and the assembled nobility and representatives of the different provinces acclaimed Charles as their lord.[2] Maximilian had planned that Charles would then travel to join him in Innsbruck where he could be formally made heir to his Austrian lands. This, he hoped, would also mean that he would be able to control Charles and leave Margaret in charge of the Low Countries. Once it became clear that this was not going to happen, Maximilian wrote to Charles emphasising the need for him to follow Margaret's advice because of her close family ties. It was all too late. Charles's long-time chamberlain, Chièvres, and Jean Le Sauvage, who was appointed Grand Chancellor, had taken charge and they were to remain the most important influences over Charles until their deaths in 1521 and 1518 respectively. These years saw Charles come into his inheritance in Spain, and his election as Holy Roman Emperor.

Charles was invited to the coronation of Francis I in Rheims cathedral on 25 January 1515 but did not attend. He was advised that he should not be seen in a subservient position to the new French king. Instead, Henry of Nassau and Michel de Sempy were sent as his representatives. They negotiated an agreement with Francis over disputed border areas, promised to put pressure on Ferdinand to return Navarre to French control and discussed plans for Charles to marry Renée, second daughter of the former king, now that his marriage to Mary was no longer possible. By removing the threat of war, thus protecting trade, the settlement was popular in the Low Countries and it suited Francis because his real focus was on Italy. He recognised that the surest way of gaining the esteem of his people and restoring France's position in Europe was to regain Milan, lost by his predecessor to the Swiss Confederacy who had installed Maximilian Sforza as duke.

Francis lost no time. By July a French army, led by the king, was ready to move into Italy and by September it was advancing on Milan. A negotiated handover of the dukedom was agreed but the arrival of fresh Swiss troops led to renewed resistance. On 13–14 September they were defeated in the Battle of Marignano, 10 miles south-east of Milan, by the French and their Venetian allies, and the duke was captured. Their reputation as the finest troops in Europe never fully recovered. Francis could now make good one of the titles he took at his coronation – Duke of Milan. The victory won him the renown that he so much desired and Henry VIII's exploits at Tournai were overshadowed. In December 1515 Francis met Pope Leo in Bologna and agreed a Concordat giving Francis the right to nominate all major church appointments in France. Although the Pope did not like the French domination of northern Italy, and had created Wolsey a cardinal partly to encourage English opposition, he recognised that for the moment Francis's star was in the ascendant.

With their French alliance effectively at an end on the death of Louis XII, Henry VIII and Wolsey were doing everything in their power, short of going to war, to weaken the French position so that when they eventually came back to the negotiating table, they would be more willing to make concessions.[3] English ambassadors Richard Pace and Robert Wingfield encouraged Emperor Maximilian and the Swiss by providing them with substantial funds to retake Milan. However, in March 1516, just when success looked possible, Maximilian withdrew his troops – Venice was his real enemy, not the French. Once again, he had proved an unreliable ally.

Everything seemed to be working out for the French king. His success in Milan had been followed in January 1516 by the death of that long-term enemy of France, Ferdinand of Aragon, opening up the possibility of Francis making good his claim to the throne of Naples and control of southern Italy. This had been disputed between Aragon and France for many years though the French defeat at the Battle of Cerignola in 1503 had left it under Ferdinand's control. His death also meant that his grandson, Charles, would at some point need to travel to Spain in order to be acknowledged as king in Castile, Aragon, Catalonia and Valencia. As a first step Charles's former tutor, Adrian of Utrecht, was sent to Spain to represent his interests. But before Charles could travel, peace would be needed, both to protect the Low Countries from attack and to ensure a safe voyage.

In April 1516 English diplomats in Brussels signed a treaty of peace and friendship that promised to send help if the Low Countries were attacked, sorted out remaining trade issues and assured Charles that he could be sure of a friendly welcome in England if his fleet should require a safe harbour on its voyage to Spain. Charles and his advisers also needed an agreement with France. In the Treaty of Noyon of August 1516, his negotiators made concessions to Francis in return for a French promise not to assist Charles's enemies in the Low Countries, namely Charles of Egmond, Duke of Guelders, long a thorn in the side of the Dukes of Burgundy. Charles was to marry Francis's own infant daughter, Claude, instead of Princess Renée, and pay 100,000 crowns a year until the marriage in recognition of Francis's claim to the kingdom of Naples. He also promised to restore Francis's ally, John of Navarre, to his lands within eight months of arriving in Spain.

The generally pro-French Chièvres and Sauvage, sometimes referred to as 'the regents', who negotiated the treaty were obviously putting the needs of the Low Countries ahead of any wider dynastic considerations. Just how realistic were the terms of the treaty? The idea of Charles marrying Claude, fifteen years his junior, meant that he would not produce an heir until the 1530s and this would be unacceptable in Spain, as was the return of Navarre. Indeed, Cardinal Cisneros, the governor of Castile until Charles's arrival, believed that far too much had been conceded, taking his lead from Ferdinand's belief that 'The nature of the French is never to keep any part of the promises they make, except to the extent that they are forced to.' In a 'Memoir on the Last Acts and Intentions of King Ferdinand the Catholic' it was written that the king 'knew by long experience that the French always have disturbed and will disturb the peace of Christendom ... that they are striving to render themselves masters first of Italy, and then of the whole world.'[4] The Bishop of Badajos wrote to Cisneros that although 'the Prince [Charles] had good parts ... he knows too little of Spaniards. He does not understand a word of Spanish. He obeys his councillors implicitly.'[5] He went on to raise concerns that Chièvres and Charles's other advisers were not only pro-French but that they would sell offices of state and appoint non-Spaniards. He believed that the king of England who 'has behaved as a trusty friend' would be a more reliable ally.

The Treaty of Noyon was a major blow to English hopes of constructing an anti-French agreement, though they held Chièvres and Sauvage rather than Charles to be responsible. It made it difficult for Henry and Wolsey to use the threat of an alliance with Charles to put pressure on Francis. English diplomats in Mechelen wrote to Henry VIII early in 1517 that the treaty meant 'the prince of the greatest inheritance for the last 500 years would be at the beck of France; the natural authority of the Emperor and his daughter overshadowed, the French established in Italy, and France would attain the crown of the empire.'[6] To make matters worse for Henry, having provided more money for Maximilian's campaigns in northern Italy, the emperor opened negotiations with the French in December 1516 and in the Treaty of Brussels he acknowledged French control of Milan and Venetian claims in Lombardy.

Maximilian viewed things differently, demonstrating not just his own but perhaps the prevailing attitude towards international treaties. He accepted 40,000 florins (£6,500) from Henry to assist England's interests, 60,000 from the French to join the Treaty of Noyon and 20,000 from Venice to hand over Verona, which he had been committed to defending![7] Ambassador William Knight reported to Wolsey in February 1517 that the emperor had told his grandson, Charles, 'My son, you are going to cheat the French, and I am going to cheat the English', thus implying that Charles would ignore the terms agreed at Noyon while he would take English money and do nothing. Knight's opinion of Maximilian was clear. He asked Wolsey: 'Thinketh your grace that the Emperor, being always prodigal, and consequently in necessity and need … will keep any promise that he hath or shall make unto the King?'[8] He went on to advise Wolsey to forget about building an anti-French alliance. A meeting between Henry and Charles would be of little value because any agreement would be over-ruled by Chièvres and the money involved would be better spent on either attacking Scotland, which since 1515 had been ruled by a pro-French regency, or strengthening Tournai.

What now became important to all sides was Charles's journey to Spain. The regents wished to make sure that Charles took power in Spain thereby making it possible for them and their supporters to take advantage of some of the rich pickings to be had. Maximilian hoped that by Charles taking Chièvres and Sauvage with him to Spain, he and Margaret could once again control the Low Countries. Wolsey calculated that once in Spain Charles would be more likely to return to Ferdinand's anti-French policy, the influence of Chièvres and Sauvage would be reduced and the terms agreed at Noyon ignored. He hoped to use the threat of assisting Charles's voyage to Spain to gain concessions from the French. When, in July 1517, a delegation from the Low Countries, led by James of Luxemburg (Chièvres' son-in-law and a close friend of Charles), arrived in London to persuade Henry to provide funds and naval assistance for Charles's voyage, they were pushing at an open door. They were received with great pomp, though it has been suggested that the ceremonials were as much to impress the French ambassador as it was the Burgundians.[9] Henry loaned Charles 100,000 gold florins to be repaid over three years.[10]

Charles eventually sailed to Spain in September 1517 having promised to return within four years and that he would send his brother Ferdinand, born in 1503 and brought up in Spain, to the Low Countries. He was already facing the problem that was to be a major issue throughout his nearly forty years in power: how to meet the conflicting demands of the numerous territories that he ruled. He was leaving the Low Countries of his birth for the first time, heading for a land whose language he did not speak and whose customs would be unfamiliar. On the voyage itself there were the dangers of shipwreck, disease and even the threat of privateers if a vessel were to be isolated from the fleet. Charles was at first seasick, saw two ships destroyed by fire and then, in a major storm, the fleet of forty vessels was scattered, with Charles landing well to the west of Santander the intended destination. A few years later the Polish ambassador to Charles, Dantiscus, on describing a similar voyage to Spain, wrote: 'If I were to gain the empire of the world for the price of that voyage, I should never again enter upon such a perilous venture.'

The risks and hardships of journeys by sea and land were to become part of Charles's life. It has been estimated that over the next forty years he spent one day in four travelling, sometimes within his territories but often on long journeys between them. As he reminisced in 1555, he had been to Germany nine times, Spain six, Italy seven, the Low Countries ten, four times to France, twice to England and twice to Africa. He had sailed on the Atlantic Ocean on three occasions and on the Mediterranean ten times. Travel by land was safer than by sea, given his large escorts, but it was usually slow. In 1530 he spent two months travelling from Bologna to Innsbruck, while his return to Spain from Vienna in 1532–33 took almost six months. Henry VIII might have moved regularly between his palaces – Greenwich, Whitehall, Richmond, and his smaller hunting lodges, mainly in the south of England – but his occasional forays further north and across the Channel to northern France were very limited in comparison.

There was no guarantee of a friendly welcome when arriving in a foreign land, even as the new monarch. On the coast of Spain, the local inhabitants at first thought that Charles and his entourage were pirates and fled to the safety of the mountains. Most people across Europe were at best suspicious and at worst openly hostile towards outsiders. In remote rural regions, that could mean those from another valley and in more populated urban areas, it was those who used a different language. Foreign merchants were often blamed for unemployment and hardship amongst the local people, such as in London on 'Evil May Day' 1517. Ignoring a curfew ordered by Wolsey, a mob of apprentices, carters, watermen and others rampaged through the streets attacking foreigners and destroying their shops and business premises in St Martin's-le-Grand, Cornhill and Whitechapel.[11] As in all such riots there was the danger of the violence spreading. Troops had to be sent in to restore order. At the time Henry was out of London, first at Richmond and later at Greenwich, having left the capital when a major epidemic of sweating sickness broke out earlier in the spring.

Charles had to face different problems. He needed to be recognised by the cortes (representative assemblies) of the various Spanish kingdoms, all of whom were keen to preserve and possibly extend their traditional rights and freedoms vis-à-vis the king's power. The negotiations in Castile and Aragon each took many months. There was no doubt as to his right to the throne, although Charles's advisers in Castile were careful to announce that he was the joint monarch with his mother, Juana, still in Tordesillas, popular though unable to rule. The Spanish were understandably wary of this new, inexperienced king. They feared that they might be of secondary importance to a ruler whose main interests were elsewhere. There was even talk that his younger brother Ferdinand would be a more suitable monarch having been brought up in Spain, though after amicable meetings between the brothers, Ferdinand was sent off as planned to the Low Countries. They particularly resented the influence of Charles's Burgundian advisers, especially when they began to be appointed to prestigious and lucrative posts, both secular and religious. Given the need to establish himself in Spain it suited Charles and his advisers to have peace and not to immediately challenge the terms they had agreed at Noyon.

England was therefore diplomatically isolated, especially after the signing of a defensive alliance between Francis, Maximilian and Charles in March 1517. Wolsey was not going to achieve success for Henry VIII by war against France, so it increasingly made sense to come to terms with Francis. The gains that he had made in Italy were of no major concern to England and talks started later in 1517. Meanwhile Pope Leo revived a plan calling for a five-year truce amongst the Christian states of Europe in order to launch a crusade against the Ottoman Turks: 'It is time that we woke from sleep lest we be put to the sword unawares.' Sultan Selim had recently achieved great victories in Egypt and the Middle East, taking control of Palestine. The Ottoman Empire had captured Constantinople in 1452 and already included much of the Balkans. It could now pose a real threat to central Europe and the whole of the eastern Mediterranean. In March 1518 Leo published his plan, which involved the arbitration of any existing disputes between European powers, and then sent legates across Europe to win approval for it.

England, however, refused entry to Cardinal Campeggio until Leo awarded Wolsey legatine powers equal to those of Campeggio. Wolsey then sidelined his fellow legate and used his new authority to take over the international negotiations. If glory could not be achieved by war, then it might be attained through peace. In October 1518 the Treaty of London was signed by all the major rulers – Pope Leo, Francis, Maximilian, Charles and Henry – and many lesser ones. It stated that it was the 'duty of all Christian princes to postpone their disputes with one another, and to defend the Holy Church and the Christian religion.' All members were to be 'friends of the friends, and foes of the foes' of any other member.[12] They pledged to avoid war, not to hire foreign troops or provide protection to rebels, and to act swiftly against any who broke the agreement, with a commitment to defend Europe against the Ottoman threat. Both Henry and Wolsey received the plaudits as the peacemakers of Europe. Bringing peace to a war-weary continent could win as much respect as military victory in the eyes of many, especially those humanist writers who had influenced the education of the young monarchs. Pope Leo, on the other hand, considered that his initiative had been hijacked, leaving only the promise of future action against the Turks. His cousin and adviser, Guilio de' Medici, commented 'from this we can see what the Holy See and the Pope have to expect from the English Chancellor.'[13]

Henry and Francis then ratified the treaty that had been agreed during the summer. Tournai was to be returned to France on the payment of an annual sum of £5,000, and the existing pension of £10,000 per annum received by England from France was to be continued. Wolsey received a considerable amount, £1,200 a year, as compensation for the loss of the see of Tournai (from which he had failed to receive much when bishop), and Francis would end French support for the anti-English party in Scotland by preventing the Duke of Albany's return.[14] In addition Henry's daughter Mary, born in 1516, was to be betrothed to Francis, the first son of the French king born in February 1518. Both sides declared their wish for the kings to meet and this was initially planned for 1519. Peace had been achieved on terms that at first glance looked favourable to England. However, far more than these sums had been spent by the English on the campaign of 1513 (over £600,000), on garrisoning Tournai between 1514 and 1518 (£176,000) and the construction of a citadel there (£50,000)[15], even though a small amount had been extracted from its citizens. This, though, is to miss the point. The capture of Tournai had been both an important symbol, showing that England under Henry VIII was a force to be reckoned with, and a powerful negotiating counter, because since his accession Francis had been very keen to restore it to French control.

By the end of 1518 Charles had become the ruler of all the Spanish kingdoms and with increasing maturity was bound to become a more significant figure in his own right. Peace, or at least the promise of peace, had been established across Christendom on terms that were generally favourable to Francis I. Henry VIII was widely recognised as one of the leading European monarchs, with his status enhanced by the peace, which was considerably cheaper than doing so by war. No-one believed that this situation would remain completely unchanged for the five years of the agreement, but few expected events to cause such a rapid transformation over the next couple of years.

Chapter Five

The Imperial Election and Royal Meetings

What changed the situation was the death on 12 January 1519 of Charles's grandfather, Emperor Maximilian at the age of 59. Only three months after signing the Treaty of London as king of Spain, Charles now inherited the hereditary Habsburg lands in central Europe as Archduke of Austria. However, as the Imperial crown was not hereditary but elective, it was more than likely that there would now be a bitter contest to become emperor. The Holy Roman Empire was already an ancient institution, founded when Charlemagne was crowned in Rome by Pope Leo III on Christmas Day 800 CE. It was anything but a unified state. It consisted of over 300 independent principalities, duchies, free imperial cities and other areas ruled over by dukes, counts, margraves, archbishops, bishops and city councils. Its territory included most of the present-day states of Germany, Austria, Switzerland, Liechtenstein, the Czech Republic, Slovakia, Slovenia, the Netherlands, Belgium, northern Italy (excluding Venice), western Poland and eastern France (Alsace, Lorraine, Franche-Comté and Savoy).

The emperor was recognised as the supreme judge in law, bestowed titles and determined items for discussion at the Imperial Diets. These were meetings of the rulers within the Empire, divided into three 'estates', the prince-electors, other ecclesiastical and secular princes, and the imperial cities. In return the emperor was expected to protect the Empire from invasion and uphold the traditional rights of the states. However, it was difficult to enforce any decisions made at a Diet since there was no permanent army and no effective Empire-wide system of taxation. The emperor was often in dispute with other princes of the Empire over territorial claims and about the resources that he could call upon. Each ruler wished to have greater independence from Imperial power and yet still have the security that unity provided against external enemies.

Any emperor had to deal with these numerous problems, but the title was regarded as the highest honour that a Christian ruler could receive, one of the twin pillars of Christendom alongside the Pope. For hundreds of years the emperor had been elected by the prince-electors, of whom in 1519 there were seven: the archbishops of Mainz, Cologne and Trier, the king of Bohemia, the Duke of Saxony, the Margrave of Brandenburg, and the Count Palatine of the Rhine. Once elected, the term 'king of the Romans' was used until such time as there could be a coronation by the Pope, though Maximilian had never been able to go to Rome and so he had been given the title 'emperor-elect'. From then on, those elected were called 'emperor' and if during their lifetime a successor was chosen, they would be referred to as 'king of the Romans'.

Maximilian had attempted to get Charles so elected, and spent a considerable amount on bribes in the process, but no election had taken place. Although the Habsburg family had held the imperial crown for two generations, Maximilian's death meant that an election could no longer be avoided. This was likely to upset the new veneer of unity across Europe. Charles's heritage and upbringing convinced him that it was his destiny to be 'God's standard-bearer', to defend Europe from the external threat of 'the Turk' and against heresy within. When it was suggested that, given all his other responsibilities, he might give way to his brother Ferdinand, he forcefully argued that such a division of power was exactly what the French wanted. He wrote at length from Spain to Margaret of Austria, stating that he had most to offer because the extent of his lands would provide him with greater resources to fulfil the role. He believed that once elected he would be able to 'accomplish many good and great things, and not only conserve and guard the possessions which God has given us, but to increase them greatly and, in this way, give peace, repose and tranquillity to Christendom.' He made clear that 'there is nothing in this world we want more' as his reputation and honour depended on it.

He was not the only contender. Francis wished to extend his title of 'Most Christian King' and take the Imperial crown. He would then be seen as the premier ruler in Europe and prevent the spread of Habsburg influence. Henry VIII certainly did not wish to see Francis as emperor and would rather not have Charles either, so a third candidate would be preferable. Why not the king of England? Some at home warned against Henry's involvement, arguing that if he became emperor this would mean that England must be part of the Holy Roman Empire, which it never had been, and that could have serious implications in the future, since after Henry's death another, foreign, emperor would be elected. Nevertheless, Henry wished to be seen as a candidate alongside his rival monarchs, or at least to force a stalemate or perhaps both. Richard Pace was sent to canvas the prince-electors and push Henry's case, although he was never supplied with the diplomatic or financial powers to have much impact.[1] Failing his own unlikely victory, Henry, like the Pope, would have preferred one of the prince-electors themselves to take the throne so as to prevent either Charles or Francis becoming too dominant. Duke Frederick III (the Wise) of Saxony was the most obvious candidate but, in the end, he declined to put his name forward.

Francis argued that it was undesirable for one family to be repeatedly elected and that Charles would end up with so much power that he would be a threat to the German princes. He was encouraged by some of the electors. As early as 1516 he believed that he had won the support of the archbishops of Trier and Mainz in any future election, and, by June 1517, two of the secular electors had also indicated their backing. However, they had a vested interest in a contested election so as to be able to take bribes from all sides. Francis also believed that there was an indication of papal support, but as the Florentine diplomat Francesco Guicciardini wrote, he 'deceived himself more every day' since Pope Leo did not wish to see a further extension of French influence in Italy. Charles's campaign was carried out by his representatives in Germany and the Low Countries, co-ordinated by Margaret of Austria. His propaganda argued that having a 'non-German' emperor, such as Francis or Henry, was against custom and would not be tolerated by the majority of rulers within the Empire. Charles was presented as the 'national candidate', despite the fact that he had yet to learn to speak German or even visit Habsburg lands in the Empire. It was emphasised that only he had the resources to defend the Empire against Ottoman incursions and had an interest in doing so given his land holdings in Austria.

But what mattered most in this election was money. None of the candidates had sufficient ready cash but Charles had access to loans from the Fugger and the Welser banking houses of Augsburg. Wolff Haller, the Fugger agent in Antwerp, already known to Charles, travelled to Spain to negotiate with him. In total Charles spent 835,000 florins on the election, of which 65 per cent came from the Fuggers. Francis could not match that level of spending. When the electors met in Frankfurt on 28 June 1519, a combination of greed, ambition, fear and genuine support resulted in a unanimous vote for Charles. Four years later Jacob Fugger, when writing to Charles to complain about the failure to repay loans, reminded him that: 'It is well known that Your Imperial Majesty could not have gained the Roman Crown save with mine aid.'

Besides not becoming emperor, which had never been a realistic expectation, why did this matter to Henry VIII and England? Although both Henry and Francis congratulated Charles on his victory, with Henry reminding him of the traditional friendship between England and the Low Countries, the truth was that the level of rivalry between the monarchs had been heightened. Antonio Giustinian, the Venetian ambassador to France, summed it up very well: 'These sovereigns are not at peace; they adapt themselves to circumstance, but hate each other very cordially.' What was claimed by Charles to be his duty and destiny was regarded by others as naked ambition, the furtherance of his power and that of his dynasty. Mercurino Gattinara, soon to become Charles's chief adviser after the death of Chièvres in 1521, wrote to him that 'God has by His grace elevated you above all other Christian kings and princes ... you are on the road to Universal Monarchy and on the point of uniting Christendom under a single shepherd.' This was hardly to be welcomed by other monarchs even though what this really meant was a universal peace within Christendom, such as had just been achieved by the Treaty of London, not an attempt to recreate the ancient Roman Empire.

On the broader canvas it was a matter of geopolitics. While hardly needing to worry about an invasion by the Ottoman Empire as some areas of Europe did, England had its own concerns. Traditionally Scotland was the natural ally of France when it was at war against England, forcing the English to have some troops ready to repel an invasion from the north. This, in turn, meant that England often allied itself to Spain so that France's southern border could be threatened in the same way. Charles's election as emperor meant that France was now in danger of being surrounded by Habsburg territories, with Charles ruling in Spain, Germany and the Low Countries. While he held Milan, Francis was not completely hemmed in but he knew that Charles had ambitions there too. Even though France had the advantage of being a single, more unified, state compared with Charles's diverse lands, Francis I could never willingly accept this situation. He would always be looking for ways to undermine Charles's control of these lands. There were opportunities that might be exploited in several areas. Duke Charles of Guelders could usually be encouraged to oppose Habsburg dominance of the Low Countries. Many German princes would have disputes with the new emperor, the more so once the unity of the Roman Church broke down. Charles was also having trouble establishing his authority in parts of Spain, which resulted in open rebellion in 1520.

But whatever their problems these two major powers had resources considerably greater than those available to Henry VIII. For a king who wished to stand alongside Francis and Charles as an equal, this fact posed a major problem. England's population of approximately 3 million was small compared with France's 15 million. Charles's territories included populations of 8 million in Spain, 2.5 million in the Low Countries and perhaps upward of 20 million in the Holy Roman Empire, although the Empire, given its structure, was difficult to tax and unreliable in terms of raising troops without considerable expenditure. In other words, England was one of the most important of the lesser states, so it needed to over-achieve in the international sphere if Henry's ambitions were to be realised. Previously, when a greater number of smaller rather more equal states were involved in European diplomacy, England could look to build broad alliances. Charles's election meant that a Habsburg-Valois conflict was likely sooner rather than later and that it might continue intermittently for many years. For Henry VIII and England this provided both opportunities and problems.

The major benefit was that the ongoing enmity between Charles and Francis meant that both would wish to have England's support. The question then became who to back? Henry could hold out for significant concessions on England's other foreign policy priorities, promising to support the highest bidder. On the other hand, there was the question of the balance of power. While the advantage was with neither side, England's position was strong. When it became imbalanced the weaker of the two sides was likely to offer most for England's support. However, by backing this weaker side England would run the risk of facing defeat and finding itself in the difficult position of being confronted by a very powerful enemy. There was one other consideration. England's location as an island on the north-western edge of Europe, but with a base in Calais, meant that it was possible to mount an invasion of France. To invade Charles's more distant lands in Spain or the Empire was beyond Henry's resources, and conflict with the nearby Low Countries would be very damaging to the nation's trade and therefore unpopular at home. A delicate, subtle handling of foreign policy was going to be required.

Those are not characteristics usually associated with Henry VIII but his often remarked on inability to make a rapid decision was sometimes beneficial. In a quickly changing diplomatic situation, so long as national security was not in immediate danger, the waiting game often paid dividends. It certainly made it possible to time one's intervention so as to achieve the maximum advantage. There is no doubt that Henry enjoyed grandiose plans but they were always tempered by a reality that came from his chief ministers, first Wolsey and then Thomas Cromwell, and his wider council. It had taken him four years as king before he led his first expedition to France in 1513. English armies only did so twice again in the remaining thirty-four years of the reign – in 1523 led by the Duke of Suffolk and in

1544 led by the king. It has been convincingly argued that given the unstable nature of English politics and the changeable and unpredictable world of Habsburg-Valois rivalry in Europe, Henry's 'foreign policy' was more a case of implementing short-term tactics rather than following a long-term strategic plan.[2] For much of the time Henry's relations with foreign powers, even with the marital and religious crises that were influential factors for considerable periods, consisted of attempting to capitalise on the problems of other rulers and, most of all, ensuring that the two great powers, Emperor Charles V and King Francis I, did not make common cause against England.

This had seemed a possibility after 1515 with many rulers coming to terms with a victorious Francis and Charles's advisers taking a pro-French stance. However, the active diplomacy of England's representatives abroad, together with the Pope's call for a general peace and the signing of the Treaty of London prevented it. The new circumstances after Charles's election victory meant that there was little chance of Charles and Francis working together and that the peace was unlikely to hold for long. A new round of negotiations would soon have to take place, with England being pushed into a position of having to choose between the emperor and the French king. Henry and his minister had no intention of making an impulsive, rushed decision. Rather they intended to maximise the prestige to be gained from being 'honest brokers', to keep their options open and then to benefit from any concessions to be had from their eventual ally.

There was one other practical impact of Charles's election as emperor. He would need to travel to the Empire for his enthronement in the cathedral of Aachen (Aix-la-Chapelle). Just as his subjects in the Low Countries had not wished him to depart for Spain back in 1517, now his Spanish subjects objected to him leaving the country. They extracted a promise that he would return within three years. When he needed money for the voyage, they were very reluctant to grant it (in fact, it was never collected) and his appointment of Adrian of Utrecht as regent in his absence provoked outrage, as it broke the promise Charles had made earlier not to make foreign appointments.

When he sailed from Spain in May 1520, he left a country that was about to experience a serious challenge to royal authority. Since 1519 there had been protests and riots in Valencia resulting from existing social and religious tensions. The following year, open revolt broke out there and in Castile, where many major cities, such as Toledo, Salamanca and Segovia, refused to send representatives to the cortes or to pay new taxes, and expelled (and in Segovia lynched) their corregidor (royal representative). The rebels even captured Tordesillas and set up a rival government in the name of Queen Juana. It was not until 1521 after timely concessions had split the rebels that they were defeated and the situation was brought under control. Charles wrote in 1529 that because of his youth, inexperience and over-reliance on Lord Chièvres, he had 'spent very little time here [in Spain] and ... being unmarried and without an heir, it is not surprising that there was scandal and disturbance.'

Charles must have been well aware that preparations for the delayed meeting between Henry and Francis had been under way since February. This concerned him. A closer understanding between Henry and Francis would almost certainly be to his disadvantage. Shortly before his departure from Spain, a treaty was signed with Henry VIII agreeing that Charles would land in England on his way to the Low Countries. He would be met by Henry and Catherine of Aragon 'who has the most ardent desire to see the king of the Romans, her nephew' and they would travel together to Canterbury for a short stay.[3] Later, in July, there was to be a second meeting 'in a place half-way between Calais and Gravelines' at which Charles would be accompanied by 'Madame Margaret', his aunt, and Henry, once again, by Catherine. It was written into the terms that both sides would be 'unarmed, except for the usual guards of each of the Kings. Both the Kings will have an equal number of followers.' It was also agreed that Charles would send 'five well-armed vessels' to cruise between Spain and Southampton and Henry five vessels cruising between Southampton and Flanders, 'to protect the lives and goods of merchants against the attacks of pirates and enemies.'

Charles's voyage across the Bay of Biscay and along the Channel was less eventful than his earlier one to Spain. On 26 May he was met by Cardinal Wolsey at Dover where they spent the night in the castle. Henry rode from Canterbury to greet Charles early the next morning. They returned to Canterbury and were given a rousing welcome by the people of the city. The monarchs celebrated Mass and prayed at the shrine of St Thomas Becket, after which Catherine was delighted to meet her nephew at the Archbishop's Palace. Henry, Catherine, Charles and Mary, now Duchess of Suffolk, dined privately, served by England's highest nobility. The evening banquet was a much larger affair which, as so often with Henry, ended with dancing into the early hours, though Charles, rarely one for being the life and soul of the party, remained at the table. Nevertheless, he wished to please his hosts – he wanted an alliance with Henry, or at least to prevent an Anglo-French treaty. A day of talks followed, during which it was confirmed that the second meeting would take place in July.

This was important. Henry had been at Canterbury because he was on his way to the meeting with Francis outside Calais, between English-held Guînes and French-controlled Ardres, at what became known as the Field of Cloth of Gold. Had Charles arrived in England just a few days later he might have missed the king altogether. The meeting of Henry and Francis was to become one of the most written about events of the sixteenth century. The organisation, led for Henry by the Earl of Worcester and for Francis by Gaspard de Coligny, took over four months. The numbers who attended were enormous. Each monarch had an entourage of around 6,000, ranging from the highest nobles to the most humble of servants, from the secular and spiritual leaders of their countries to those that fed their horses and cleaned their clothes.[4] The English contingent of almost 1,000 'persons of substance' and 5,000 servants of various sorts crossed from Dover in a large fleet that included the *Mary Rose* and *Henry, Grace à Dieu*. The costs for both countries were vast. It has been estimated that Henry spent a total of £36,000 on this meeting, more than the usual costs of the royal household for a year.[5]

This was the coming together of international relations and conspicuous consumption. Immediately outside Guînes and linked to the castle by a covered walkway, a temporary palace, measuring 100m square, was built for Henry. Its walls were made of brick to the height of over 2m and above that of wood and painted cloth taking it to almost 10m. Its sloping roof was of oiled canvas painted to look like slate.[6] There was splendid decoration throughout. Enormous pavilions were erected for the elaborate entertainments and a field was prepared for a tournament, including combat on foot and, most importantly, the jousting in which the kings would take a leading role. The whole extravaganza, lasting over two weeks in June, with its declarations of mutual friendship, has often been regarded as an expensive exercise in one-upmanship and deception. After all England and France were at war within two years. However, it was genuinely intended to be a celebration of the Universal Peace declared in London, as well as a chance to impress attending ambassadors who would report back to their masters. Although the monarchs were undoubtedly rivals and potential enemies, there was also a degree of admiration and bonding between them that was not completely false. The banquets and jousts were both signals of friendship and indications of the other's power. Peace with honour was a chivalric ideal that both recognised.[7] But the fact remains that in terms of concrete outcomes, rather more was achieved in Henry's lower key meetings with Charles than at the much-vaunted Field of Cloth of Gold.

While Henry, like Francis, was no doubt enjoying his chance to display his jousting skills, courtly charms and his ability to entertain his guests, Charles was visiting Ghent and Brussels. It had been arranged that Henry would meet him at Gravelines on 4 July, but in late June it was suggested to

Henry that the meeting should be moved to Bruges, as it had more suitable accommodation. This was angrily rejected by the English since it suggested that Charles's business with his German and Flemish visitors was more important than that with Henry. In the end Wolsey met for discussions with Chièvres and Gattinara. These talks involved identifying what each side considered possible and clearing up misunderstandings before the formal meeting of the monarchs. The emperor's advisers were keen to tempt Wolsey to favour a close alliance, offering to replace his French pensions with ones of their own.

Although rather later than intended, on 10 July Henry and Catherine rode to meet Charles at Gravelines and the next day Charles, accompanied by Margaret of Austria, returned to Calais with them. Although the planned banquet under canvas was disrupted by strong winds, good terms were established. Notes on the treaty signed on 14 July comment that the time available to Henry and Charles had been limited and therefore not all matters of importance had been covered, but they agreed that neither would 'within the space of two years, conclude any treaty with the King of France concerning marriage or other affairs.' They also stated that they would hold a congress in Calais within two years 'to confer on their future line of policy and decide what measures are most advantageous to them.' A 'permanent and standing embassy' was to be established at each other's court and it was confirmed that they would assist each other if their 'dominions are invaded by an enemy.'[8]

However, this was not the full Anglo-Imperial alliance that Charles had wished for. It did not require Henry to break any existing agreements with France, just not to extend them. England already had a permanent ambassador at the French court so the arrangement with Charles was just a matter of catching up. Furthermore, two years seems a long time before another meeting. This provided plenty of scope for Henry to adapt to any changes in the diplomatic situation that occurred in the meantime. While it is often asserted that by mid-1520, Henry knew that he would eventually end up in an anti-French alliance with Charles, the outcome of these royal meetings seems to be much less clear-cut. England had retained some room for manoeuvre.

Chapter Six

Taking Sides

Henry now had treaties with both Charles and Francis, as well as a vested interest in maintaining the peace of Europe as established by the Treaty of London. As a sign of good faith and to show that there had been no anti-French alliance, Henry instructed his ambassador to France to give a full account of the negotiations that had been held with Charles at Calais. This was also intended to show Francis that England had other options available if he did not keep the peace. Henry's problem was that if either of the two major powers decided to challenge the status quo, England's position would be severely tested, perhaps to breaking point.

After his meeting with Henry, Charles spent some time in the Low Countries. While there he received the first Aztec treasures dispatched by Hernando Cortes from Mexico, which had been sent on from Spain. They were displayed in Brussels Town Hall and Albrecht Dürer was one of many to see them. He wrote: 'I saw the things which have been brought to the King from the new land of gold, a sun all of gold a whole fathom broad, and a moon all of silver of the same size, also two rooms full of armour of the people there, all manner of wondrous weapons … very strange clothing, beds, and all kinds of wonderful objects of human use. All the days of my life I have seen nothing that rejoiced my heart so much.'[1] These were the first of many valuables followed by large quantities of bullion that Charles received from Mexico and, later, Peru during the course of his reign. As the king of Castile, he was due one-fifth – the Quintus – of all the wealth generated and plundered from his lands in the New World. By the 1540s the value of these shipments and the loans taken out using them as collateral made a significant contribution to Charles's always-troubled finances.

In the autumn he moved south to Aachen, arriving on 22 October. He took the coronation oath that evening and was crowned by the Archbishop of Cologne in the cathedral the following morning. He was accompanied by the electors, princes and noblemen from throughout his realms. Though personally less extrovert than his fellow monarchs, Charles too knew the importance of pomp and ceremony. Albrecht Dürer, who had followed the royal progress to Aachen, 'saw all manner of lordly splendour, the like of which those who live in our parts have never seen.'[2] Three days later the official blessing of Pope Leo X arrived, giving Charles the right to use the title 'elected Roman Emperor'. Leo wrote to him that: 'As there are two luminaries in the heavens, the sun and the moon, which outshine all the stars, so are there two great dignitaries on earth, the Pope and the Emperor, to whom all other princes are subordinates and owe obedience.'[3] While this kind of statement might have concerned Charles's fellow rulers, they probably recognised it for what it was. Such high-flown language rarely matched reality. Charles's relations with the five Popes of his reign were often fractious.[4] He was always careful to treat them with the respect that their position warranted, but he was frequently critical of their putting personal and family ambitions before the good of Christendom and their lack of trustworthiness in the political sphere.

Francis feared that Charles's elevation would encourage him to challenge for control of Milan and resist French plans to take Naples. He rightly understood that the longer he left it before he made his move against his rival, the stronger Charles was likely to become. He still felt that he had the upper hand, saying of Charles in 1519 that 'he is young and has no practical experience of war', whereas Francis himself had already led a victorious campaign to capture Milan. Also, in 1516, Charles had agreed to the Treaty of Noyon, very much to Francis's advantage. But if Francis expected the same response over four years later, he was very much mistaken. Charles believed that his honour depended on protecting his territories and handing over his inheritance to his successor undiminished; he was prepared to go to war to do so.

Peace ended in early 1521. Seeking to take advantage of the uprisings in Charles's Spanish lands, Francis encouraged his allies to take military action in support of their claims against Charles, hoping to distract his attention from Italy. Robert de la Marck, Duke of Bouillon and Lord of Sedan attacked in Luxembourg; Henry d'Albret invaded Navarre in an attempt to regain his family's lands; and Duke Charles of Guelders supported a rebellion in Friesland. The emperor reacted aggressively, probably the more so because of the deaths of his generally pro-French advisers, Sauvage and Chièvres. He also needed to end any perception that Francis or others still might have of his personal or political weakness.

Although Charles himself did not take to the field of battle, his commanders demonstrated that they had the wherewithal to defend his positions and then to launch counter-attacks. At first Henry d'Albret and his French allies successfully occupied Navarre but when they advanced further south, they were decisively defeated by Spanish troops at the Battle of Noáin, near

Pamplona. Robert de la Marck was repulsed in Luxembourg by troops commanded by Henry of Nassau, who went on to besiege and capture Tournai in December 1521. The city, recently returned to the French after its capture by Henry VIII in 1513, was never again to be under French control.

From the start both sides claimed that they were the subject of unprovoked attacks and requested England's backing under the terms of the Universal Peace. In March Charles suggested an offensive alliance against France, with the offer to marry Princess Mary, Henry's 4-year-old daughter already betrothed to Francis's infant son, when she came of age. The terms were rejected by the English, largely on financial grounds, not on principle. This supports the idea that Henry's foreign policy was usually about 'honour and profit', where profit might be a gain in either prestige or money. Charles's offer was also reported to Francis, hardly an action that would have been taken if England was already a confirmed ally of the emperor. Cuthbert Tunstall, Henry's negotiator (later to be Lord Privy Seal and Bishop of Durham) was also instructed to point out to Charles that an Anglo-French alliance, by controlling both the Channel and Milan, could block the communications between Charles's various lands. The rejection of Charles's initial proposal did not, however, mean that England would side with France. Wolsey advised Henry not to be rushed into the war and proposed a conference be held in Calais to restore peace, with him acting as arbiter. Charles accepted this plan, but Francis at first refused until June when things started to go wrong for the French.

As talks continued with Charles's representatives, it was to prove very useful for Wolsey to keep open both his role as peacemaker and the possibility of an alliance with Francis in order to put pressure on Charles to offer improved terms. However, that position could only last if Charles still needed Henry's support. If he came to believe that he could defeat Francis without Henry's assistance, then England could hardly expect a favourable offer. If, on the other hand, England backed France there was the danger that it would end up supporting what many still believed to be her natural enemy in a losing cause while opposing its successful traditional ally.[5] At some point, probably in the spring of 1521, Henry signed a document that outlined six different possible outcomes of negotiations with Charles, ranging from a renewed universal peace through to an all-out war against France. If none of these could be agreed upon, then the only other option was to join France against the emperor.[6]

Besides defending his possessions in the Low Countries and Navarre, Charles also went on the offensive in Italy. Since 1494 Italy had been the major battleground in the conflict between the European powers. The ancient claims of the French monarchs to both Naples and Milan had been revived by Charles VIII and continued by Louis XII and now Francis. These claims had been contested by the emperor in Milan and by Ferdinand of Aragon in Naples. Charles's accession to the Spanish thrones and his election as emperor meant that this opposition to Francis was brought together in one person. As Charles said: 'My cousin Francis and I are in complete accord; he wants Milan and so do I.'

The numerous Italian states had previously indulged in a complex combination of diplomacy, ever-changing alliances and limited wars fought mainly by mercenary soldiers. The equilibrium had been destroyed by the arrival of foreign powers with large armies, sometimes invited in by local rulers but increasingly of their own volition. The small but wealthy states had little effective defence and provided rich pickings for foreign rulers and their troops. The instability was increased by the Italian ducal families' attempts to increase their own territories. There was widespread devastation caused by long sieges and foraging soldiers, who also both suffered from, and spread, diseases – cholera, the plague and syphilis, the first major outbreak of which in Europe was amongst French soldiers at Naples in 1494. By the 1510s Machiavelli described Italy as being 'leaderless, lawless, crushed, despoiled, torn, over-run'.

An additional complication in Italian politics was the fact that the Pope was based in Rome. As well as being the spiritual head of Christendom the papacy also ruled territory in central Italy. Most Popes, who often came from leading families such as the Medici and Farnese, were always keen to add not only to papal lands but to those of their own family. Often with children, some acknowledged and others not, their authority enabled them to pursue policies that were in their own interests, while at the same time arguing the need for Christian unity and peace. Control and influence over the papacy could, and did, provide another weapon in the conflict between the major powers. However, as Pope Clement VII (1523–1534) later explained most Italians did 'not wish the eagle [Charles] to land in Italy or the cock [Francis] to crow there.' The result was that if one foreign power gained the upper hand, then before long the papacy and other Italian states would come to fear their domination and look for alliances with another power in order to challenge and remove them. Thus, when Francis took Milan in 1515 and gained the pre-eminent position in northern Italy, it was only a matter of time before the right circumstances came about for an anti-French coalition to attempt to drive them out.

It was therefore no surprise that in May 1521, Charles signed a treaty with Pope Leo that had the aim of removing the French from Milan and

Genoa, which would be restored to the Empire, as well as from Parma and Piacenza, which would come under papal control. The cost of the mercenary troops employed to achieve these tasks would be shared. Charles promised to protect Leo's city, Florence, and he would become king of Naples. Leo committed to crowning Charles as Holy Roman Emperor. Despite being the originator of the idea of the Universal Peace, Leo was more a Renaissance prince than a shepherd of Christian harmony. The fall of Belgrade in August 1521 to the Ottoman Turks under Suleiman the Magnificent, who had become sultan the previous year, did nothing to bring the warring parties of Christendom together.

Charles's agreement with the Pope was yet another factor that had to be considered by Henry VIII. If he joined a papal alliance, it would be easier for him to convince his subjects to pay for an expensive war, as it could be represented as 'just'. It has also been argued that both Francis and Charles hinted that they would support Wolsey's candidacy in the next papal election in an effort to win his support for their cause. It seems unlikely that he was so naive as to believe them, and there is no evidence that they ever did so when they had the opportunity. Also, there is little to suggest that Wolsey made any significant attempt to build up support amongst members of the College of Cardinals who would make the decision. However, relations with the Pope were warm when Henry received papal approval of his book *Assertio Septem Sacramentorum* (A Defence of the Seven Sacraments). Dedicated to Pope Leo, it strongly defended the Catholic Church against the ideas of Martin Luther that had spread rapidly through Germany and into neighbouring countries since the publication in 1517 of his Ninety-Five Theses against the sale of indulgencies. In October 1521 Leo gave Henry the title 'Defender of the Faith' used to this day by British monarchs. He could now stand alongside Charles, the 'Most Catholic Majesty', and Francis, the 'Most Christian King'.

Six months earlier Charles had confronted Luther at the Imperial Diet held in Worms. Although intended as a discussion document, the nature of Luther's questions in the Ninety-Five Theses were confrontational. Why, he asked, when the Pope was so rich, did he 'build the basilica of St Peter's with the money of poor believers rather than with his own money?' When called upon to retract his views, he defended them vigorously and put forward other arguments that clashed with the Roman Church. He believed that salvation could only be received by the gift of God's grace through the believers' faith and not through good deeds such as pilgrimage, penance, the sacraments and buying indulgencies. In June 1520, Pope Leo issued a papal bull condemning Luther's writings, which were to be burnt, and threatening him with excommunication. Luther refused to revoke his views or to be silenced and publicly burnt a copy of the bull. In January 1521 the threat was carried out and responsibility for his arrest and punishment fell to the secular authorities, ultimately Emperor Charles.

The members of the Diet insisted that Luther be given a last chance to repent so he was promised safe conduct if he came to Worms. He arrived on 16 April and two days later, the famous confrontation took place. Luther forcefully put his case before Charles, concluding, 'I am neither able nor willing to recant, since it is neither safe nor right to act against conscience. God help me. Amen.'[7] This was not the climb-down that Charles had expected. In reply he made a clear statement of his position. His ancestors, he said, had all been 'true sons of the Roman Church' and he intended to follow their example. To allow this heresy 'would be a disgrace to me and to you, the noble and illustrious German nation'. It was 'certain that a single monk must err if his opinion is contrary to that of all Christendom.'[8] He regretted not having acted sooner but kept his word in allowing Luther to leave Worms. The schism in the Church was to become an ever-greater issue for Charles once this first attempt to deal with it had failed. But in the summer of 1521, he had a more immediate problem – the war with France and whether he could gain Henry's support.

It is difficult to determine exactly when Henry and Wolsey finally decided to make an alliance with Charles. The Calais conference that started on 2 August has often been characterised as a plot to deceive the French – that Henry and Charles had already agreed terms and that the meetings in Calais were merely a means of delaying the open declaration of England's position. By the time the conference ended in the autumn, this was true. But at its start it seems likely that Wolsey, with Henry's approval, was retaining his room for manoeuvre, though strongly inclined to Charles's cause. Early in the conference there was a dispute between Wolsey and Charles's delegation, with Wolsey failing to get the terms that he wanted. When he left Calais on 14 August to travel to Bruges to have direct talks with Charles, he told the French that he needed to persuade the emperor not to abandon the peace negotiations completely. However, an agreement was reached with Charles and the Treaty of Bruges was signed on 25 August 1521, though not immediately made public.

By the terms of the treaty, England would declare war on France by March 1523. The delay brought time, possibly to achieve peace but more likely to prepare for war. England was to provide ships and money for Charles's voyage back to Spain. Arrangements were made for Charles to cover the costs of the French pensions received by Henry, and detailed plans were set out for the dowry that was to be paid when Henry's daughter Mary married Charles. The sums were large. Henry would pay 200,000 gold crowns (worth about £40,000) at the time of the marriage and the same amount within a year. If Henry were to have a male heir, the total amount would increase to one million gold crowns (£200,000). If there was no male heir and Mary became queen of England, then Charles would have to repay the marriage portion that he had received. Both the king and the emperor would seek dispensation from the Pope for this marriage, which was required because Charles and Mary were cousins. Charles undertook to renew the betrothal vows when Mary reached the age of 12 and not to marry until then. Henry bound himself not to promise Mary in marriage to anyone else. If either of them broke this agreement, then they would pay a fine of 400,000 gold crowns to the other.[9]

This part of the treaty always seemed unrealistic. Mary was still only 5 years old and Charles, who was now 21, would be 30 by the time she came of age. Many of his subjects would be very unhappy at the thought of waiting so long for a possible heir. From Henry's point of view, it was very expensive but perhaps he was already thinking about how to secure his daughter's accession if he had no male heir. Charles would be powerful enough to insist upon it but too occupied in his other territories to wish to dominate the affairs of England.

Having concluded the deal with Charles, Wolsey then spent another three months at Calais in talks supposedly aimed at achieving a truce, against the wishes of the Pope who had yet to achieve his war aims. Charles's reason for continued involvement in these talks, despite having just gained English support, was because their aim was a truce with a temporary cessation of fighting and not a final peace settlement. As such it could be used to buy time before the resumption of hostilities, time that Charles needed to travel to Spain and to restore his finances already stretched by the cost of the war. It is noticeable that his enthusiasm for such a truce fluctuated during the course of the war – when he was doing well it waned, but when things were going badly it picked up. Naturally, when he was keen for a truce the French would see little benefit in it. There was really little hope of any agreement. As for Wolsey this was no longer the point. He wanted to bide his time before England was fully committed to a costly conflict that Henry, having made the decision, seemed keen to get on with. Another motive was that he wished to be seen to have made every possible effort to avoid it when England eventually did declare war.

In November the Imperial and papal troops took Milan, and handed the city back to the Sforza family. Another defeat for France in April 1522 at the Battle of Bicocca, just north of Milan, confirmed the loss. There had, however, been one threat to the growing series of anti-French alliances. In December 1521, Pope Leo X died. This would cause a real problem for Charles if his successor took a more pro-French line and cancelled the papal treaty with the emperor. The conclave of the College of Cardinals summoned to elect the next Pope was deadlocked. The leading candidate was Giulio de' Medici, who had risen rapidly during his cousin Leo's papacy. Although he controlled more votes than any other candidate, those who opposed him – Italians jealous of Medici power and French cardinals unhappy with the way Leo had turned against their king – worked together to prevent him achieving a majority. He backed down and on 9 January 1522 cardinals from all sides voted for the relatively unknown Adrian of Utrecht, who became Pope Adrian VI. As Charles's former tutor and currently his regent in Spain, the emperor was delighted. He thought that they would be able to achieve 'many good and great things, for we shall be as one and act in unanimity'. Not for the last time he was to be disappointed.

After these successes Charles was now ready to make the journey back to Spain, thereby fulfilling his promise to return within three years. He would have plenty of work to do in the wake of the rebellions that had flared up after his departure and he expected that he would need to spend a considerable time there. But he did not leave his other lands unattended. He was careful to appoint regents with clearly defined responsibilities in readiness for his absence.

In the Low Countries he turned once again to his aunt, Margaret of Austria, who had already shown her ability and dedication to his and the family's interests. While there Charles had met his brother Ferdinand, now 18, and it was decided that Ferdinand's marriage to Anne of Hungary, arranged years before by Maximilian, should go ahead. Ferdinand was granted the five Austrian dukedoms of the Habsburgs (Upper and Lower Austria, Styria, Carinthia and Carniola) and made an Archduke. The marriage took place in Linz in May 1521. In the following month Charles's sister, Mary, travelled from Innsbruck to Hungary to join her husband, Anne's younger brother, King Louis of Hungary and Bohemia, who she had formally married back in 1515 when she was 9. There was a clear understanding that should Louis die without an heir, Ferdinand would become king in his place. Charles was securing the position of his dynasty in central Europe.

To complete the arrangements for his departure he needed to decide upon a regent in the Empire. Ferdinand was the obvious answer. Not only would this give him a role appropriate to his status, but as a Habsburg he would be seen by others as a suitable replacement. Although Charles hardly knew his brother, he had already recognised that Ferdinand had a loyalty to the family that meant that he would be less likely to challenge Charles's authority. The need for all these measures reveals both the strengths and weaknesses of Charles's position. On the one hand he had family members that he could trust to act in his best interests, but on the other the very extent of his territories meant that he could never give his personal attention to all of them at once. This is shown again and again through the forty years of his reign. His subjects often demanded his presence, since that persuaded them that they were his main concern and only he could make some of the grants, appointments and promotions that they wanted. To deal with the ever-increasing threat of religious divisions he needed to be in Germany, but he also had to defend territories in central Europe and the Mediterranean against attack by the Ottoman Turks and continue to deal with an aggressive king of France in Italy and the Low Countries. However, by May 1522, he was as ready as he ever could be to leave for Spain and visit his new ally Henry VIII in England on the way.

Chapter Seven

Charles in England

Both Henry and Charles had reasons to be pleased with their new alliance. Charles's war with Francis was likely to continue for some years and he believed that Henry could provide valuable support. Henry, having committed to the Imperial cause, was now keen to plan for the invasion of France, believing that with Charles's help he would be able to make substantial gains and even make good his claim to the French crown. The enthusiasm with which Henry pursued this claim fluctuated considerably during his reign. When Francis was in difficulties, as in 1521–1522, Henry's speeches and letters were full of references to his rightful inheritance, while at other times his 'God-given right' appeared to be something that could simply be traded for increased pensions and other concessions.

If the idea of peace could be extravagantly celebrated at the Field of Cloth of Gold, then the visit of an ally with whom Henry had recently signed an aggressive alliance had to be equally memorable. Wolsey had been received with great honour by Charles at Bruges in 1521, riding, dining and praying with him, as well as lodging in the palace.[1] The emperor's visit to England was to be a much grander affair than his short stay two years before. In March 1522 a joust and a banquet attended by both Henry and Wolsey was organised in honour of Lachaulx, Charles's ambassador, who had arrived in England to discuss the detailed arrangements for the visit. His reception contrasted sharply with that of the French ambassador who received no such welcome.[2]

The treatment of ambassadors at a foreign court was important because any obvious lack of respect was taken, and usually intended, as an insult to the monarch that the diplomat represented. Equally the status of an ambassador in his own country sometimes indicated the value that his monarch placed upon good relations with the host country and his likely reception there. When the highly regarded and well-placed Sir Richard Wingfield was sent to the court of Francis I in 1520, he was given privileged access to the king. Increasingly Henry VIII used members of his privy chamber on important overseas missions, both to show respect to the receiving court and to try

67

to ensure that they would be readily accepted by courtiers and others from whom they could get information.

Charles wished to visit England at the first possible opportunity, hoping to persuade Henry into an early declaration of war on France. Wolsey was keen to delay matters, knowing that England had not yet prepared for a war on the scale that was required. However, if the English king had any doubts about the alliance with the emperor, they were removed by the ending of previously agreed pensions paid by Francis, the arrest of English merchants in Bordeaux and the successes of Charles's army in Italy.

The negotiations in advance of Charles's arrival reveal much about the protocols of state visits. Charles, having heard about the extravagance of the planned celebrations, wrote to say that there should be no unnecessary spending, claiming that he liked to travel simply and that the money would be better spent on other things, such as preparation for war. But it was almost impossible for him to travel without a large entourage. There were too many nobles, commanders and diplomats who expected to accompany him, especially when his whole court was moving from the Low Countries to Spain. In any case he surely expected to be received in a manner that befitted his status. When he arrived in late May there were over 200 nobles from 'Spain, Flanders and Germany'[3], 100 officers and 1,700 servants. They would all have to be housed and fed during the stay which was expected to be for well over a month.

The emperor's reception in London started to be planned as early as March. Nothing was left to chance. The Lord Mayor shouldered much of the responsibility. The houses of all citizens of status were assessed for the number of visitors that they could sleep, ideally in feather beds, while inns and stables were to be taken over to provide for servants and the large number of horses that would arrive. Besides lodgings, other considerations included lighting, wood, coal, tables, chairs, kitchen equipment and, most importantly, food. The city authorities made enquiries as to how much meat and poultry was prepared each week and were reassured that, given two weeks' notice, there would be no problem in supplying the required amount. On top of the practical arrangements there were the street decorations and pageants to be planned, produced and paid for. It seems that many of the city guilds that were to foot the bill were slow to make their contributions, and many who were instructed to do the work were reluctant because they knew that payment for their work would be tardy.

On Sunday, 25 May, Charles was greeted by the Marquess of Dorset near Gravelines. Outside Calais they were met by Sir Edward Guildford, the Lord Warden of the Cinque Ports and Marshall of Calais, accompanied by fifty men at arms and 100 mounted archers and the emperor's entry to the town was celebrated by cannon-fire.[4]

The following day Charles and his party had, according to some reports, a rough crossing to Dover, arriving at 4.00 pm. He was met on the sands by Cardinal Wolsey, with 'three hundred lords, knights and gentlemen of England' and they rode to Dover Castle where they spent the night, while the rest of Charles's company was lodged in Dover 'according to their degree'. Having complained about the crossing, Martin de Salinas, Archduke Ferdinand's ambassador to Charles's court, again found reason to be critical – this time, about the standard of the food.

Henry had originally planned to meet Charles on the Downs as the Imperial party travelled to Canterbury but they were delayed for two days by the late arrival of much of the baggage. On Wednesday an impatient Henry therefore rode the 17 miles from Canterbury to Dover. Although Wolsey had been warned, Henry appeared unannounced to Charles so that his guest might believe that Henry's arrival 'was of his own mind and affection towards the emperor'. These unexpected entrances were something that Henry never seemed to grow out of. They did not always have the anticipated result, as witnessed years later in January 1540 when he appeared before his unprepared bride-to-be, Anne of Cleves. Charles, however, took it all in his stride. The next day was spent quietly with the monarchs in conversation and preparing for the coming journey through Kent. On Friday morning Henry proudly showed Charles around the English fleet that had assembled at Dover. They went aboard the warship *Henry Grace à Dieu* and were rowed through the harbour so that Charles could see the quality of workmanship and the fine armaments on board.

That afternoon the monarchs rode to Canterbury on the first stage of their journey to Greenwich. They were received outside the walls by the mayor and aldermen, and on entering the city were met by Archbishop Warham and twelve bishops, who escorted them to the cathedral for prayers. Charles spent the night in the Archbishop's Palace while Henry stayed at St Augustine's, a short distance away. On Saturday 31 May they travelled to Sittingbourne, where they stayed overnight, and then moved on the next day to Rochester. Given the distance covered between early afternoon on Friday when they left Dover and Sunday afternoon when they arrived at Rochester – over 40 miles – this was rapid progress. Henry and Charles rode ahead with a relatively small group while the rest of the company took considerably longer to reach their destination each day. The royal visitors and their immediate entourage were given the finest lodgings prepared in readiness, while the majority would be billeted in whatever, often overcrowded, accommodation was available.

On the Monday morning they travelled the 8 miles to Gravesend where they were met by barges belonging to the king and other noblemen. As they were rowed up the Thames to Greenwich all boats on the river, decorated with banners and streamers, lined the banks to welcome the emperor.[5] Arriving at 6.00 pm they were received by Queen Catherine, Princess Mary and the full court. Charles knelt before Catherine and expressed 'his great joy to see the Queen, his aunt, and especially his young cousin the Lady Mary'. Charles stayed in the king's lodgings which, according to Edward Hall, was 'so richly hanged that the Spaniards wondered'. On the first evening they were 'highly feasted'.

For the entertainment and enjoyment of the company, a tournament was prepared and jousting arranged for Wednesday, 4 June. Hall describes the events of the day. 'On the one part was the king, the earl of Devonshire and ten more companions on horseback, their apparel and bardes [the ornamental coverings of the horses] were of rich cloth of gold, embroidered with silver letters, very rich, with great plumes on their heads. This company took to the field, and rode about the tilt. Then entered the Duke of Suffolk, the Marquess of Dorset and ten with them and their apparel was russet velvet, embroidered with sundry knots of gold. The emperor and the queen, with all the nobles stood in the gallery to behold the doing. The king ran at the Duke of Suffolk eight courses and at every one broke his spear. Then every man ran his courses and that done, all ran together volant [flying], as fast as they could discharge and when the spears were broken, then they disarmed and went to supper.'[6]

This was not the end of the day's festivities. After supper the dancing began. Hall describes how 'the emperor beheld the ladies dancing and suddenly came to the chamber six noble men apparelled in crimson velvet and cloth of gold ... and danced a great while with the ladies.' Then 'six other maskers entered ... apparelled in long gowns and hoods of cloth of gold, of which number was the king, the Duke of Suffolk, the prince of Orange, the count of Nassau, [and two others].' After much dancing and praise for each other's costumes 'every person departed to their lodgings.'[7]

Preparations were well under way to continue the tournament the next day when King Henry was informed that there was a messenger from France. Henry read the letters and immediately instructed Sir William Compton, a friend and senior member of his privy chamber, to ask the emperor to join him. Charles, without delay, 'came to the king, who showed him the letters from Sir Thomas Cheyney, his ambassador, wherein was contained the definitive answer, made by the French king, to the king's requests.' These were the demands made by Henry that Francis should pay him the pensions that he owed him and desist from attacks on Charles that had broken the Treaty of London and therefore made Francis his enemy. Henry had added that he was loathe to shed Christian blood and wished to be a mediator. To all this the French king had answered to Cheyney: 'We have well considered your master's desire to which we nothing agree, nor hold us content with his request.' Francis went on to deny all the grievances that had been listed by Clarenceux, King of Arms, herald of the English king, specifically that he had made war on Charles, failed to pay his dues, sent the Duke of Albany to stir up anti-English feeling in Scotland and unlawfully imprisoned English merchants. He then granted safe conduct to the English diplomats so that they could leave his country. Hall's account ends with the statement that 'Thus now was the war open of all the parties.'[8]

After a while the emperor called for his horse, the king was armed and the tournament commenced, this time in the form of a melee, the combat of two teams of horsemen (though it was sometimes on foot), rather than jousting. Hall recorded that all fought very valiantly until being called to disarm. On this final evening at Greenwich, the monarchs had supper and then Henry took Charles to the finely decorated great hall, where more masked dancers 'revelled lustily' before the guests took wine and spices. Not everyone was pleased by the expense and frivolity. De Salinas found his lodgings expensive and of a poor standard and considered that neither ruler was getting down to business. His main interest was to win support against the Ottoman Turks after their taking of Belgrade, but he wrote that 'the emperor and his councillors are so much occupied in festivities that they have no time for business and it has not been possible to get an audience.'[9] He should not have been surprised. Henry had little concern for what was happening in Hungary; as Wolsey remarked, the real 'Turk' was Francis and that it was the French king who was a threat to the country.[10]

On the morning of Friday, 6 June, the king and emperor with the rest of their company set off for London. A mile or so south of the capital, in a pavilion of gold cloth, Henry and Charles prepared for their formal entry, changing into similar clothes to demonstrate their brotherhood. The procession was organised by the heralds with Englishmen alongside those who had arrived with Charles, each in their allotted position according to rank. They were met by the mayor, and then Sir Thomas More stepped forward and made an 'eloquent oration in praise of the two princes, and of the peace and love between them and what comfort it was to their subjects to see them in such amity'. They entered Southwark and outside the Marshalsea Prison, Henry, at Charles's request, pardoned a great number of prisoners. From there the procession travelled north to London Bridge where nine pageants, each with colourful tableaux and dramatic presentations, started. The rest were spread along a route of almost a mile and a half, over the bridge, north along Gracechurch Street to the junction of Leadenhall Street and Bishopsgate, from there turning left into Cornhill and thence onto Cheapside ending at St Paul's Cathedral.

The pageants had been newly constructed to celebrate the friendship of Charles and Henry, full of classical illusions and references to the ancient lineage of their families.[11] On a large scale and with themes of shared ancestry, friendship and unity in defence of the Church, they were intended to show how much Henry and Charles working together would achieve. At the south end of London Bridge the first pageant consisted of two giants, Hercules and Samson, representing the power and strength of the emperor. On the tablet beneath them the Latin inscription proclaimed: 'Carolus Henricus vivant. Defensor uterque. Henricus Fidei. Carolus Ecclesiae' – 'Charles and Henry live. Defenders both. Henry of the Faith, Charles of the Church'. This was repeated in every street along the route of the procession. Halfway across the bridge the next pageant showed Jason holding the Golden Fleece honouring the Order of which Charles was so proud. In Gracechurch Street the pageant focused on Charlemagne, the first Holy Roman Emperor, whose crown Charles now wore.

At the end of Gracechurch Street where it turns into Bishopsgate, the fourth display was designed to emphasise the joint descent of Charles and Henry from John of Gaunt, Duke of Lancaster. Charles was descended from John of Gaunt through the duke's daughter, Catherine, who married Henry III of Castile. As they turned into Cornhill a mock castle had been constructed across the street. This pageant balanced the reference to Charlemagne with one celebrating King Arthur. There was a gateway on either side, each with a tower above. One had several trumpeters and on the other, musicians played sackbuts (a form of trombone) and shawms (an early woodwind instrument). King Arthur sat at the Round Table between the towers, with kings and nobles from across northern Europe paying homage. Further along Cornhill another display celebrated the friendship of the two monarchs.

The first of three pageants in Cheapside consisted of two gateways supporting a square structure with four towers that were connected by galleries decorated with gold and silver cloth bearing the coats of arms of emperors and the kings of England. The galleries were filled with musicians and singers. As the monarchs approached a large rose was lowered. When it opened up, a girl holding two roses stepped out to hand the white rose to Charles and the red rose to Henry. There then followed verses praising the emperor and the defence of Christendom against the infidels. Further along Cheapside was a second genealogical pageant, this time with the descendants of the thirteenth-century king of Castile, Alphonso X. A tree came from his chest and the branches had platforms for the various kings leading up to Charles, Henry, Catherine of Aragon and Princess Mary. The link to the English royal family was that Alphonso's half-sister Eleanor had married Edward I. The final pageant had a religious theme, dedicated to the Virgin Mary, consisting of angels and saints in heaven. As the procession ended outside St Paul's Cathedral, the Archbishop of Canterbury and twenty-one bishops welcomed Henry and Charles who attended a short service of blessing.[12]

Charles was reportedly very content with his reception, writing to the Abbot of Najera that 'the procession was very brilliant, the welcome hearty', and even Martin de Salinas considered it impressive. The emperor was lodged at Blackfriars Priory and many of his nobles in the nearby new Palace of Bridewell. Both were highly decorated and connected by a long gallery. Others of Charles's party were lodged in the houses of wealthy citizens. It is not reported whether Londoners considered this an honour or an imposition. Charles was in an outgoing and optimistic mood. His letter had already praised Henry 'who treats [me] with all the love of a father and pays all the expenses of [my] household with royal liberality' and he continued: 'The war [against the French] will be carried out with so much vigour that it will not be difficult to expel the French entirely from Italy. Peace will thus be restored to Italy … and a common war of the Christian princes with the Turk can be undertaken.'[13]

On the Saturday, Henry and Charles took on the Prince of Orange and the Marquis of Brandenburg at tennis. Hall comments that 'they departed even hands after eleven games fully played.' That evening Wolsey held a banquet for resident ambassadors, at which he was highly critical of the French and justified Henry's claim to the French throne. On the morning of their last full day in London, Whit Sunday, the monarchs attended St Paul's. De Salinas, who clearly believed that Wolsey was full of pride, wrote that 'the Pope [adding between the lines 'who is the Cardinal'] said Mass.'[14] They feasted at the Bridewell Palace after which they took a barge to Westminster, heard evensong in Westminster Abbey, visited Westminster Hall, at which the emperor marvelled, and returned to Bridewell for supper.[15]

Much of the next week was made over to hunting, enjoyed equally by Charles and Henry. On Monday, 9 June, they dined with the Duke of

Suffolk in Southwark, hunted and then rode to Richmond where they stayed the night. The next day they went to Hampton Court 'where they had good cheer' and on Thursday, moved to Windsor[16] where there was more hunting on Friday and Saturday. On Sunday evening they watched a play in which the main characters, Friendship, Prudence and Might, worked together to tame a wild, unruly horse. The meaning would have been very clear to the audience. The horse represented Francis, or the war that he had caused, and those that brought it under control were the members of the Anglo-Imperial/Spanish alliance.

This set the tone for the negotiations that took most of the next three days, which Henry, Charles and their advisers spent in council. The councillors had been at work during the previous three weeks discussing the terms and the wording of the treaty, though a few remaining details needed to be finalised. The Treaty of Windsor, signed on 16 June, confirmed the main points of their earlier treaty signed in Bruges. It began with a blistering criticism of Francis and a justification of their decisions. 'The Turks, being the irreconcilable enemies of Christendom, have conquered new territories from the Christians, and are more dangerous than ever. Some of the Christian princes, instead of employing their forces in repelling the Turks, are only trying to gain advantages by the troubles … The King of France is the worst of them, and gives a bad example to others. The King of England, therefore, renounces his friendship with the King of France, and regards his treaties with him as not concluded. As the Emperor and the King of England, who is the Defender of the Faith, are in duty bound to defend the Catholic Church, they have concluded an everlasting alliance.'

The treaty was not just one of defence. They agreed that they would 'assist one another with all their power in defending their dominions, those which they at present possess', but added 'as well as those which they hereafter may conquer in accordance with this treaty.' They would seek to 'reconquer from the King of France all their former dominions which have been wrested from them.' They promised 'to make a common war upon France by land and by sea, and not to desist from it until they have reconquered all that France unjustly withholds from them.' If either of them suffered a defeat or losses they would restore the strength of their forces within one month. They would not 'conclude a peace or truce, or begin negotiations with the King of France, without the knowledge of the other.'[17] The enemies and rebels of one were to be regarded as the enemies and rebels of the other and were to be handed over. They decided to invite Pope Adrian to become the head of the League, but even if he refused the treaty would remain unaltered as far as Henry and Charles were concerned. Invitations to join the League were to be sent to Venice, the Swiss and other rulers.

On 19 June more details were agreed in a separate secret treaty. The future marriage of Charles to Princess Mary, and its associated financial settlement made in August 1521, was confirmed. On military matters, both rulers committed to invade France, though the main attack was put back a year to 1524. Charles would invade from the Spanish frontier and Henry from Calais, each with 30,000 foot soldiers and 10,000 cavalry. If needed Henry would pay for horses that would be delivered from the Low Countries. They knew that Francis often used a significant number of mercenary soldiers from Germany so they decided that they would enlist as many German soldiers as possible so that Francis would struggle to strengthen his army. They also agreed to each have 3,000 fighting men at sea.

The issue of the loss of English pensions from France was dealt with. Charles agreed to pay the cost of the pensions, as well as to cover French debts to England that would be forfeited by the attack. These were no small sums. In November 1519 the French had paid Henry 25,000 livres tournois (Lt) – approximately £2,500 – as the half-yearly instalment due for the return of Tournai the previous year. He also received a larger amount as a result of the peace treaty of 1514. At the same time Wolsey received 1,400 Lt and an additional 6,000 Lt as compensation for the loss of revenue as Bishop of Tournai. Others had been receiving French pensions for years – for instance, Suffolk and Norfolk, 875 Lt each; and the Earl of Worcester, 1,700 Lt. All these sums were paid half-yearly. In total Charles agreed to pay 66,802 crowns (worth approximately £13,360) every six months from November 1522. When Henry took possession of French towns and provinces, the net revenue of those lands would be deducted from the amount to be paid. Payments would end when a peace treaty had been concluded in which Francis agreed to restore all payments. An annual sum of £26,720 made a significant contribution to Henry's finances when his ordinary revenues amounted to about £110,000 a year.

Negotiations having been completed, Henry and Charles went to St George's Chapel on Corpus Christi Day – Thursday, 19 June – where they both received the sacrament, and after Mass they 'swore to keep the promises and league each to the other … [and] great joy was made on both parties.'[18] There followed a feast that evening before they set out for Winchester the following morning. The journey of nearly 50 miles was spread over three days with, of course, hunting taking place on the way. The company stayed at Winchester for over a week. The ancient Round Table in the castle had been repainted, with a Tudor rose in the centre, and re-hung in the hall where it was proudly displayed during a banquet. From Winchester they moved on to Bishop's Waltham Palace near Southampton. While there, Charles's will, initially drawn up in Bruges, was completed, witnessed and signed in readiness for his voyage. At the end of June, thirty English ships, commanded by Admiral Howard and accompanied by several courtiers close to Henry, such as Nicholas Carew, Anthony Browne and Francis Bryan, had left Southampton with orders to patrol the seas along the French coast for any enemy vessels. They also had orders to carry out a raid on Brittany when they had completed their initial task. Charles's fleet arrived at Southampton and on 6 July, having received rich gifts and a substantial loan from Henry, he set sail for Spain, arriving at Santander ten days later.

Charles's visit to England was the high point in his relations with Henry. He had been received in fine style and appreciated the warmth of his welcome. The king and the emperor had confirmed their war plans for an invasion of France. As Charles departed it seemed that the old alliances between England, Spain and the Low Countries had been renewed with enthusiasm. Charles was confident that he could now deal with the threat of France and Henry thought that he was in a powerful enough position if not to take the French throne, then at least seize substantial territories to give himself a strong bargaining position in the future. They were never to meet again and the next few years were to demonstrate once again that little remained the same for long in sixteenth-century Europe.

Chapter Eight

The 'Great Enterprise'

Charles spent the next seven years in Spain, not leaving until July 1529 when he joined his fleet in Barcelona to travel across the Mediterranean to Genoa. It was the longest uninterrupted period of time that he was to spend in any of his lands and it is generally accepted that this was when he firmly established himself in the country that he later called his 'bedrock'. He had plenty to do there. The rebellions of 1520 and 1521 had only recently been defeated. He needed to learn its language, understand its customs, and get to know the nobles and bureaucrats who would help him to rule. He was yet to be regarded as 'their' monarch rather than a foreign one. He also needed to establish a system of government that would function efficiently when he left for his other lands as he surely would have to do. Although he was at war with France and had just made commitments to Henry about how the war would be conducted, these were never his only concerns.

In the original treaty of August 1521, the joint invasion of France was to take place in 1523, though the Treaty of Windsor had delayed the 'Great Enterprise' by a year. The reason given for the postponement was that more time was required for military preparations. In England a 'general proscription' or survey was carried out during 1522 by sending commissioners to each county to discover what resources Henry could call upon for the war. The early reports were so incomplete that new instructions were issued to clarify what details were required. However, by the end of the year, an estimate of the number of able-bodied men available for military service and the weapons that they could be expected to provide had been made, along with information about the size of the retinue that could be raised by individual nobility and gentry. The collection of so much detail was itself quite an achievement and many feared that it would be used to determine how much money could be collected, and from whom, in the form of a parliamentary subsidy and forced loans.

They were to be proved correct. No monarch in the sixteenth century could afford to wage war using only their ordinary income. Henry's was small by the standards of Francis I and Charles V, and even they were constantly struggling to find the ready cash that was needed to meet the ever-increasing costs of maintaining an army in the field. Troops that weren't paid, especially the mercenary soldiers upon which many armies depended, were unreliable. There were also the costs of providing supplies, both of military equipment and the vast quantities of food and drink that an army of tens of thousands required daily, besides the provision of horses and carts for transport. Finance was thus central to the creation of an effective fighting force and the outcome of many a campaign was determined by the ability of a ruler to fund it for as long as was needed. Henry made good use of the information gathered by the survey of 1522. By the spring of 1523 he had raised forced loans to the value of £200,000 from the laity and another £55,000 from the Church.[1] When Parliament met in April 1523 it was initially asked for an unprecedented and unrealistic £800,000[2] but eventually agreed to grant a subsidy of £152,000 over a four-year period.[3]

Although war had been formally declared in May 1522, the military action against France in that year was restricted to a raid on Morlaix in Brittany by the fleet commanded by the Lord Admiral, the Earl of Surrey, and an expedition from Calais into Picardy. Two unsuccessful sieges, foraging for supplies and some looting by the soldiers caused considerable damage to the locality, but the campaign lacked any specific objective and was never likely to achieve much without the backing of troops from the Low Countries. No land remained under English control once the troops had returned to Calais.

For Henry, renewed anxiety about the security of England's northern border was one reason for the limited military action against France. King James V of Scotland had become king at the age of 1 on the death of his father in 1513 at the Battle of Flodden. His mother, Henry VIII's sister Margaret, was at first the regent but her position was challenged by the pro-French faction led by John Steward, Duke of Albany, next in line to the Scottish throne. Brought up by his mother in France, Albany renewed the 'auld alliance' between France and Scotland. As Anglo-French relations deteriorated, Albany was encouraged in his ambitions by Francis, who supplied soldiers and ships for his return to Scotland in November 1521. By the summer of 1522 it became necessary for Henry to send a large force to defend against cross-border raids and a possible Scottish invasion. In 1523 the Earl of Surrey, probably England's most experienced commander, was sent north to oversee the defences. The other threat to Henry came from the continued French support (when it suited them) for Richard de la Pole, but plans for him to lead an invasion of England never came to fruition and instead he served in the French army.

There was also pressure on the monarchs, particularly Charles, because of the success of the Ottoman Turks under Suleiman the Magnificent. In 1522, having taken Belgrade the previous year, his forces attacked Rhodes, the base of the Knights Hospitaller since the loss of Acre in Palestine back in 1291.[4] Against overwhelming odds the Knights held out for six months. The new Pope was unable to contribute to the defence of this Christian stronghold because of the vast debts left by his predecessor. Despite his requests and the pleas of the Knights themselves, the leading monarchs of Europe, involved as they were in their own struggles, provided nothing but fine words. The Knights, having sustained great losses, eventually came to terms with Suleiman. They surrendered and the survivors were permitted to leave Rhodes unmolested on 1 January 1523.

In that month Pope Adrian exhorted Charles, Francis and Henry to 'conclude an immediate truce of three years and to undertake a common war against the Turks'.[5] By March he was using more forceful language when he wrote to Charles that 'He had hoped that he [the emperor] would be the first to obey his exhortations, but was deceived. He and other Christian princes preferred to indulge in their private passions, inordinate cupidity, and lust for power, neglecting their duties to the Christian religion.'[6] Charles used the excuse that he could not enter into negotiations with Francis unless Henry consented to it – implying that the English king prevented him from doing so. He also argued that the Pope had refused to provide money to pay for 'so numerous an army and navy as are required in a war with the Turks' and that the Pope should be the one to organise 'a general conference, where the manner in which the war with the Turks is to be carried on shall be discussed.'[7] In April 1523 Francis also rejected the Pope's plans for a truce.

Such concerns about events in the Balkans and the eastern Mediterranean, however, do not explain the delays in the organisation of the 'Great Enterprise'. More significant was the increasing lack of trust and co-ordination between the allies. Their failure to support the English campaign in Picardy raised the issue of how committed Charles and his regent in the Low Countries, Margaret of Austria, really were to the invasion of France. Henry realised that without such support the chances of a successful campaign were limited. Although he was still keen to pursue his claims to French territory there seemed to be no urgency in the English preparations for a campaign in 1523, despite being pressed by Charles. By June Charles was being advised by Louis de Praet, his ambassador in England, that so little had been done that the emperor should not count on English help in any plans that he had for that year. Similarly, the English representatives in Spain were dubious about Charles's plans, reporting that he had little money to spend, that he was really much more interested in Italy than invading France, and that he had been complaining that Henry was merely using their alliance to help in his difficulties with Scotland. Well before the date agreed for the major invasion, both monarchs were having doubts about the reliability of their ally.

It was the defection of Charles, Duke of Bourbon, that provided the impetus that was needed. As the Constable of France, Bourbon was the highest-ranking military officer under Francis I. As a 'prince of the blood' he was close to the royal family. His marriage in 1505 to Suzanne of Bourbon brought together the vast estates of both the senior and junior lines of the Bourbon family, with Charles as the undisputed head. He had fought at Marignano and jousted at the Field of Cloth of Gold. His wife's death in 1521 led to a bitter dispute between Bourbon and Louise of Savoy, Francis I's mother, who claimed the lands that Suzanne had bequeathed to the duke. Francis refused to support Bourbon against his influential mother. A furious Bourbon started talks with Charles V's representatives. When, in 1523, Louise seized much of the disputed land even before the resolution of the legal process, Bourbon offered to make war on Francis. Although Henry was at first unimpressed about what Bourbon could offer, the possibility of a full-scale rebellion against Francis encouraged Wolsey and the king to reassess the situation.

In early July a new agreement was reached between Charles and Henry after much hard bargaining over such details as the numbers of soldiers and horses to be supplied and who would pay the mercenaries that would be employed. Both would have armies ready by mid-August. The English would attack from Calais with 15,000 troops assisted by 3,000 soldiers, supplies and money provided by Margaret from the Low Countries. Charles's force would advance from Spain into south-west France (Guienne) with 20,000 men. Neither would discontinue their attack before the end of October, except by common consent.[8] By early August Bourbon had been brought into the plan. English money would be sent to help him raise forces for a rebellion in his lands in eastern France and he would then advance into Champagne. Henry wanted Bourbon to recognise him as the rightful king of France, but the final decision on this was to be made by the emperor. Bourbon was given to believe that he might marry Charles's older sister, Eleanor, the widow of King Manuel of Portugal.

Elsewhere English, Spanish and Imperial ambassadors were working hard to bring Portugal, as well as Venice, Milan, Savoy, Florence, Genoa and other Italian states into a broad anti-French League. Charles himself was attempting to gain the support of the Pope for the invasion of France.

In a letter of 22 August to Adrian VI, he began that 'his whole life bear him full witness that he has always been and still is animated by the love of peace' and that 'neither he nor the King of England harboured any selfish plans, but were only anxious to secure public tranquillity and security.' He wanted nothing more than to have a three-year truce but 'the King of France is, from his very nature, a despiser of the Christian religion and consequently did not desist from agitating and disturbing "land and sea". He increased his army, raised tumults in Italy and … continually harassed the coast of Spain. Under such circumstances, he [the Emperor] thinks neither his honour nor his Christian devotion can be exposed to any danger of misrepresentation if he, in common with his august ally, the King of England, resume war on all sides.' After months of apparent inaction everything was now moving swiftly towards war.

By the end of August, the Duke of Suffolk, who had been handed command of the English army, had 11,000 soldiers in Calais ready to advance. In the original plan, agreed by both Henry and Charles, the English troops would first besiege and take Boulogne. Charles, and later Wolsey, now wished for a bolder thrust into France, with the army linking up with Bourbon and going on to threaten Paris. It is often claimed that Cardinal Wolsey needed to restrain the more warlike Henry. Certainly, Wolsey, at times, used this perception during negotiations in order to procure better terms from his French opposite number. However, in this case it was Henry who was the more cautious of the two. He argued that taking Boulogne would extend the limited lands that he controlled around Calais and that this would then provide a more secure base from which to launch the main invasion of France, the Great Enterprise, in the future. He thought that it was too late in the campaigning season to follow the more ambitious plan, that they had not prepared sufficiently to supply a fast-moving army and that if the soldiers were denied the spoils of war, which as an army of liberation from Francis's rule they were supposed to be, they would soon lose motivation and demand to return home.[9] He also feared that given an open rebellion led by Bourbon and with his crown at stake, Francis might well bring troops back from Italy thus leaving the English isolated in French territory confronted by a much larger force.

Against this Wolsey came around to favour the idea of taking advantage of the present circumstances. If all went well, one concerted assault on France could bring about the great victory that Henry wished for and thus save what was bound to be the enormous expense of launching an invasion in 1524 or 1525. By mid-September Henry was persuaded and it was agreed to follow the more aggressive plan, the so-called 'march on

Paris'. By then the French alliance with Venice had collapsed and Pope Adrian, after attempting to remain neutral in the face of much pressure from Charles, seemed at last to be favouring his former pupil. On 16 September, Francis formally declared Bourbon a traitor. It is possible that Bourbon had agreed to acknowledge Henry as the king of France without Charles V's knowledge and that this both forced Francis to make his declaration and influenced Henry to follow the higher-risk strategy. Suffolk advanced south from Calais and took eight towns without too much resistance as the French avoided a major battle. This, of course, denied Henry and Suffolk the major victory that they desired, which given that it would not only increase Henry's prestige but also provide a powerful bargaining counter in any negotiations, was perhaps the main aim of the campaign. The army crossed the River Somme near Corbie and by the end of October had reached Montdidier some 70 miles north of Paris. This was to be the extent of their progress.

Much had gone wrong, particularly with the assistance that Henry had expected from his allies. Support for Bourbon's rebellion was negligible and he proved unable to lead troops north to link with Suffolk. In fact, he soon left France, retreating south to Genoa. Charles's anticipated invasion of Gascony never got off the ground, much as Henry's ambassadors had feared. Many of the promised troops from the Low Countries were diverted north to deal with a rebellion in Guelderland and those that were provided, commanded by the Count of Buren, seemed more committed to the defence of the Low Countries from any French attack than to an offensive strategy. As they remained unpaid, they also took to looting, something which it had been agreed should be avoided. Neither the artillery nor the horses and carts for transport, promised by Margaret of Austria, materialised.

As for Suffolk's army, their condition deteriorated. They experienced poor food supplies, the spread of disease, and appalling weather with 'great rains and winds' followed by 'a fervent frost so severe that many soldiers died of cold, some lost fingers and some toes.'[10] All this contributed to increased indiscipline with much grumbling, heavy drinking and mutinous behaviour. There was discontent about the order not to loot, especially as they considered that they had done most of the fighting, only to see Buren's troops taking goods away on carts that Suffolk's soldiers did not have access to. 'We beat the bush and they take the birds', they complained. Henry was uncertain what to do. His first instinct was to order the army to withdraw to a defensible position north of the Somme and winter in France while he sent reinforcements. Even if this had been possible, the intense cold, increasing mutinies and the disbandment of Buren's forces meant that Suffolk made the decision to tell his troops to make their way north, directly to Calais or through the Low Countries. Once there most did not stop and continued their journey back to England.

This had not been the campaign that Henry had intended, and in most respects his doubts about the strategy had turned out to be fully justified. Suffolk might have been concerned about what awaited him on his return, but showed little sign of this when he created sixteen knights for valour during the campaign, including Edward Seymour and John Dudley who both went on to hold the highest offices in the land under Edward VI.[11] In fact he suffered little or none of the blame for any perceived failures. Although little had been gained, he had shown how a relatively small English army could penetrate 'into the bowels of France'. The fact that he had not been able to consolidate his advance was put down to the failure of England's allies to provide any support.

At Christmas 1523 Henry was still remarkably optimistic when talking about the 'Great Enterprise' and in February, it was reported that he was as 'resolved as ever' to continue the war against France.[12] As winter turned into spring, with more time to consider the previous year's events, he was in a different mood. He was aware that much of the money raised for the war had been spent for as yet little gain. He now doubted whether his allies would give him the support he needed for a successful invasion of France. His ambassadors had been right when they had warned him that Charles's real goal was to drive the French out of Italy. Bourbon had been unable to deliver what he had promised, despite ambitions to rule a large swathe of France himself. Henry's problem was that if he deserted his allies, he would not only risk a loss of honour but also leave England isolated. Instead, he instructed English diplomats to complain to Charles about his apparent lack of commitment to the cause and his and Margaret's failure to provide what had been agreed. Henry's discontent was made clear. During the campaign Wolsey had frequently expressed his anger to Charles's ambassador, even at one stage suggesting that given how much Henry had done and spent compared with the contribution of the emperor, it might be better if England were at war with Charles rather than Francis.

Henry, though, had not completely abandoned his ambitions. Perhaps he hoped that pointing out Charles's failings would spur him to meet his treaty obligations. In February 1524 Henry wanted Bourbon to travel to England to have urgent discussions with him about some 'secret expedition of the greatest importance against the common enemy.'[13] Bourbon never went to England and so the plan was never revealed. The policy that was then adopted by Henry and Wolsey was one of inaction. Charles and Bourbon needed to attack France first and achieve some success before Henry would send troops – essentially, he would wait and see how events unfolded but try to make sure that he did not miss out on any opportunity that might present itself. Much, of course, would depend on how the war between Charles and Francis fared elsewhere, particularly in Italy, where fortunes swung back and forth throughout 1524 and into 1525.

In early 1524 the French seemed to be at least as strong as Charles. It cannot have been a coincidence that a certain John Joachim de Passano, a friar in the employment of Louise of Savoy, had been granted entry to England in April 1524. He became involved in discreet talks about the possibility of an Anglo-French truce. The intensity of the talks fluctuated; as French fortunes in the war fell, English interest in the talks dwindled, and when their fortunes improved, the negotiations seemed to pick up. Henry and Wolsey's motivation for such talks can be seen as the need for an insurance policy in case France got the upper hand in the war, or if the emperor decided to agree an independent truce with the French. It might even have been the case that the talks were designed to extract further promises of support from Charles. Whatever the motives little progress was made. The gap between the demands of both sides was too great and terms that could be regarded as honourable to both parties were not reached. Nevertheless, lines of communication had been opened.

However, by the summer of 1524, the chances of a successful invasion of France were greater than they had been in the previous year. If Henry was only waiting for successes by his allies, he might have concluded that the time had come. In March, Spanish troops recaptured the important border town of Fuenterrabia in the Pyrenees. A failed French attack into Piedmont in the autumn of 1523 had been followed by an Imperial invasion of Provence led by the Duke of Bourbon, who was encouraged by talk of a new kingdom being created for him there. He took Aix-en-Provence in July 1524 and advanced to besiege Marseilles. Henry's diplomat with Bourbon, Richard Pace, wrote to the king that 'we shall never have again such help to do good for ourselves in France.'[14] Charles did all that he could to persuade Henry to invade France from Calais or even in Guienne in the south-west, as did Bourbon's representative. The emperor gave Ambassador de Praet the authority to promise the provision of more soldiers from the Low Countries and to convince the English king that this was the right time to take advantage of Francis's weakness.

Charles, though, still hampered by the lack of funds, was doing little to follow up his own success in the Pyrenees, preferring to concentrate his efforts in Italy. He wrote to his ambassador in Rome, the Duke of Sessa, that his army had to return to Spain from Fuenterrabia because it was in great need of reorganisation. This displeased Henry who, along with Wolsey, had learnt from the events of 1523 not to commit to military action unless absolutely sure of his ally's intentions. He made it clear that he would only do so if Bourbon redirected his attack northwards towards Lyons, and if Charles agreed to provide reinforcements from the Low Countries and contribute to the costs of the English army. Of this there was little real chance. The emperor might make promises but they were little more than good intentions. Charles had yet to pay any of the money that had previously been promised to Henry to make up for the loss of his French pensions. Henry still had concerns about a possible attack from Scotland and the activities of Richard de la Pole.

Throughout the summer there were rumours of possible truces and peace deals. On 14 May Charles produced a lengthy secret document for Gerard de la Plaine, his representative being sent to Rome. It outlined nine possible peace settlements that might be considered, involving various combinations of royal marriages; control of Milan and other Italian cities; his and Francis's rights in Burgundy, Artois and Flanders; and a settlement of the Duke of Bourbon's outstanding claims against the French king and his mother. Nothing came of these ideas and with de la Plaine's unexpected death in August, they were never seriously considered.

Nevertheless, in early September Henry sent word to the Duke of Norfolk (the Earl of Surrey had inherited the title on the death of his father earlier in the year) and wrote to the country's lords and gentlemen 'to be ready with such power as you be able to make'[15] for an invasion of France. It seems doubtful that this would actually happen especially so late in the year, and even as the letters were being sent events were turning against such an action. No invasion force was sent. Ambassador de Praet, whose relations with Wolsey were rapidly deteriorating, started to advise Charles that it would be better to come to terms with France than let Henry VIII betray him.

By the autumn Henry's decision to hold back looked like a good one. As early as July Charles had been warned that unless Henry attacked France in the north thus forcing Francis to divide his forces, Francis would successfully counter-attack Bourbon in the south, make him retreat and follow him into Italy. Charles angrily wrote about Henry and Wolsey: 'If only they would keep their promises. Their endless delays threaten to ruin entirely the enterprise.' He went on that they should either invade France or pay Bourbon the money they had promised, and that he believed that they were honour bound to fulfil the treaty that they had concluded.[16] His fears were justified. As Francis moved against him Bourbon ended his siege of Marseilles and retreated, leaving the way open for Francis to advance into Italy. By the end of October, a French army, led in person by the king, had marched over the Alps and advanced on Milan. Faced by a much larger force, Charles de Lannoy, 1st Prince of Sulmona, commander of all Imperial armies in Italy, withdrew with his troops to Lodi where he was joined by Bourbon. Instead of immediately pursuing the retreating imperial troops, Francis secured Milan and then moved on to Pavia, held for Charles by Antonio de Leyva with about 9,000 troops. Although the walls were breached in several places, the French onslaught was withstood and Francis besieged the city.

As the French king looked to be in a position to dominate the whole of northern Italy, Venice, Siena and Lucca soon made alliances with him. In Rome, Pope Adrian had died in September 1523. His austere lifestyle and attempts to reform the clergy had not been well received there. According to the Florentine diplomat and historian Francisco Guicciardini, the cardinals and priests were 'full of ambition and incredible greed' and, on news of his death, there was 'boundless joy'. A non-Italian Pope was not to be elected again for over 450 years. In one of the longest ever papal conclaves, the cardinals eventually chose Leo X's cousin, Guilio de' Medici, who became Clement VII. Henry VIII had been keen for Wolsey to be elected, and Charles in 1521 had even hinted that he would support his nomination, but in reality, he had no chance.

When Clement had been elected, Charles's ambassador in Rome had believed that the new Pope would give his support to the emperor's cause. This was not to be. Clement maintained a neutral position and wished to act as a peacemaker. The College of Cardinals wrote to Charles in March 1524 saying that they had elected Clement because 'they knew that he would employ all his energies to establish a general peace of Christendom.' They pointed out that 'former Emperors did not earn their great reputations by expelling the French ... or subjecting Italy, but by making war upon the Jews, putting heretics to death.' He should therefore follow their example by 'concluding peace with the King of France, making war with the Turks and trampling under foot and extirpating the Lutherans.'[17] In December 1524 Clement came to an understanding with Francis. There was discussion of the possible marriage of Francis's second son, Henri, to the Pope's niece, Catherine de' Medici, and some of the French army was sent south through the Papal States to challenge Spanish control of Naples. Clement explained the agreement to Charles by writing that 'since his elevation to the Papal throne his love for him [Charles] has not diminished, but his hatred towards others [Francis] has disappeared.'[18] Charles replied by asking whether it was

1. Kaiser Maximilian I (1459–1519). A seventeenth-century copy of a portrait by Bernhard Strigel (c.1507). Maximilian was Charles V's paternal grandfather and his predecessor as Holy Roman Emperor.

2. Margaret of Austria (1480–1530) at the age of about 10 by Jean Hay (the Master of Moulins). Margaret was taken to France when betrothed to the future Charles VIII at the age of 3. Charles VIII repudiated the betrothal in 1491. After the deaths of two husbands (Prince Juan of the Asturias and Duke Philibert of Savoy), she played a major role in Charles' upbringing and served as his regent in the Low Countries until her death in 1530.

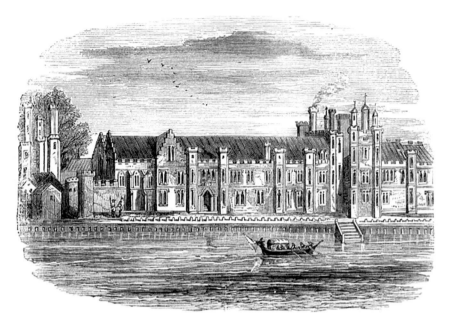

3. The Palace of Placentia, usually known as Greenwich Palace, had been rebuilt by Henry VII between 1498 and 1504. Henry VIII and both his daughters, Mary and Elizabeth, were born here. Charles V stayed in the royal apartments during his visit to England in 1522.

4. The courtyard of Margaret of Austria's palace in Mechelen, often known as the Court of Savoy. Margaret established her court here after returning to the Low Countries in 1507 to become guardian of Charles and his sisters.

5. Erasmus of Rotterdam (1466–1536), by Frans Huys (1522–1562) after Hans Holbein. Erasmus, probably the most renowned scholar of his time, had an influence on the education of both Henry VIII and Charles V.

6. Charles V in about 1520 shortly after his election as Holy Roman Emperor, by a Netherlandish painter. The insignia of the Order of the Golden Fleece is prominent on his chest. He was rarely painted without it.

7. Henry VII and his wife Elizabeth of York (rear) and Henry VIII and his wife Jane Seymour (front) by George Vertue (1684–1756) after Hans Holbein the Younger (1497–1543). Holbein's original mural, which established the pose most associated with Henry VIII, was lost in the fire of 1698 that destroyed most of the palace. However, a copy had been made by van Leemput in 1667 on which this version was based.

8. The Tournament on Horseback by Albrecht Dürer c.1517/18. Henry VIII's performance in jousts was at its peak when this woodcut was made. He revelled in his successes which continued into the 1530s.

QUESTA LAPIDE, CHE CELEBRA LA DIMORA IN BOLOGNA DI
CLEMENTE VII E DI CARLO V NEGLI ANNI 1529 E 1530 E
LA INCORONAZIONE DI CARLO V A IMPERATORE NELLA
BASILICA DI S. PETRONIO DEL 24 FEBBRAIO 1530, FU, DALLA
FRONTE DEL PALAZZO DEL COMUNE, IN OCCASIONE DEI
RESTAURI, QUI TRASPORTATA NELL'ANNO 1887.

9. The plaque on the wall of the Palazzo Comunale (Palazzo d'Accursio), Bologna, commemorating the meeting of Charles V and Pope Clement VII from November 1529 to February 1530 and the emperor's coronation in the Basilica of San Petronius on 24 February 1530. The plaque was erected in 1887.

10. Francis I (1494–1547) by Titian. Francis was the main rival of both Charles V and Henry VIII after he became King of France in 1515. This made war between Charles and Henry less likely as both knew that Francis would take advantage of such a situation.

Henry Second Roy de France

11. Henri II, King of France between 1547 and 1559 by Jean Morin (1600–1650) after Francois Clouet. Henri died, aged 40, as a result of infection of an eye wound sustained while jousting at a tournament held to celebrate the Peace of Cateau-Cambrésis.

12. Emperors Charles V and his brother Ferdinand I (c.1531). In January 1531 Ferdinand was crowned King of the Romans, Charles' designated successor as Holy Roman Emperor.

13. Emperor Charles V. A woodcut by Lucas Cranach. Note the use of the emblem of the Order of the Golden Fleece; and, in the top right, is Charles's motto, 'Plus Oultre' ('Plus Ultra') meaning 'Further beyond' on his symbol of the two pillars, representing the Pillars of Hercules.

MARIA REGINA HONGAR. GVBER. BELGII SOROR IMPERAT. CAROLI QVINTI.

14. Mary of Hungary (1505–1558), Charles' younger sister. She was married to King Louis II of Hungary until his death in 1526 at the Battle of Mohacs. She became Charles' regent in the Low Countries in 1531. She travelled to Spain with Charles in 1556 and died only one month after him in October 1558.

15. Armour, probably of Henry VIII, produced in the Royal Workshops at Greenwich in 1527. The armour, made of steel, gold, leather and copper alloys, stands 185.4 cms high and in total weighs 28.45 kg (62lb 12 oz).

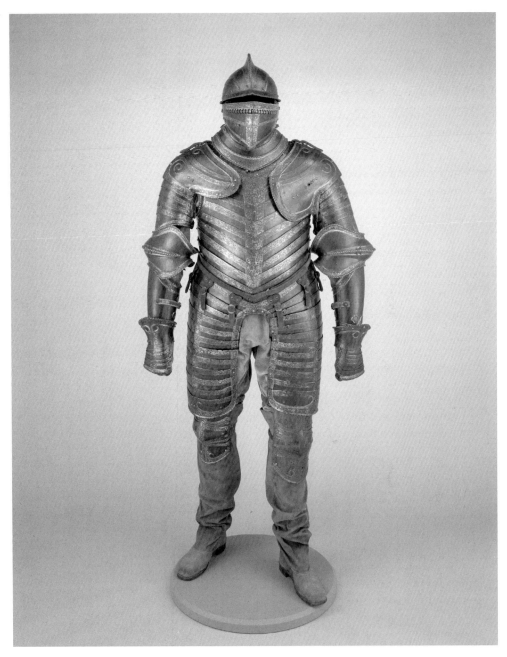

16. The Field Armour of Henry VIII, produced in northern Italy, used by the king in the campaign to capture Boulogne in 1544. Weighing 22.91 kg, it is lighter than the earlier armour but it very clearly demonstrates Henry's greatly increased girth in his later years.

17. Charles V. This engraving was produced in Antwerp during the 1620s by Lucas Vorsterman. It shows the emperor as he would have looked in his formal armour during the 1530s.

18. Henry VIII by Wenceslaus Hollar, produced in 1647 based on an earlier Holbein sketch. In this engraving Henry is shown in his early forties during the 1530s.

19. Henry VIII in 1547 – an unflattering engraving by Cornelis Massys. This image shows clearly how overweight Henry became. Shortly before his death he was hardly able to walk independently.

20. The future Edward VI (1537–1553), a portrait from the workshop of Hans Holbein, reworked after he became king in 1547. (Holbein died in November 1543). Edward was keen to introduce further evangelical reforms in the Church and wished to prevent his Catholic sister Mary succeeding him.

21. The victory of Goleta, near Tunis (in 1535), from the Triumphs of Charles V. Charles led the successful campaign to drive the Ottoman Admiral Barbarossa out of Tunis in 1535. Goleta was the fortress protecting the harbour of Tunis.

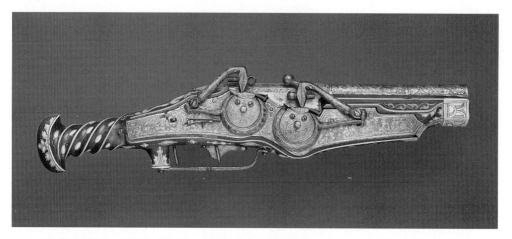

22. Double-barrelled wheel-lock pistol made for Emperor Charles V by Peter Peck, Munich c.1540–45. The pistol was made of steel, gold, cherry wood and staghorn. It is 49.2 cms long and weighs 2.55 kg.

23. Emperor Charles V after the Battle of Mühlberg (1547) was painted by Titian while the emperor was in Augsburg in 1548. This copy was produced by Franz von Lenbach in 1868. The image of the armoured Charles as the conquering warrior was how he wished to be remembered – the reality by the late 1540s was different.

24. The future Philip II of Spain as King Consort of England, 1555. The inscription reads: King Philip, Prince of Spain, 28 years of age.

25. Queen Mary of England, 1555. The image is very similar to the well-known painting by Anthonis Mor. The inscription reads: Mary I Queen of England, France and Ireland, Defender of the Faith.

26. A view of Charles V's rooms at Yuste from his gardens. He lived here for the last eighteen months of his life and died in his bedroom which adjoined the monastic church.

hatred to defend Italy and the Holy Church, and that Clement's predecessors Leo and Adrian had judged differently.

By February 1525 English negotiations with French diplomats had been renewed. In Spain Charles was depressed by his situation. While jotting down notes to help clarify his thoughts he wrote that he had always wished for peace, but that 'it cannot be had without the enemy's consent.'[19] He considered that his friends had 'forsaken me in my evil hour', by which he meant Henry VIII in particular, and that 'all are equally determined to … keep me in my present distressed state.' His allies were deserting him and his alliance with Henry had reached a low point. Both sides believed that they had been let down, Henry in 1523 and Charles in 1524, as indeed they had been. Neither had any more money to spend on the war. Henry had easily spent the £400,000 that had been raised by forced loans and parliamentary grants, and Charles recognised that he had no money even to pay his existing army, let alone employ more soldiers.

The level of distrust between the erstwhile allies can be clearly seen in a letter from Charles de Lannoy to Margaret of Austria in which he wrote: 'If the English King had done his duty towards the Emperor, his ally, and remitted sooner his contribution in money, the affairs in Italy would be in a more prosperous state.' In England an incident involving the arrest of a messenger and the opening of letters sent by Ambassador de Praet to Charles and Margaret of Austria broke any remaining trust between Wolsey and the Imperial ambassador. The letters contained unfavourable remarks about Wolsey and they were immediately taken to him. He summoned de Praet and objected to the language used and what he claimed was the misleading information that de Praet was giving the emperor, forbidding him to write again unless Wolsey first read the correspondence. De Praet in turn complained in the strongest terms about the interception of his letters, saying that 'great injury had been done to the emperor's honour and reputation' and arguing that never before had an ambassador of an ally been prevented from communicating freely with his king. He added that he believed that this had not been the first time that letters had been opened and that Wolsey's motives were to find information that could be used against Charles.[20] Needless to say, de Praet was withdrawn as Charles's ambassador to England within months. There was little point in having a representative that had lost the trust of its host country, as he would have little access to useful information.

Charles knew that in Italy a major battle could not be 'postponed for much longer'. His army under Lannoy and Bourbon was advancing from Lodi towards Pavia. The commanders knew that they had to attempt to break the siege immediately before they ran out of money to pay their troops. Although some reports reaching Charles suggested that the French were weaker than many people thought, at the beginning of February, de Praet had advised Charles that 'Things are going badly – there is no hope left but in battle.'[21] Lannoy believed that Charles 'had done enough for his honour and ought to conclude peace', though he was determined to follow Charles's instructions to the best of his ability. On considering the coming conflict the emperor concluded: 'my prospects are bad'. Wolsey was sanguine about the outcome of the battle. If the emperor won, then England was already his ally and relations could be restored. If the French were victorious, he believed that the cost to Francis would be so high that he would need English friendship and because they had been in negotiations for many months, the concessions that Henry would have to make would be limited.

In his notes Charles commented that regardless of the outcome of the battle, he wished to go to Italy himself in the future to revive his fortunes and to put right the fact that he had done little as yet 'to cover myself in glory'. He thought that one way to fund such an expedition and to help deal with the governance of Spain in his absence was to marry his cousin, Princess Isabella of Portugal. Although these were his own private thoughts and not communicated to Henry, this was perhaps the moment at which Charles decided that marriage to another cousin, Henry's daughter, Princess Mary, to whom he had been betrothed for several years but which could not be finalised for a few more years because of her age, was both of decreasing diplomatic importance and increasing impracticability because of the wait for an heir. The 'Great Enterprise' that had started with such enthusiasm had disintegrated amid widespread distrust and accusations of deceit with the result that Henry and Charles could hardly any longer be regarded as allies.

Chapter Nine

Rapidly Changing Alliances

At about midday on 10 March 1525, urgent messages arrived for Charles in Madrid. They carried news about the long-awaited battle that had taken place at Pavia two weeks earlier, on 24 February, Charles's twenty-fifth birthday. On receiving the information, he turned pale, remained silent and retired to his rooms for private prayer and contemplation. After about 30 minutes he emerged and asked for further details. He was told that on the night of 23/24 February, with their enemy distracted by an artillery barrage and heavy rain, the Imperial army had advanced from their position towards the Mirabello hunting-park where most of the French army believed themselves secure behind sound walls. Engineers were able to create three breaches in the defences, thereby allowing their troops to enter the park and have some element of surprise on their side as the battle commenced at dawn. They were joined by the soldiers of Antonio de Levya, Duke of Terranova, who overcame French troops in the siege lines and attacked from the town. The numbers of troops on each side were roughly even but well before midday, the battle was over and though not a long one, the outcome was decisive. Not only had the French had been defeated with heavy losses, but King Francis was now Lannoy's prisoner.

How this had come about has been described elsewhere but it was clear that the ability of Charles's generals to adapt their tactics to the changing nature of warfare, especially the firearms that were becoming more widely used on the battlefield, won the day.[1] Francis's undoubted bravery in leading a cavalry charge that initially broke through the Imperial lines had not been enough. Because of the disposition of their troops after this charge, the French were unable to make their superior number of cannons count, while the 3,000 Spanish arquebusiers could direct their deadly fire on the French. Francis's horse was shot from beneath him after which he continued to fight on foot until surrounded and captured as were other commanders – Anne, Duke of Montmorency, Marshal of France; Henry II of Navarre; and Robert III de La Marck. Thousands of others fell on the battlefield or were drowned in the River Ticino as they fled. Casualties among the French nobility matched those at Agincourt over 100 years before. Francis wrote to his mother that all was lost to him, except his honour and his life.

Charles's reaction to these events was one of relief after months of apprehension and increasing concern about his diplomatic and military position. He remained calm and announced that noisy rejoicing with bells and fireworks was inappropriate after a battle won against Christians as opposed to infidels. Prayers of thanksgiving and acknowledgement of the victory as being the will of God were ordered. The fact that it had occurred on his birthday did not escape his notice and he took this to be another sign of God's grace. He ordered Lannoy to take good care of his royal prisoner and to send regular reports about Francis's health to his mother in France. Charles believed that he had now been given the opportunity to achieve peace in Italy and throughout Europe, to pardon his enemies, though he was certainly known to harbour grievances against those who opposed him, and reward his friends. What he failed to realise was that a peace based on Habsburg dominance was hardly acceptable to his fellow rulers and was more than likely to be challenged. This was despite the fact that Pope Clement and many other rulers who had recently come to terms with Francis hurried to send their congratulations to Charles.

Rumours of an Imperial victory were first heard in England on 4 March but the scale of the victory was only confirmed to Henry five days later. It is told that the king rose from his bed and dressed quickly, read the message, cried out with joy, fell to his knees in prayer and then called for wine. He quizzed the messenger about the capture of the French king and was reassured that he had slight wounds, had been disarmed and was now in the hands of Lannoy and Bourbon, who were treating him with the dignity that befitted his rank.[2] Particularly pleasing to Henry VIII was the news of the death of Richard de la Pole, on hearing which he is supposed to have wished God to have mercy on his soul, cried out that all the enemies of England are gone and told his servants to give the messenger more wine.

On the same day an audience arranged with French envoys was cancelled, giving an indication that Henry hoped to make the most of the Imperial victory. The king attended High Mass at St Paul's, officiated by Wolsey, on Sunday, 12 March,[3] and celebratory bonfires were lit throughout the country. It might be surprising to learn that John, Lord Berners, Lord Deputy of Calais, initially asked for instructions on whether or not to celebrate Charles's victory at Pavia. This was a result of the unpredictable nature of English foreign policy and the knowledge that right up until the outcome of the battle was known, negotiations were taking place with French diplomats. Indeed, many in England were expecting peace to be made with France. Wolsey, however, on behalf of the king, immediately wrote to Charles congratulating him on the victory, expressing his 'greatest pleasure and satisfaction' and the expectation that 'they shall be able not only to recover all their rights, most unjustly detained by the said king (Francis) but to establish ... the peace and tranquillity of the Christian world.'[4]

The war, though, had not ended with Francis's capture. His mother, Louise of Savoy, became regent of France and she intended to defend the country, uphold royal authority and negotiate her son's release. Henry lost no time in wishing to open talks with Charles about their next move. He believed that the time was right for them to 'devise means of getting full satisfaction from France' and that not an hour should be lost. He recognised that this was his opportunity to follow in the footsteps of Henry V and take much of France. He received encouragement from the Duke of Bourbon who believed that 'now is the time for the king to obtain all his inheritance.' He considered 'that Henry will get by a peace some part of his right ... but still he thinks it better to take and enjoy all.'[5] Henry's first proposal to Charles argued that it would be folly to restore Francis to even a reduced France and, instead, they should put into effect the plan of the Great Enterprise and divide France between them. Henry would be crowned king of France, and take much of the north and centre; Bourbon would be restored to all the lands that he had previously controlled so long as he recognised Henry as king; while Charles would take Burgundy, Provence and Languedoc. Henry also reminded the emperor that by marrying Princess Mary he might, in time, inherit much more.

Henry was aware that Charles might not accept these plans. The victory, after all, had been Charles's, not Henry's. The English had signally failed to provide any assistance to Charles during 1524 and had played no part at Pavia. Relations between the allies had been deteriorating for over a year and the recent row about the opening of Ambassador de Praet's mail was continuing. On 26 March Henry therefore provided Sir Richard Wingfield and Cuthbert Tunstall, Bishop of London and Lord Privy Seal, who were about to travel to Spain to negotiate with Charles, with a clear set of instructions.[6] First they should ascertain whether Charles intended to keep Francis in Italy or move him to Spain. Next, they should determine whether he planned to deprive Francis of his kingdom altogether or restore him upon a ransom. They must argue forcefully in favour of the former, saying that 'No tranquillity can be expected from a tyrant who seeks means of sowing dissension' and 'if he be restored he will not fail to seek opportunities of revenging himself ... therefore he and his successors should be utterly abolished.'

If Charles agreed to remove Francis, then the question of who should rule France would become important. They should 'put the Emperor in mind of his secret promise made to the King's Highness and Wolsey at sundry times and places, all tending to the expulsion of Francis, and setting up the King in his place.' They were to encourage Charles to invade France in person as soon as possible. If, on the other hand, Charles did not 'consent to exclude the French king', they must emphasise that the existing treaty does not allow Charles to 'make an agreement with Francis without the consent of the other [Henry], and they shall demand, on the king's behalf, Normandy, Gascony, Guienne, Brittany and Picardy.' Failing that 'they are in all cases to stick to the claim on Picardy with 100,000 crowns pension.' The final section of these instructions permitted the envoys to resort to an unsubtle threat: 'They are to show the Emperor that if the King were minded to forsake his alliance, there want not offers for that purpose.' In other words, if Henry did not get at least some of what he wanted, then he would consider looking elsewhere for allies, and that could only mean France.

Any attempt to permanently deprive Francis and his heirs of the throne would require a large invasion force. It was proposed that if Charles would not personally invade France, then he should provide the funds for Bourbon to lead an army and, failing that, Henry would subsidise the duke. It is difficult to know what exactly Henry really hoped for, but he was serious in his anticipation of something substantial. Before the end of March commissioners were appointed to collect yet another tax, called the Amicable Grant, from across the country. It would be explained to the taxpayers of England, who had already paid substantial sums for Henry's war, that this grant would enable the king to recover what was rightfully his, for his honour and theirs. Such was the propaganda put out in April 1525 – Henry wanted the crown of France or at least those lands formerly held by kings of England. Plans for an invasion were rapidly made, with the Duke of Norfolk being appointed to command the vanguard. He was to cross to Calais with 20,000 foot soldiers and 2,000 cavalry and from there, advance towards Normandy. It was believed that Picardy was too strongly defended and a large army would be unable to forage sufficient supplies. The king would follow with another 20,000 troops soon afterwards.

Henry was to be thwarted on every front. His call to arms failed to create a wave of anti-French sentiment. Most people were tired of war and resented the fact that they had to pay for it. There was considerable hostility to the Amicable Grant, as those commissioned to organise it soon realised. Their first task was to gain the agreement of as many people as possible to pay amounts based on the estimates of 1522. Only then were they to collect the money, by mid-summer, and hand it over to the treasurer. The tax amounted to between one-third and one-quarter of the wealth of the clergy and between one-sixth and one-tenth of that of the laity.[7] None was ever paid. There was much unrest involving serious disturbances in many counties, particularly Kent, Essex, Norfolk and Suffolk, as well as in London. As early as 1 April the Duke of Norfolk wrote to Wolsey that he was 'afraid there will be great difficulty in raising the money generally throughout the country'.[8]

More damning was Archbishop Warham's note to Wolsey on 5 April[9] that 'It will be hard to raise the money', and he provided an insight into the attitude of many people in Kent 'for the secret ear of the Cardinal'. He informed Wolsey that they believed this was not a loan that would ever be repaid and they were very unhappy with constant tax demands; that the commissioners feared the people and did not press them to pay; and that many claimed that they were willing to pay but were too poor to do so. So much for the normal objections to taxation. There were, however, more fundamental issues raised. They objected to all the money being spent in France and in Flanders, and said that if Henry became king of France 'he will be obliged to spend his time and revenue there.' Warham continued that 'They are sorry, rather than otherwise, at the captivity of Francis I' and believed 'that all the sums already spent on the invasion of France have not gained the King a foot more land in it than his father had'. They believed that the king's father had the money and wisdom to win France 'if he had thought it expedient'.

The opposition to the Amicable Grant was not surprising. Part of the parliamentary subsidy granted in 1523 was still being collected and none of the 'loans' of 1522–23 had been repaid. The scale of the resistance became clear in early May when several thousand protestors from Suffolk and neighbouring counties gathered in Lavenham (Suffolk). The Dukes of Suffolk and Norfolk raised troops to use against them and though bloodshed was avoided, ringleaders were arrested in the aftermath. Given the widespread discontent, efforts were made to make the demands more tolerable, but they leave the distinct impression that the authorities were panicking, making policy on the hoof with no real direction. The result was confusion.[10] There was an attempt to persuade people that it was a loan that would be repaid, but most knew better than that. In London it was announced that the grant was to be changed to a benevolence, in other words people could pay what they believed they could afford. Once rumour of this was heard, it made collection of the grant elsewhere almost impossible. Many commissioners were not informed and were still attempting to raise the full amount, while others decided to reduce the sum being demanded. Eventually the whole Amicable Grant was cancelled in the middle of May. Henry publicly took no responsibility for the debacle, denying knowledge of the original demand while taking some credit for its abolition and pardoning those arrested as ringleaders after their submission. Whether it was the Council, Wolsey or Henry who originally approved the plan is impossible to know, but Wolsey shouldered most of the blame. Its failure might have resulted in a major setback to Henry's hopes of glory in France if those plans had not already been dealt a far more serious blow.

Emperor Charles had made it very clear that he was not going to be involved in the invasion and dismemberment of France. Although he did not openly admit it and gave other reasons for the decision, he simply did not have the money to carry out such a plan. As early as 26 March he wrote to Ambassador de Praet that Louise of Savoy wanted peace and that he too desired 'peace, but requires the restitution of all that justly belongs to himself' and that he wished for peace 'by fair means, and not to make war upon a prisoner who cannot defend himself.' He intended to 'use the virtues of magnanimity and clemency.' De Praet was to tell Henry that the emperor would not disarm in case his demands were rejected but to add that 'If the English wish for war, [he] leaves to them the responsibility for it.'[11] It must have become very plain to Henry that Charles was not going to depose Francis, but instead secure a peace that met his demands and then restore him.

The same message was given to the English envoys in Spain. They also reported that Charles was very angry with Wolsey for words that the cardinal had allegedly used, calling Charles a liar, Margaret of Austria a ribald, Archduke Ferdinand a child and Bourbon a traitor.[12] The envoys denied that Wolsey would have said such things and that perhaps the emperor had been misled by de Praet. He, however, was defended by Charles in a personal letter to Henry writing that he 'does not believe his ambassador would have written anything with a bad purpose'.[13] Sir Richard Wingfield informed Wolsey in June that he had worked hard to pacify the emperor and that eventually Charles had accepted that the words had been spoken in anger and might be excused, and that henceforth he would give credence not only to words but to deeds. Wolsey was also warned that any negotiations that he had with the French would immediately be known to Charles because Louise of Savoy would inform him of them in an effort to try to divide the king and the emperor.

That was not to prove a difficult task. The Anglo-Imperial/Spanish alliance had all but collapsed after four years. It was now clear that what Charles wished for was a settlement with Francis on his own terms, despite his assurance that Henry's demands would be taken into account. In his first proposals to Louise of Savoy, he wanted all French claims to Burgundy,

Artois, Flanders, Milan and Naples to be renounced; a commitment to end any assistance to Charles's enemies elsewhere; and the restoration of Bourbon to all his lands. There was nothing about Henry's claims in France. Although Charles's demands were unlikely to be met in full, the danger for England was that Charles would reach an agreement with Francis and leave England without an ally. Louise of Savoy sent envoys to Spain for negotiations that eventually lasted over nine months. By June her representatives in England, Jean Brinon and Jean-Joachin de Passano, had renewed talks with Wolsey, who now welcomed the opportunity to negotiate.

For Wolsey, England's foreign policy was more complex than a straightforward choice between Charles and Francis. The question of how to enhance Henry's status in Europe was always finely balanced. He needed to consider whether it was best achieved by war or peace, avoiding being on the losing side in case of war, and whether to work for a balance of power between Charles and Francis that could maximise England's influence. The benefits gained by an alliance with one or the other were constantly shifting. In 1521, given Henry's ambitions in France, there was more to be gained by siding with Charles. By 1525, Henry's knowledge that Charles was not going to help him take the French crown and a fear of being isolated in a Europe dominated by the emperor meant that an 'honourable' peace with France, so long as it did not mean war with Charles, seemed the most favourable option. When it became clear that Charles had all but abandoned the idea of marriage to Princess Mary in favour of a Portuguese bride, Henry might have been insulted but Wolsey perhaps saw that it opened up the possibility of a French marriage, another bargaining counter in negotiations with France. For her part, Louise of Savoy was keen to prevent any English assistance to a possible attack by the Duke of Bourbon from Italy, either by means of a diversionary invasion in the north or helping to finance it.

On 30 August, the Treaty of the More, consisting of five separate agreements between England and France, was signed at Wolsey's manor in Hertfordshire. Peace was agreed and a defensive alliance established, together with Henry's commitment to use his influence with Charles to achieve the release of Francis on reasonable terms, even though with hindsight it seems unlikely that he had any influence left with the emperor. Next, a substantial pension of 100,000 ecus (approximately £22,000) each year up to a total of 2 million ecus, was promised to Henry in return for giving up territorial claims, along with smaller but still significant amounts for others in England. The king by now had more faith in the French willingness to pay than in Charles who had failed to recompense Henry for the loss of the pension over the previous three years. Other agreements cleared up maritime disputes between the countries, prevented the return of the Duke of Albany to Scotland and provided compensation for Henry's sister Mary, the widow of Louis XII and now Duchess of Suffolk, for any losses caused by the war.

There was always the danger that the treaty would antagonise Charles. Henry's ambassadors in Spain certainly thought so. Wolsey, however, argued that there was nothing in the treaty that damaged the emperor's interests. The extent of the Imperial victory at Pavia and the capture of Francis had given Charles plenty to think about. He felt under no obligation towards Henry, but how could he best take advantage of this new position? When what he called his 'just and reasonable' demands were dismissed by Louise of Savoy as completely unacceptable, it became clear that there would be some difficult negotiations ahead. He instructed Lannoy to move Francis from Lombardy to Naples, but Francis persuaded the viceroy that if only he could meet Charles face to face, he would make substantial concessions and all their difficulties would be easily settled. In June Lannoy therefore directed his fleet to sail to Spain and by August 1525, the king was in the Royal Alcazar of Madrid. The emperor, however, did not wish to deal directly with Francis, whose attempt to gain the confidence of Charles's sister Eleanor was rebuffed, when she told him that she would only do as Charles wished. The French king also bribed his guards to improve the conditions of his captivity and even made a failed escape attempt. Unknown to the emperor, Francis also signed a secret document stating that any concessions that he made as a prisoner were invalid because they would have been made under duress.

Charles was uncertain as to what to do and his advisers were divided. Some, such as his confessor, suggested that a generous settlement would be more likely to bring about a lasting peace, with Francis bound to him as a result of his magnanimity. Others, particularly his Chancellor, Gattinara, and the respected military commander the Duke of Alva, argued that it was best to take full advantage of the present opportunity. They warned that the fruits of victory consisted of using it well and that there was the danger that he would end up, like Hannibal against the Romans, with a major military victory and nothing to show for it. They had little faith in Francis's virtue and believed that he would renege on any deal and seek revenge. It was only when Francis became seriously ill in the autumn that Charles visited him. Despite Charles's kind words and Francis's charm, a friendly relationship did not develop. What the incident made Charles realise, however, was that if Francis were to die all his advantage would be lost. Francis later bluffed that he was perfectly willing to remain a prisoner and even directed Louise of Savoy to begin the process of arranging for the accession of his son, Francis.

In the negotiations one of the major sticking points was Burgundy, which Charles believed to be part of his natural inheritance, but had been taken by the French in 1477 with the defeat and death of his great-grandfather, Charles the Bold, at the Battle of Nancy. With Gattinara leading the talks for Charles there was little headway, but when the more conciliatory Lannoy took over progress was made. In reality Francis hated his captivity and was impatient to return to France. The Treaty of Madrid was signed on 14 January 1526. Francis gave up his rights as feudal overlord in Flanders, Artois and Tournai, renounced his claims to Milan and Naples and promised to persuade the Paris *Parlement*, the most important court in France, to agree to the return of Burgundy to Charles. Francis was to marry Charles's sister Eleanor. According to Henry's representatives in Spain, this encouraged Francis to agree 'more readily to many articles at which he would otherwise have sticked'.[14] The Duke of Bourbon, who had expected to marry her, was displeased. Charles had to explain the necessity of the change and Bourbon was offered 'great recompenses', namely being promised control of Milan, to which he 'said with his tongue he was content, whether he was in his heart or not.'[15]

As a guarantee that Francis would fulfil the terms of the treaty, his two eldest sons, Francis and Henri, were to be handed over in exchange for the king. The boys were young – Francis had just reached his eighth birthday and Henri was just short of his seventh at the time of the exchange. In February Charles left Toledo and met Francis at Illescas, south of Madrid, where they exchanged solemn promises to uphold the agreement and the French king was introduced to Eleanor. Lannoy wrote to Margaret of Austria that 'I am to attend Francis and receive the Princes. It is a great and weighty charge.'[16]

On paper this was a great success for Charles, but Francis had on the previous day repeated his secret oath that it had no validity because it had been achieved by coercion. Gattinara believed that Charles did not have sufficient guarantees to ensure its implementation and refused to sign it. Nevertheless, on 17 March, Lannoy supervised the exchange of Francis for his sons on the French border with a parting reminder to the king: 'Do not forget your promise', to which Francis replied: 'I shall fail in nothing.' So five years after the outbreak of war between Charles and Francis, a war in which Henry had been keen to join on the emperor's side, peace had supposedly been achieved very much on Charles's terms and Henry was now allied to France.

Chapter Ten

Personal Matters

While these military and diplomatic manoeuvres were being played out during 1525 and into 1526, it should not be forgotten that both Charles and Henry were also dealing with domestic politics and family issues. Charles was still working on winning over the people of Spain. With the death or removal of his earlier Burgundian advisers, he now appointed Spaniards to key posts. Many of his Spanish subjects were beginning to recognise that they could benefit from having their king as emperor as it opened up both military and bureaucratic opportunities across Europe. Meanwhile, in England, Henry had now to accept that his wife Catherine, over five years older than him, was past childbearing age. The question of how he could deal with having no male heir was beginning to loom large.

On Charles's arrival in Spain in 1522, he first needed to deal with the aftermath of the revolts of the previous two years. In Castile he took a generally lenient approach. Most of those arrested were pardoned, with only 270 being imprisoned and twenty-three executed. In Valencia, where the challenge to the existing social order had been even more threatening, the nobility pushed for greater severity. Under the viceroy, Germaine of Foix, the widow of Ferdinand of Aragon, there were nearly 800 executions. There was also an ongoing religious issue in Valencia. A substantial number of Muslims lived there and many had been forcibly converted to Christianity. Some people questioned the validity of these conversions but they were declared to be acceptable because the individuals concerned had been given a choice – even though in many cases the choice offered had been either conversion or death.

Charles strengthened his relationship with the cortes of each kingdom. They had attempted to weaken his authority when he became their king, but now a more confident Charles expected them to provide him with the funds he requested before he attended to their grievances. He introduced measures to improve the efficiency of the administrative, judicial and financial functions of government. He wished to be seen as a king who was just and who would reward those who had been of service. Corrupt officials were removed from office and he appointed men who people trusted to the

Royal Council. He created a number of new councils – of War (1522), of Finance (1523) and of the Indies (1524) – to administer specific aspects of government.

This system of councils was also used to administer lands outside Castile – Aragon, Catalonia, Valencia, Sardinia, Sicily and Naples that had belonged to the kingdom of Aragon, and then New Spain (Mexico) and Peru as Spanish conquests in the New World expanded. A viceroy, appointed by Charles from amongst the high nobility, represented him in each of these lands. Each viceroy's work was overseen and administered by the relevant Council, which produced consultation documents for Charles before final decisions were made. The secretary of the council would then draft letters for his signature and dispatch them to the viceroy. The system had the checks and balances needed for a consistent and effective decision-making process but could be very slow, a problem when there was some urgency. It required Charles to work hard if he was to keep up with the demands made upon him. He was usually regarded as diligent and thoughtful in his application to the work involved.

For their support the higher nobility was rewarded by appointments to viceroyalties, councils and army commands. Many of the lesser nobility and landowning classes gained opportunities as officers or minor officials, especially in Italy and the New World. Others trained as lawyers and some were able to rise high in royal service, with appointments increasingly made on the basis of ability. The most successful aspired to join the ranks of the higher nobility, although this could cause resentment from the ancient noble families. Those in power often used their position to build up a network of officials who owed loyalty to them, but Charles was fully aware of the power of patronage and never delegated major appointments. If some individuals felt undervalued there was always the risk that they would take bribes. Nevertheless, Charles was able to establish a reasonably efficient system of government, although his efforts to increase his revenues by imposing taxes on the nobility, who were traditionally exempt, were resisted and came to nothing.

Perhaps what mattered most for many people in his Spanish lands was the issue of his marriage. Charles had already fathered a number of daughters as a result of various relationships in the early 1520s.[1] The eldest was born in 1522 to Johanna van der Gheynst, a servant of Charles de Lalaing with whom Charles had stayed during the siege of Tournai the previous year. Christened Margaret, she was later acknowledged by the emperor and brought up in the Low Countries by his aunt, Margaret of Austria, and then his sister, Mary of Hungary. She was later used by Charles in diplomatic marriages and went on to become the Governor of the Low Countries under Charles's successor. Other liaisons produced two other daughters born in 1523. Tadea was born to Ursolina della Penna of Perugia, who had been at Charles's court in the Low Countries. The girl spent her youth in a convent in Italy, briefly met Charles in the early 1530s and eventually became a nun in Rome. Much less is known of a third daughter, Juana, born in Valladolid. Sent to a convent with her mother immediately after her birth, she died in 1530. None of this, though, provided Charles with an heir.

At the age of 25 he remained the most eligible bachelor in Europe, despite his frequently remarked on large lower jaw. However, the number of potential brides was limited to royal princesses and any marriage was expected to bring significant political and financial benefits. He had been betrothed several times, most recently to Henry's young daughter, Mary. His subjects wished for a quick marriage. The death of his father Philip, at the age of 28, and that of his uncle Juan, aged only 19, showed that death could sometimes be sudden, even for those in their prime. The last thing that the Spaniards wanted was his demise with no legitimate heir, or a very young successor that would mean a long period of minority rule with all the problems associated with either situation.

As relations with England deteriorated during 1524, Charles had serious doubts about his betrothal to Henry's daughter. On receiving the English ambassadors in Spain after the Battle of Pavia, he accepted a valuable ring sent on Mary's behalf saying that 'he would wear it for her sake'. He then requested that the 9-year-old princess should travel to Spain immediately so 'that she might be brought up in Spain, and learn the language and manners of the country'. Also, the first instalment of her dowry should be sent with her so that he could reassure his councillors and subjects that plans were moving forward.[2] The English envoys objected to this on the grounds that the journey to Spain would be damaging to the health of so young a princess. In any case Henry did not have the money. Charles threatened to cancel the engagement and marry elsewhere if he did not get his way. He already had a suitable alternative bride in mind: Isabella of Portugal, the sister of King John III. She was the daughter of King Manuel I and Maria of Aragon, the sister of both Charles's mother Juana and Catherine, the queen of England. Only two years younger than Charles, the marriage could be consummated immediately, would bring a larger dowry and she would be a very popular choice among his Spanish subjects.

In February 1525 King John of Portugal had married Charles's youngest sister, Catherine, and he was keen for the match, as was Charles's brother, Ferdinand. Negotiations were concluded by October 1525, even before the emperor had officially informed Henry of his decision to call off his betrothal to Mary. The marriage to Isabella was to take place in Seville and the dowry was to be one million ducats (about £200,000). The required dispensation from the Pope did not arrive until February 1526 and Charles used various subterfuges to slow down the wedding preparations without offending King John or Isabella. As Francis was being escorted north from Madrid by Lannoy, the emperor was travelling south through Extremadura to Seville where Isabella had arrived on 3 March. The city had been captured from the Moors in 1248 and the Alcazar had been the favourite residence of many Castilian monarchs. Having been granted a monopoly of the trade with the New World the city's size and wealth were growing rapidly.

Charles was welcomed by large crowds on the evening of 10 March and the marriage took place at 2 o'clock the next morning in what is now known as the 'Salon de Carlos V' in the Alcazar, newly refurbished with a fine coffered wooden ceiling for the occasion. The Portuguese ambassador wrote that 'the bride and groom ... have eyes only for one another.' Years later Charles recorded in his memoirs: 'The Emperor left Toledo in 1526 for Seville, where he married, and during the journey he received news that the Queen of Denmark, his sister, had died.' In a letter to his brother Ferdinand, he wrote: 'I have now entered upon the state of marriage, which pleases me well.' Charles was rarely one to reveal his emotions about personal issues in letters. Isabella seems to have charmed Charles with her intelligence, beauty and good nature. He had every reason to be pleased with his choice of wife. She proved to be an excellent regent for him when he left Spain. She had seven pregnancies and, although two ended in stillbirths and two sons, Ferdinand and Juan, died in infancy, three children survived to adulthood – Philip (born in 1527), Maria (1528) and Juana (1535).

After the wedding the couple travelled to Granada, no doubt enjoying the Andalusian spring. They rested briefly in Cordoba, the once great Moorish city which, in the reigns of Abd al Rahman III and his son Al Hakim II before 1000 CE, reputedly had fifty hospitals, 600 public baths, 1,000 mosques and a vast library with 400,000 volumes. They would have visited the former Mesquita or Great Mosque that had been converted into a cathedral and where the construction of a new capilla mayor [main chapel] and choir was just starting in the centre of the complex. Charles had given permission for this new building work but was reputed to have said when he saw it: 'You have destroyed something that was unique in the world.'

Once in Granada they stayed in the Alhambra Palace with its delicate plasterwork, patterned tiles, magnificent ceilings and lovely gardens cooled by flowing water. Charles and Isabella remained there for over six months, longer than originally expected. The emperor commissioned a new Renaissance palace to be built in the grounds to display the new styles of architecture that were being developed in Italy. It was never completed and though having many features that can be admired in isolation, it was always out of place. Charles was never to return to Andalusia; there were simply too many demands on his time elsewhere. As the couple travelled north at the end of the year, Isabella was pregnant but the international situation had turned against the emperor.

Henry VIII, on the other hand, had by 1526 been married to Charles's aunt Catherine of Aragon for seventeen years. On his accession Henry had been keen to marry her and, for years, had shown her much affection. She was well regarded and popular with the English people. There was, of course, one central problem. Their son, Henry, had survived for only a few weeks. Their daughter, Mary, was born in 1516, but Catherine's four other known pregnancies had resulted in the stillbirth of two daughters and two sons. There had been no pregnancy since 1518 and, by the early 1520s, they no longer shared a bed. There would be no more children. Henry had taken lovers during this time, though he was by no means the lothario that many have assumed him to have been, unlike his fellow monarch Francis I. Elizabeth Blount became Henry's mistress in 1514 and the relationship lasted for six or seven years. In 1519 she gave birth to a son conceived when Catherine was in the latter stages of her pregnancy in 1518. Although Elizabeth left court during her pregnancy and confinement to avoid scandal, Henry freely acknowledged the boy as his own, presented him at court and named him Henry FitzRoy (son of the king). Blount married Gilbert Tailboys in 1522 by which time Henry had turned his attentions to the older Boleyn sister, Mary. She had lived at the French court for some years and is supposed to have had an affair with Francis I before returning to England and marrying William Carey.

The lack of a legitimate son was of major concern to Henry. Although affectionate to his daughter, he was keenly aware that there had never been a queen regnant in England. Her marriage to a foreign prince could lead to England being ruled by that prince, while if she married an English nobleman his family would be the envy of all others. In either case the Tudor dynasty would end, civil unrest might ensue and the work of Henry's father would have been in vain.

Henry FitzRoy's first six years had been very comfortable but generally out of the public eye. In 1525, however, Henry decided that he should be given honours appropriate for a king's son. He was raised to the highest rank of the peerage, being created Duke of Richmond and Somerset, much to Queen Catherine's dissatisfaction. The significance of these titles was not lost on the many nobles who attended the ceremony. The lands granted to him were mainly from Margaret Beaufort's estate. She was descended from John Beaufort, Earl of Somerset, the legitimised son of John of Gaunt, Duke of Lancaster, and was the mother of Henry VII, who had held the title of Earl of Richmond. FitzRoy was also made Lord High Admiral of England and Lord President of the Council of the North. Henceforth, he lived at Sheriff Hutton Castle in Yorkshire, until brought back to Windsor in 1530. In May 1525 Wolsey sent to the king heraldic 'arms devised ... for his entirely beloved son, the Lord Henry FitzRoy'.[3] Henry perhaps considered making FitzRoy his heir at some point in the future and it was also mooted that if FitzRoy were to marry Princess Mary, the Tudor dynasty would be secured, but Henry never accepted this dubious solution.

The king became convinced that the failure of his marriage to produce a son was because the marriage itself was invalid in the eyes of God. If this was the case then Mary's position changed dramatically. Henry had always regarded himself as a true son of the Church. Until this time his beliefs were essentially traditional, hence his defence of the Papacy against Luther's criticisms. Although it has been suggested that he always wished to carry out ecclesiastical reforms, influenced by Erasmus and other humanist scholars,[4] there is also plenty of evidence supporting Henry's belief in the importance of pilgrimages, praying at the tombs of saints and the value of monasteries.[5]

His conviction that his marriage should never have taken place was based on the passage in Leviticus (Chapter 20, Verse 21) where it states that a man who marries his brother's wife shall be childless. Henry chose to interpret 'childless' as meaning without a son. He therefore concluded that Pope Julius II had been wrong to grant a dispensation for him to marry Catherine and that Pope Clement should now put this right, not just by allowing a divorce but by an annulment. Although Henry often left the details of policy and implementation to Wolsey and, later, Cromwell, preferring to spend time on his leisure activities, this problem was an exception. It brought together two aspects of government in which he was particularly interested: religion and foreign policy. As it was a matter of vital personal concern to him, he was bound to be intimately involved in resolving it.

What brought the matter to a head in 1526 was that Henry had fallen for Anne Boleyn and she resolutely rejected the idea of becoming a mere royal mistress. She wanted a marriage and though he was frustrated by her refusal to accept anything less, he recognised that a new marriage could provide him with a legitimate son. Anne was the daughter of Thomas Boleyn, a diplomat, and Elizabeth Howard, the sister of the Duke of Norfolk. Boleyn had been on missions to the Low Countries to persuade Margaret of Austria to support Henry's war with France in 1512, to France between 1518 and 1521 where he played a role in setting up the meeting at the Field of the Cloth of Gold, and to Charles V in Spain in 1521 and 1523. While in the Low Countries he had met Margaret of Austria and, in 1513, she had accepted his younger daughter Anne as a maid of honour in Mechelen. Anne then accompanied Henry's sister Mary to France for her marriage to Louis XII and stayed there for seven years, becoming a maid of honour to Queen Claude after Francis I became king.

In early 1522 she was recalled to England by her father to marry an Irish cousin, James Butler. The negotiations floundered and the marriage plan was abandoned. Slim, of middling height, with dark hair and eyes, opinions about her beauty vary, but she impressed the court with her charm, intelligence, quick wit and French style. She enjoyed the attentions of the courtiers and formed an attachment to Henry Percy, son of the Earl of Northumberland. This was ended by the opposition of both Percy's father and Cardinal Wolsey. Anne left court for a while, but soon returned as lady-in-waiting to Queen Catherine. There the poet Sir Thomas Wyatt is said to have fallen in love with her before he had to back down, given the growing interest of the king. By the end of 1526 Henry had decided that he wished to marry her. Both believed that this would be possible within months, with Catherine retiring to a convent and Pope Clement granting an annulment of the king's marriage to her. Such decisions were not uncommon. In March 1527 Pope Clement granted the petition of Henry's sister Margaret for a divorce from her second husband, the Earl of Angus. Earlier Charles Brandon had divorced his first wife, Margaret Neville, in 1507 and had his betrothal contract to Elizabeth Grey overturned in 1514 so that he could marry Henry's sister Mary. Neither Henry nor Anne anticipated just how long the process would take or how fundamental the changes required to bring it about would have to be. Once again the relationship between Henry VIII and Charles V was to be seriously challenged, and the outcome was to have profound implications for England and much of Europe.

Chapter Eleven

Hopes Destroyed

It must be doubtful whether anyone really believed that the terms set out in the Treaty of Madrid signed by Charles V and Francis I in January 1526 would be respected for long. Within days Sir Robert Wingfield, the English ambassador in the Low Countries, expressed the view that some of the terms were 'not in his [Francis's] power to perform' and others 'so great, that, being once at liberty, it is not like that he intendeth to perform them.'[1] He also reported that the peace was very unpopular in France and that preparations for war were being made in Italy. Even before the exchange of Francis for his sons, a distrustful Charles instructed Ambassador Louis de Praet, no longer welcome in England but his new ambassador in France, to 'become perfectly well acquainted with the physiognomy of the French princes, that there may be no trickery, especially as they are unknown to the Viceroy [Lannoy].'[2] Wolsey wrote to Louise of Savoy that 'The king and the whole country are pleased to hear of her son's deliverance' and 'doubts not that she will take care that the dishonourable and unreasonable treaty violently extorted from him will not be observed in any part.'[3]

Francis wasted no time in engineering its collapse. Soon after his release he claimed that the publication of the terms by Charles had made the task of persuading his subjects to approve the treaty much more difficult. French envoys in England informed Wolsey that Francis argued the treaty had been 'extorted by the Emperor through fear and menaces' and that 'neither he nor his subjects are bound in conscience, law or reason' to carry out its terms. Charles instructed de Praet to remind Francis of his obligations. Francis responded by saying that he needed to discuss the terms with his council as he had not had the chance to do so while he had been Charles's prisoner. The emperor then sent Lannoy to put pressure on Francis. On 16 May Lannoy reported back from Cognac that Francis had told him the treaty was invalid because it had been signed under duress and that he would never return Burgundy to the emperor. It is thought that Francis tried to induce Lannoy to desert Charles by offering him Bourbon's lands in France, playing on Lannoy's fears that Charles might be angered by the total failure of his policy of reconciliation. Lannoy was not tempted and suffered no recriminations on his return to Spain. Charles's commanders and advisers often showed great loyalty to him, and were rewarded by rarely having to suffer the dire consequences of a failed policy all too often meted out by other rulers at the time.

Within six weeks of leaving Spain, Francis, encouraged by English diplomats, had established the anti-Habsburg League of Cognac, signed on 22 May. France was joined by the main states of northern Italy – Venice, Florence, the Papacy and the Sforza of Milan – who feared Habsburg domination. Their aim was the removal of Charles's forces from Italy. The emperor responded by appointing Hugo de Moncada, an experienced soldier and former viceroy of Sicily, as his commander there. Renewed war was inevitable and Francis intended to use the situation to gain revenge for his defeat, retake Milan and possibly even capture Naples. Although Henry VIII did not at this stage join the League and avoided making any financial or military commitment, he was called its 'protector'. Henry and Wolsey had in mind the restoration of Henry as a major figure in European affairs in the role of honourable peacemaker, as he had been in1518, once Charles's position had been weakened.

In an act of provocation, the emperor was invited to join the League on terms that were known to be totally unacceptable to him, including the release of the French princes for a reasonable ransom,[4] the payment of his debts to Henry VIII and the disbanding of his army in Italy. Charles reacted angrily, for once allowing his emotions to show. He accused Francis of acting dishonourably and told the French ambassador that he would not take money for the princes, that he no longer trusted the king and called into question Francis's honour 'for he has deceived me, and that like no noble prince'. If he could not fulfil his promises then he should 'return again hither into prison.'[5] As far as Charles was concerned his plan to go to Italy for a coronation by the Pope in Rome had been shattered; it was as if the Battle of Pavia had never taken place. Later, in answer to peace proposals from Henry VIII, Charles claimed that 'he [Henry] is not well informed upon these affairs, and that the way proposed will not lead to peace.' He would send all the relevant papers to Henry to prove it. Charles continued that he was willing to consider reasonable arrangements with the League and that it was not ambition that drove his wish for the coronation but a wish to do 'some good to Christendom against the Turks, Infidels and Lutherans'.[6] Events were soon to make Henry's role as arbiter impossible. It was another three years before peace was restored and, by then, Henry's plans to end his marriage, which came to dominate English foreign policy, had been seriously damaged.

The other setback that Charles suffered while in Granada was news of the defeat of King Louis II of Hungary, Croatia and Bohemia by Sultan Suleiman. Louis, married to Charles's sister Mary, had defended his thrones against internal opponents while at the same time being on the front line of Christian Europe's defences against Ottoman attacks. Suleiman's plans to invade Hungary in 1526 were widely known as early as February. In March Louis wrote to Pope Clement expressing the hope that 'while peace is being secured in Christendom, the Pope will procure aid for Hungary against the enemy, who is sure to come' and to Henry VIII asking 'at least for a supply of money to raise troops'.[7] Charles told his brother that he had received a letter about it from the Pope, but commented that 'Such reports are often spread. I know not what to believe.'[8] Despite Louis' appeals for assistance from Christian leaders little was forthcoming and, on 19 August, he was overwhelmed by the much larger Ottoman army at Mohacs, 100 miles south of the capital. The king, along with most of the Hungarian nobility, perished. Budapest was ransacked with great loss of life – some reports talked of tens of thousands – before the Turks withdrew, returning to Istanbul for the winter.

Henry VIII commiserated with Pope Clement claiming that he 'wept over the loss of Hungary, which is owing to the dissensions of Christendom' and like others promised that 'when other princes have agreed, I will not be behindhand in joining the Crusade.'[9] Nevertheless, the warring Christian monarchs readily blamed each other for refusing to make peace and thereby failing to prevent this defeat, though as emperor and Louis' brother-in-law Charles felt the greater weight of responsibility. Francis wrote to the German princes, in an effort to stir up more difficulties for Charles, that while he (Francis) had offered 'to resign his just rights in Italy that there may be no impediment to peace' the result of the emperor's refusal to accept 'reasonable terms' was that 'Christian fields and cities are being devastated and burnt'[10] leaving southern Hungary a wasteland.

If Charles had been in any doubt, he now knew the extent of the challenge that he would face from Suleiman's forces, both in Hungary and in the Mediterranean. His brother Ferdinand, married to Louis' sister Anne, was elected king of Bohemia and claimed the disputed Hungarian throne. He was to bear the brunt of defending east and central Europe from further Ottoman attacks for the next forty years. Although at times Charles was able to divert his time and resources from his other major problems, with France and the growing challenge to the Catholic Church, he was never able to give the Ottoman threat his full attention for long. This exemplifies the different stages on which the two monarchs, Charles and Henry, were performing.

Henry's focus was England's security: enhancing his status and, if possible, gaining territory in France; and, increasingly from the mid-1520s, on the succession. Charles had local and regional difficulties but his work was on a European scale, even a global one if the Spanish lands in the Americas are taken into account. This was the reason that he never even visited the new palace that he had commissioned in Granada – he was simply on the move too much to be able to settle anywhere.

The war in Italy did not progress as Francis and the Pope would have hoped. Although their Italian allies, led by the Duke of Urbino, took the town of Lodi in June 1526 they did not follow up this success, blaming the French for failing to send troops. Imperial reinforcements prevented an attack on Milan and the next month, Duke Francesco Sforza had to surrender the fortress there to Bourbon. A papal army failed to capture Siena and then troops commanded by Cardinal Pompeo Colunna, a bitter enemy of Pope Clement, marched into the Papal States from the south and entered Rome. The Pope took temporary shelter in the Castel Sant'Angelo until they withdrew after a truce was negotiated with Moncada and Colunna. In October Clement requested 30,000 ducats each from Henry and other rulers and indicated that he had little intention of keeping the truce as he wished for vengeance on Colunna. The money promised by Henry actually arrived in Rome early the following year, much to the astonishment of the cardinals.[11] Unfortunately for the League, its best commander, Ludovico di Giovanni de' Medici, known as Giovanni delle Bande Nere (Giovanni of the Black Bands), died of wounds. The Imperial army under Moncada, Bourbon, Ferrante Gonzaga and Philibert, Prince of Orange, was joined by 14,000 German landsknechts under Georg von Frundsberg and 9,000 troops sent by the Viceroy of Naples, Charles de Lannoy.

Early in 1527 the enlarged Imperial army began to march south, through Lombardy and into Tuscany. Alarm spread through the cities on their route but no attack came. Having been unpaid for months and with no sign of new funds arriving, the troops were in mutinous mood. Their generals attempted to reason with them but to no avail. Von Frundsberg suffered a stroke from which he never recovered. The soldiers decided that the cause of all their problems was the Pope living in splendour in Rome. As they marched south their anger, together with their various prejudices, whether it was loyalty to the imperial cause, anti-clericalism, Lutheran hostility to the Roman Church, or straightforward desire for loot, grew. They believed that they could get all they wanted in Rome.

Pope Clement was indecisive. Having broken the earlier truce and attacked Colunna-controlled territories, he then bemoaned the failure of

Francis to send troops to support him. In January he rejected proposals for another truce put forward by Lannoy, despite the growing advantage of the Imperial forces. When Clement again requested French aid, Francis sent encouraging news that he was on the verge of a treaty with the English king and promised money and military support. Although Henry was still considered a possible mediator, events had moved beyond that point. Henry and Wolsey were now ready to make a greater commitment to the cause of the League. Lengthy negotiations between Wolsey and Francis's representatives had been taking place for months, with the English side pushing for favourable terms especially as they were 'deserting their old ally in favour of their old enemy.'[12] These talks eventually resulted in the Treaty of Westminster, signed on 30 April 1527. It included a treaty of 'perpetual peace' between England and France, the agreement to declare war on Charles if he refused their demands to release the French princes and pay his debts to Henry, and a French marriage for Princess Mary, to either the king or his second son, Henri. The two kings agreed to another meeting though 'it is not to be so pompous and costly as the former one'[13] at the Field of Cloth of Gold.

Clement realised that any French troops would arrive too late. He managed to negotiate a truce with Lannoy whereby the Pope would pay off the Imperial troops in return for handing back Milan to Sforza and all armies would return to their original positions. However, since the Pope did not have the money to pay, and Bourbon and the other commanders of the advancing Imperial army had not been consulted, the plan was a non-starter. Cities between the Imperial-Spanish army and Rome provided some soldiers for the League's commander, Urbino, but their priority was to protect their own cities from attack, not Rome. Charles's army therefore advanced unchallenged, and arrived at the walls of Rome in early May. Its defenders were greatly outnumbered, which might not have mattered had its physical defences not been so antiquated. The attacking army did not have the resources for a lengthy siege so the assault on the city started on the morning of 6 May. Almost immediately Bourbon was shot and killed. The Prince of Orange took command and the overwhelming numerical superiority of his army won the day despite brave resistance by the Swiss Guards, most of whom died. The Pope, together with fourteen cardinals, fled once again along the covered passageway from the Vatican to the safety of the Castel Sant'Angelo where they remained besieged. Once the victorious troops were inside the city there was little hope of controlling them.

What followed became known as the 'Sack of Rome'. Details of the atrocities carried out could cover pages – a few examples will serve to give an idea of the ordeals that the inhabitants had to suffer.[14] Churches, monasteries and palaces were ransacked with many items of value removed and others vandalised or destroyed. Murder and rape were widespread, only easing with the realisation that ransoms could be demanded from the wealthy. Some victims were ransomed twice, once by the Spanish troops and then by the Germans. Even then some cardinals were subjected to ridicule and public humiliation as local people took advantage of the situation to act on old vendettas. Those who could not or would not pay were subjected to cruel tortures – branding, having their teeth pulled out, their ears and noses chopped off, being dragged around the streets by their testicles, or suspended from upper-floor windows by one arm. The population was terrified and it is estimated that 4,000 died and many others injured. The Prince of Orange attempted to restore order on the third day but his wishes were ignored until the soldiers had exhausted all sources of loot.

Of course, what happened in Rome in May 1527 was not unique. The sacking of cities and towns that had refused to surrender was common practice. But the fact it had happened to Rome came as a real shock as the news spread across Europe. In Italy others took advantage of the defeat of the Pope and his allies. Venice occupied several papal cities and, in Florence, the Medici family were removed from power and a republic re-established. Elsewhere, as the horrendous details became known, reactions were predictable. In Valladolid the first news of pools of blood in the streets of Rome and rooms in the Pope's palace being used as stables must have put a chill on the celebrations following the birth of Charles and Isabella's first child, Philip, on 21 May. This was a public relations disaster for the emperor. Even though he had never intended such an outcome, it had been carried out by his troops. The failure to send money to pay them had been the result of his lack of funds. In response, a major effort was made to let people throughout Christendom know that he had not ordered it and that real responsibility lay with those who had made war on him and repeatedly broken their promises for peace. Over twenty years later he was still defending his actions, writing in his memoirs that the fault lay with 'those who had compelled him to raise for his defence so many soldiers who did not obey him well.'[15]

Others naturally took an entirely different view. This was a stick with which to beat the emperor. Charles could be portrayed as an enemy of the Church, and those ranged against him its protectors. They received widespread support and again prepared to challenge his position in Italy in what they could now portray as a just war. A French army under Marshal Lautrec entered northern Italy in August and took Lombardy, with the exception of Milan which was defended by Antonio de Leyva. Andrea Doria, an experienced naval commander acting for the French, seized control of his home city of Genoa. Wolsey travelled to France and the Treaty of Westminster was confirmed and ratified at Amiens in August 1527, with an indication that Princess Mary's marriage would likely be to Francis's second son, Henri, who remained a hostage in Spain.

Of even more importance to Henry VIII was what was referred to in the diplomatic correspondence as his secret or private matter. Wolsey, while in Amiens, wrote to Henry that 'I have foreborne at present to speak of your private matter, deferring the same till I have put your affairs in perfect train.' He continued that 'I hope he [Francis] will agree, and for this I study the means day and night.' Already, in May, a secret tribunal had been set up to hear the case of the king's marriage, without informing Queen Catherine. It was expected that the marriage would be declared unlawful and it was hoped that the decision would be accepted by the Pope. The matter was not to remain a secret for long. It is likely that the leak came from Henry himself who, in June, visited his queen and informed her that they had never been properly married and that they had been living in sin for eighteen years. Catherine was upset and then angry. She believed that she had been a true wife to Henry, had borne him several children and that it was beyond her control that all but one had been 'called to God'. She looked to her family for support and managed to send a message to Spain about Henry's intentions. From France, Wolsey told the king that an English envoy in the Low Countries had informed him that 'it has come to my Lady Margaret's knowledge that you intend to be divorced … therefore, the Emperor has knowledge of it.' The cardinal then succinctly outlined what was to be the underlying problem facing Henry's foreign policy and his relations with Charles V, as well as being behind much domestic policy, for the next decade. Charles would 'do all he can at Rome to prevent it.'[16]

Henry was to make his appeal to the Pope for the annulment of his marriage at exactly the wrong time. Charles would never accept such a dishonour to his family and he wrote to Catherine offering her his full support. It was important for Henry, therefore, that the situation in Italy be changed. Firstly, Clement needed to be freed from Charles's control, and secondly the emperor's position in Italy needed to be so weakened that Clement had the freedom of action to carry out Henry's wishes. Both would require the support of France and this meant backing the revival of Francis's influence in Italy. In the later months of 1527 Wolsey planned to gain the Pope's approval for a meeting of cardinals in Avignon that could act on his behalf while he was still besieged in Rome. The cardinals would then, guided by Wolsey, agree to Henry's request. Nothing came of this; the Pope decided that he was in no position to anger Charles and refused his permission. At the same time Henry sent the diplomat William Knight to see Clement. His instruction was to get from the Pope a dispensation for Henry to remarry, regardless of his existing marital status.[17] This was to damage Henry's case because it suggested that he wished to take another wife, whether or not his marriage to Catherine could be shown to be invalid. Knight returned empty-handed.

Henry's plans to marry Anne Boleyn were making no progress because of the emperor's power over the Pope, and Francis had still failed to persuade Charles to release his sons. In January 1528, in order to put more pressure on Charles, the French and English heralds were instructed to declare war, listing Charles's misdeeds, particularly his imprisonment of the Pope. Charles replied that he was surprised that Francis should now do so since he had been waging war against him for several years without any such formality. He went on to point out that Clement was now free. Charles had permitted him to escape from Rome to Orvieto in the previous month on the promise of a substantial sum to pay the Imperial troops. He later repeated a challenge made earlier to Francis to settle their dispute by personal combat instead of a war with all the death and destruction that would bring.

Having been Charles's ally until 1525, England was now officially at war with him for the first and only time in Henry's reign. But this was a 'phony' war. Henry would give financial support to the French army in Italy, but the only parts of Charles's territories that he could attack directly were in the Low Countries and he had little intention of doing so. No English army was sent overseas and the major warships never left port. Even if plans for an invasion were drawn up, the commercial interests of both England and the Low Countries made any such action unlikely. When, after the declaration of war, Margaret of Austria ordered the arrest of English merchants and the seizure of their goods, thus closing down the cloth trade, there was much unrest in England. It was necessary for the government to insist that cloth production continued and that the merchants purchased the goods regardless of whether they could sell them, in order to avoid widespread unemployment and possible riots. This was not something that could last for long and a truce with the Low Countries was soon agreed. Such economic dependence on the Low Countries was later to encourage England to look for markets elsewhere.[18]

Henry would have to rely on the weakening of Charles's position in Italy. The hand-to-hand combat between Charles and Francis was never going to happen, although it was said in Spain that Francis's failure to respond proved he was no gentleman. The war would continue. Early in 1528 Lautrec's army moved south from Lombardy to invade the kingdom of Naples, bypassing Rome which the Imperial army abandoned in order to strengthen the defences of Naples. By April the French had besieged the city whose port was already invested by the Genoese fleet under Doria's nephew. The former viceroy, Lannoy, had died of a sudden illness in September 1527 and his replacement Hugo de Moncada's attempt to break the naval blockade on 28 April ended with his death and the destruction of his fleet.

Francis was confident of victory but once again his failure to keep the loyalty of a military commander caused him problems. Andrea Doria was dissatisfied with the way Francis had failed to reward his efforts in the French cause and ignored the Genoese claim for Savona. On hearing this Charles acted quickly to offer Doria the title of Captain-General of the Sea to seal his allegiance. In July Doria ordered his nephew to remove his fleet from Naples, thus ending the sea blockade. This was followed by a major outbreak of disease, either cholera or the plague, which swept through the French army, killing thousands including Lautrec in August. Their much-reduced army retreated from Naples but it was intercepted at Aversa, a few miles north. The Prince of Orange, the new governor of Naples, was able to report to Charles that the war in southern Italy had been won. Events continued to go Charles's way. In June 1529 Leyva defeated the French army at Landriano, south of Milan, and captured its commander. Italy was now dominated by Charles.

This, of course, was very bad news for Henry VIII. It is not the intention here to follow every twist and turn of Henry's efforts to end his marriage to Catherine and marry Anne Boleyn – much has been written on that topic. However, the tactics that Henry used were influenced by events in Europe and were, in turn, bound to have an impact upon England's relations with Charles. The efforts of English envoys in Rome to make progress on Henry's divorce during 1527 had failed. Things were moving at a snail's pace to the great frustration of the king. In the spring of 1528 Stephen Gardner and Edward Foxe were twice sent to negotiate with the Pope. With Charles's forces in Italy under pressure, their aim was to gain approval for a decretal commission that could make a final and irreversible decision on the marriage issue.

Eventually, after the second visit, the Pope issued a commission to Wolsey and Cardinal Campeggio, but a secret instruction was given to Campeggio telling him to use every opportunity to delay things. It was in Pope Clement's interest that there should be no decision because while the marriage issue was still active, it provided a bargaining counter that he could use in negotiations with both Henry and Charles. He knew that Henry would be prepared to sacrifice much for his support while he could perhaps use the threat of granting a divorce to gain something from Charles. Campeggio reached London in October 1528 and he first went to Catherine who again refused to consider retirement to a convent. This could have been a straightforward solution, leaving Henry free to marry while not calling into question the validity of her marriage and the legitimacy of her daughter, Mary. But Catherine had no intention of giving up what she believed to be her rightful position as queen of England.

Henry, for his part, was aware of the popularity of the queen and keen to explain his position to the nation's elite. He talked of his love for Catherine, her virtues and his honest doubts about the sanctity of their marriage. Henry was surprised that he failed to convince many of them because he had certainly persuaded himself that in the eyes of God he had sinned. Campeggio commented that even an angel from heaven would be unable to change his mind.[19] With both king and queen determined not to budge from their genuinely held positions and the Pope unwilling for any decision to be made, the likelihood of a long drawn-out dispute increased. The winter months were taken up with arguments about the validity of a new text of the original dispensation that had come to light in Spain. It was claimed that this strengthened Catherine's case but the Spanish refused to send it to England for authentication for fear of it being destroyed.

It was not until June 1529 that the proceedings of the commission began at Blackfriars. Henry's case was never particularly strong and Catherine's supporters presented her arguments well, but everyone involved knew that the decision would not depend on that but on the wider political issues. Catherine and Henry appeared in person, the queen delivering an attack on the competence of Wolsey and Campeggio to deliver a verdict and announcing her intention to appeal to Rome. In July Clement decided to recall the case to Rome, which would remove the powers of the commission in England. At the end of the month, to ensure that it would never reach a conclusion, Campeggio announced that the sittings would be adjourned until October, by which time the paperwork announcing that the case was to be decided in Rome would have arrived in London.

The reason why Clement took that action was obvious. With Charles's military victory in Italy the ongoing peace talks had reached a conclusion. The Treaty of Barcelona between Charles and the Pope was signed on 29 June. The language of the treaty could easily mislead. It talked of them 'joining hands out of grief at the divisions of Christianity, to beat off the Turks and to make way for a general peace.'[20] More practically it returned

Ravenna, Cervia, Modena and Reggio to papal control, and Charles promised to use military force to defeat the Florentine Republic and hand the city back to the Medici. This eventually took a siege of ten months (October 1529–August 1530) and cost the life of one of Charles's most able generals, the Prince of Orange. In return Clement agreed to Charles's coronation when he travelled to Italy and absolved those responsible for the Sack of Rome. Charles and Ferdinand would henceforth receive one-quarter of the Church's income in their lands to assist in the fight against the Turks. As in most treaties there was also a marriage agreement. Clement's nephew, Alessandro de' Medici, would marry Charles's natural daughter, Margaret, when she came of age. Clement declared that he 'had quite made up my mind to become an Imperialist', though in reality he had accepted that he could not drive Charles out of Italy and that it was much better to come to terms.

The treaty was another setback for Henry and Wolsey. Although they had no involvement in its creation, it was to have a momentous impact, initially on the man who had been the architect of England's foreign policy over the previous fifteen years, then on the rest of Henry's reign and, ultimately, on English history for many centuries. Together with the Treaty of Cambrai, agreed between the emperor and Francis, it signalled the collapse of Wolsey's policy and his attempts to obtain the annulment of Henry's marriage. This, together with the enmity of much of the English nobility who were jealous of his power, led to his downfall. Within a few years of his fall England had broken away from the Roman Church, never to return, creating enemies across Europe and religious controversies at home.

Chapter Twelve

Coronation and Divorce

The failure of England's foreign policy in the second half of the 1520s and its resultant isolation was made obvious to all by the Treaty of Cambrai. Signed on 3 August 1529 and sometimes referred to as the 'The Ladies Peace' as it was mainly negotiated by Margaret of Austria and Louise of Savoy, it ended the war between Charles and Francis. England's financial claims against both of them were given a very low priority, although Francis had to take on Charles's debts to England. The main terms confirmed those in the Treaty of Madrid (1526) whereby Francis had to abandon all claims to territories in Italy and give up his rights to sovereignty in Artois, Flanders and Tournai. In the one significant change Charles accepted that Burgundy would remain part of France. The emperor would release Francis's sons on payment of two million ecus au soleil (about £433,000) and Francis would marry Charles's sister Eleanor. Neither the princes nor Eleanor would leave for France until the ransom had been paid. Raising such a large sum took time and there were frequent disputes about the weight and quality of the coins provided.[1]

The original exchange date, 1 March, was postponed and it eventually took place on 1 July 1530. The two princes had by then spent over four years in Spain. The conditions of their captivity were sometimes harsh, in austere castles, with few servants to converse with and restricted access to the outside world, especially after the French declaration of war in January 1528. Margaret of Austria had to remind Charles that they should not be held responsible for the failings of their father and that Charles's own honour was at stake. Nevertheless, the experience certainly marked Henri, the younger of the two, who became Francis's heir on the death of his older brother in 1536 and later became king of France as Henri II. Perhaps not surprisingly, his relationship with his father was not easy and he certainly never forgave Charles.

Eleanor and Francis had already been married by proxy, though another ceremony was held with them both present on 7 July. This was a diplomatic marriage par excellence. Eleanor was treated with the appropriate courtesies in public but the couple had no children and she never had an influence on policy. Even though the Constable of France, Montmorency, considered her a 'beautiful and virtuous' lady[2], Francis continued to spend far more time with his mistresses, especially Anne de Pisseleu d' Heilly, Duchess of Étampes (1508–1580) who had great influence at court, particularly towards the end of Francis's reign. After Eleanor's coronation as queen in March 1531, Francis watched her formal entry to Paris from an open window in the company of his mistress.

Although Charles had approved the terms of the Treaty of Cambrai, by the time the final negotiations were concluded he was sailing to Italy for his coronation by the Pope, leaving his wife Isabella as regent in Spain. Of course, many people there did not wish him to leave and the explanation that he gave depended on his audience. To military commanders he claimed that he wished to win honour and glory; to his sister Mary, to achieve a universal peace in Christendom; to the Castilian Council of State, to wipe out heresies and reform the Church; to the Pope, to prepare to fight a Turkish invasion. Certainly, these were his ambitions. In his memoirs he recorded that he wished to deal with the religious 'errors in Germany ... assume the crowns which he had not yet received, and finally be in a better position to oppose the Turk.'[3] He left Barcelona to shouts of 'Plus Ultra', his personal motto,[4] and received a grand welcome in Genoa, where the cries of 'Carlo, Carlo, Impero, Impero, Cesare, Cesare' rang out as he approached the specially constructed pier hung with tapestries and cloth of gold. After over two weeks as the guest of Andrea Doria he travelled slowly to Bologna to meet the Pope, arriving in November.

They held wide-ranging talks during the three months they spent lodged in adjacent apartments in the Palazzo Comunale. Eventually it was decided that his coronation would take place in Bologna, not Rome. The official reason given was that Charles wished to move north to Germany as soon as possible, but there was also the fear of a hostile reception in Rome, where the sack of the city was still fresh in people's memories. His coronation as emperor took place on 24 February 1530, his thirtieth birthday (Plate 9). Thousands from across Europe crowded into Bologna during the preceding weeks and, on the day of the coronation, the city was decorated with arches and displays commemorating imperial victories, both Roman and medieval.

The papal procession left the Palace at 8.00 am and crossed the piazza to the basilica of St Petronio, soon followed by Charles, accompanied by the nobility of Italy, Germany and the Low Countries, ambassadors, commanders, chamberlains and cupbearers. On his arrival he was presented with the symbols of office and anointed emperor. After Mass, Charles and

Pope Clement walked together through the basilica to the steps outside where they had to wait half an hour for the crowds to clear before they could descend. After further ceremonies lasting most of the day, the emperor held a banquet for seventy selected guests, while outside in the piazza the crowds fed on oxen stuffed with partridges and snipe, suckling pigs and hares, geese and ducks, all roasted on enormous spits, and drank wine from the fountains. What no-one present knew was that this would be the last time a Pope would officiate at the coronation of an emperor, a tradition that stretched back 700 years.

Despite appearances, not quite everything was going well for Charles. While in Bologna he suffered from gout for the second time. The illness was to cause him considerable pain on numerous occasions for the rest of his life. We know this because in his memoirs dictated in 1550, he mentions seventeen such attacks, often recording where he was and for how long he suffered each time. There was little effective treatment available, though various changes of diet and dubious remedies were tried. At times it undoubtedly inconvenienced the emperor, making travelling more uncomfortable and distracting him from his work.

Meanwhile, in England, Wolsey's fifteen years of being chief adviser, architect of Henry's policies, even sometimes referred to as the 'Alter Rex' (another king), had come to an end. In October 1529 he was stripped of his offices of state and many of his fine residences. Thomas More became the new Lord Chancellor despite his known opposition to Henry's divorce. The king accepted this for the time being, perhaps believing that he could change his friend's mind. Although Wolsey was charged with numerous crimes including praemunire (the offence of asserting foreign jurisdiction in England), his end was not instant. Henry allowed him to remain Archbishop of York and he was sent off to visit his archdiocese. But Wolsey found it hard to abandon the trappings of power. His plans for a grand enthronement at York and his continued contacts with foreign ambassadors gave his many enemies the chance to finish him. He was arrested on 4 November 1530 and died in Leicester on 29 November while being escorted to London for a trial and almost certain execution.

Henry's overriding concern remained how to end his marriage to Catherine in order to marry Anne Boleyn. Opposed by the emperor and faced by a Pope who had decided that he could not grant his wish, it was to Francis that the English king turned for diplomatic support. When, in August 1529, Francis requested financial concessions from Henry he was at first refused. But two weeks later Henry's attitude changed. He returned the valuable jewel, the 'Fleur-de-lis', that had been in English hands since

1508, and agreed to remit the next instalment of the pension due from France so long as the money was used on the ransom for Francis's sons. What Henry wanted in return was obvious – Francis's assistance in getting his divorce by using any influence that he had with the Pope. This was to be the pattern of Henry's foreign policy over the next few years – attempts to gain Francis's support for his appeals to Rome and, failing that, to get his backing for increasingly hostile moves against papal power.

Henry had few options left. The original approach to Clement challenged the decision made by a previous Pope in a way that, if accepted, would weaken papal authority. The option of a military solution had disappeared with Charles's defeat of the League of Cognac. Henry could only resort to diplomatic means and he soon realised how limited his diplomatic clout actually was. He attempted to apply moral pressure by adopting an idea originally suggested by Thomas Cranmer of Jesus College, Cambridge, and conveyed to the king by Edward Foxe, the provost of Kings' College. Theologians from universities across Europe were asked to declare their opinion on the case. Not surprisingly their views varied, largely determined by the attitude of the ruler within whose jurisdiction the university was based. Guided by Foxe, both Cambridge and Oxford came out in the king's favour, as did the Sorbonne and most other French universities, while those in Spain and Italy did not. Clement tried to prevent any expression of opinion while the matter was still, in theory, being decided in Rome.

The only way that Henry could exert real pressure on Clement was to challenge the Pope's authority in England. Although in 1515 Henry had stated that 'Kings of England in time past never had any superior but God', he had intended this to refer to his political powers, not spiritual powers which he believed rested with the Pope. Nevertheless, if he was to challenge the Pope's right to decide the fate of his marriage, he needed to reduce the power of the Church in England and of the right of the papacy to interfere in England's religious affairs. Edward Foxe, together with Cranmer, produced a dossier that claimed to show that over previous centuries the papacy had usurped powers over matters that were rightly the domain of secular rulers. The Pope, it argued, was no more than the Bishop of Rome and Henry should restore the king's rightful powers over both laity and clergy in England. In 1528 Wolsey had warned Pope Clement that 'if the king's desire were not complied with ... there would follow a speedy ... ruin of his lordship [Wolsey] and the Church's influence in this kingdom.'[5] Two years later Wolsey had fallen and Henry was about to implement the threat to the Church's position in England. He made use of long-standing anti-clericalism. Parliament needed little encouragement from the king to pass legislation against the powers of the Church. Behind Henry was Anne Boleyn who was herself interested in some of the new religious ideas coming out of Europe and who introduced Henry to the writings of William Tyndale[6], in particular his views on the authority of a king in *The Obedience of a Christian Man.*

What became known as the Reformation Parliament first met in November 1529. By 1534 it had passed numerous acts that initially reduced papal powers in England and then removed them altogether, making the king supreme head of the Church in England. It first removed the legal privileges of the clergy and reintroduced the offence of praemunire. In April 1530 papal dispensations for pluralism were forbidden and, in September, there was a proclamation of the fourteenth-century Statute of Provisors, which recognised the rights of kings over church appointments in their lands, again weakening the power of the papacy. At the same time English envoys in Rome were instructed not to accept any mention of the Pope's jurisdiction in England's religious matters.

In January 1531 Pope Clement issued an instruction that Henry was forbidden to re-marry until the issue of his marriage to Catherine had been settled. In response the entire clergy of England were accused of praemunire and told that they would be pardoned by Henry only on payment of the vast sum of £118,000, equivalent to a year's 'ordinary' income for the king. In February it was demanded that they acknowledge Henry as 'protector and supreme head of the English Church'. They paid the fine and after much discussion and a personal interview between the king and Archbishop Warham, they accepted Henry's title but secured the important qualification 'as far as the law of Christ allows'.

While Henry was becoming ever more desperate to achieve his divorce, Charles travelled north after his coronation in Bologna, first to Innsbruck, where he met his brother Ferdinand (Plate 12) and sister Mary of Hungary (Plate 14), the widow of King Louis II, and then to Augsburg for a meeting of the Imperial Diet. In 1529 the threat of Turkish invasion had once again become a reality. Suleiman led an army of over 100,000 through Hungary and advanced on Vienna, defended by 20,000 troops under the experienced Nicholas, Count of Salm. The city's defences were strengthened and its inhabitants prepared for a siege, a pitched battle being out of the question. Fortunately for them the Ottoman army was delayed by heavy rains, making the transport of the heavy field guns all but impossible, and had been weakened by disease. It reached Vienna at the end of September, very late in the campaigning season, without effective siege equipment.

After Suleiman's call for the city to surrender had been rejected and initial attempts to breach the walls had failed, they withdrew in mid-October. Vienna had been saved, for now, but it was obvious to all that the Ottomans would return. When they did Charles wanted to play a part in resisting them.

The Imperial Diet in Augsburg was the first Charles had attended for nine years. During that time there had been considerable problems in Germany. The Knights' Revolt of 1522–23 against their declining status had been crushed by their secular and spiritual rulers, as had the widespread Peasants' Revolt of 1524–25, with as many as 100,000 killed in that conflict. Luther, a social conservative, had supported the princes in the tract 'Against the Murderous, Thieving Hordes of Peasants'. While at Augsburg Charles wished to bring those who were to become known as Protestants – in Germany mainly, though not exclusively, Lutherans – back into a single universal Church. In 1529 Catholic leaders had attempted to reimpose the Edict of Worms against those who had challenged the Roman Church. A letter of protest was issued, signed by Duke John of Saxony, the Margrave of Brandenburg, Landgrave Philip of Hesse, three other rulers and the councils of fourteen cities – hence 'Protestants'. Charles entreated the Pope to summon a general church council which he hoped might find a doctrinal solution that would prevent a schism and end abuses of church power. He thought that with his authority and goodwill on both sides, now that Europe was at peace, unity could be restored. Clement would not do so, believing that such a council would undermine his authority and enhance that of the emperor, a fear that Francis shared. At Augsburg, after an encouraging start, months of talks failed to break the deadlock. The Lutheran leaders then established the Schmalkaldic League in February 1531 to defend themselves against any aggressive move that Charles and the Catholic princes might make.

During 1530 Charles received news of two deaths. The first, in June, was that of his second son, Ferdinand, born in November 1529 shortly after he had arrived in Bologna. Then, in December, his aunt Margaret of Austria, a major figure in his youth and regent of the Low Countries for over ten years, died as a result of an infection spreading from an injured foot. In her final letter to him she expressed her sorrow at not being able to see him again, hoped that she had performed her duties well, and commended to him a policy of peace towards both France and England, advice that he was to find hard to follow. Having been impressed by his sister Mary when they met in Innsbruck, Charles persuaded her to become his new regent in the Low Countries, where she had spent her early years with him. After Augsburg he travelled to the Low Countries, visiting various provinces and spending time there with Mary during 1531, giving her the authority that she would need to successfully fulfil the role. She was to do so for over two decades.

He was now urged by Isabella to return to Spain but he informed her that: 'I must stay and take control of German affairs. The Turkish menace has increased so much that I have even considered coming to an agreement with the Lutherans in order to prevent worst disaster.'[7] At the Diet of Regensburg in the summer of 1532, this is precisely what he did. In the lengthy religious arguments both sides seemed to become more intransigent, but Charles agreed to a compromise that left the situation unresolved in order to create a united front against a new Ottoman advance. His army of over 80,000 moved down the Danube to confront Suleiman, whose advance was once again slow. Charles reached Vienna on 23 September by which time the sultan had already withdrawn his forces, wishing to avoid a repeat of 1529. Charles could claim credit for his role in seeing off the invader, though it has been argued that these campaigns were really a 'parade of strength' and 'a competition in splendour'[8], where neither side really wanted a major battle because of the loss of prestige, or worse, if they were defeated. Nevertheless, Charles's actions demonstrated that he was prepared to commit resources and be personally involved in defending Christendom, while other leaders merely talked about it.

In England there was a lull in anti-papal legislation after Henry's successful demands for the recognition of his authority by the English clergy in early 1531. He had defied the Pope and challenged papal power in England as far as he could without taking the ultimate step of removing it altogether, a step that he was still reluctant to take. At no point did Henry have a prepared plan of action that would lead to a break with Rome. He was reacting to the Pope's reluctance to give him what he wanted. Many of those around the king harboured serious doubts about the whole issue of the divorce, though few were prepared to speak out openly or even in private. His sister, Mary, was close to Catherine and now rarely attended court. His most able minister since the fall of Wolsey, Thomas More, was known to be opposed to it. Henry lacked the advice that he needed to advance his case. This opened the door for Thomas Cromwell who had already shown himself to be a capable fixer in Wolsey's service and then, as a Member of Parliament, a strong supporter of the anti-clerical statutes passed in 1529 and 1530. He was appointed to the Royal Council in the summer of 1531 and proved to be the efficient, able minister who could bring about what the king wanted.

Henry continued his efforts to gain support abroad. The alternate cajoling and threatening of the papacy by his envoys in Rome had no impact so Henry increasingly looked for support amongst the Pope's enemies, including non-Lutheran evangelical reformers in Basle, Strasburg and Zurich, and the Lutheran princes in Germany who had formed the Schmalkaldic League. Many of them were hostile to Charles V. They were attempting to overturn the emperor's brother Ferdinand's recent election as King of the Romans, in other words Charles's heir in the Holy Roman Empire. Several of their representatives travelled to England during 1531 but there was no agreement. Henry disliked their religious beliefs and they were not convinced by his arguments about why his marriage should be ended.

If foreign pressures were not going to succeed then the changes would have to continue at home, and Cromwell, with his attention to detail and step-by-step approach, was the ideal man for the job. In February 1532 the Statute for the Conditional Restrain of Annates, reducing the amount of church taxes that would be sent to Rome, hit papal revenues from England. In May the king demanded that Convocation, the assembly of clergy, agree to a complete submission of their powers to run their own affairs. Despite Convocation's shock, Henry got his way. This was too much for Thomas More who resigned as Lord Chancellor. The elderly Warham, who cannot have liked this attack on the Church's authority, died in August, after nearly twenty-nine years as Archbishop of Canterbury. He was replaced by Thomas Cranmer rather than Stephen Gardiner, the Bishop of Winchester, who, though previously high in the king's favour, had spoken against some of the recent moves to undermine the power of the clergy. Cranmer had been Henry's resident ambassador to the court of Charles V since January. While travelling through the Low Countries and Germany with the emperor, he had been attempting to persuade Charles to end his opposition to Henry's divorce, but with no success. His appointment received papal approval through the good offices of King Francis.

Foreign affairs again came to the fore. This time the pro-French policy, encouraged by Anne Boleyn, seemed as though it might bring some results. France and England together could threaten communications between Spain and the Low Countries, important to Charles. Pope Clement still wished to remove the Imperial yoke if he could and the old plan for a marriage between his niece, Catherine de' Medici and Francis's son Henri was finally agreed, but it was to remain secret until Charles returned to Spain. Francis therefore might be able to use his influence on Clement in the matter of Henry's divorce. A new Anglo-French defensive alliance and treaty of mutual aid was signed in June and the monarchs agreed to meet in October. During this meeting the chain of events that resulted in the final break with Rome began.

The retinue of about 2,000 which accompanied Henry to Calais on 11 October 1532 included the Dukes of Suffolk and Norfolk, Cromwell, Henry FitzRoy, and, most significantly, Anne Boleyn, who, before the trip, had been created Marquess of Pembroke so that she had the necessary status to meet French royalty. Not involved was Queen Catherine or Henry's sister, Mary, who refused to accompany her husband, Suffolk. Henry had last seen Catherine the previous summer, after which she was dismissed from court and moved around various palaces and castles across Hertfordshire, Bedfordshire and Cambridgeshire. After spending ten days in Calais, Henry travelled to meet Francis at Boulogne, without Anne, and four days later returned to Calais with the French king. Although the cost was nowhere near as high as at the Field of Cloth of Gold, each side was keen to outdo the other in their entertainments and gifts. It was only on 27 October that Anne made her entrance at a masked ball and danced with Francis. After he departed on 29 October Henry's party was delayed for another ten days by bad weather. It was either during their stay in Calais or soon after their return to England that Henry and Anne first slept together.

Events then moved quickly. By the end of the year Anne was pregnant and, in January 1533, the couple were married in a secret ceremony so that the child, when born, would be legitimate. This effectively ended any chance of an agreed solution. It is likely that the ceremony was conducted at York Place, Wolsey's former palace that had been taken over by Henry VIII and was in the process of being extended to become his main residence and, as Whitehall Palace, the largest royal residence in Europe. It was not until March that the marriage became more widely known and in April, Henry informed Catherine that he had married the 'other lady' and that in future she would be known as the Dowager Princess of Wales. In the same month Parliament passed the Act in Restrain of Appeals forbidding all appeals to the Pope on religious or any other matters. Any decision by the Pope now had no legal status in England. Convocation declared that Henry's marriage to Catherine broke the laws of God and, in May, a special court, headed by Cranmer, decided that the marriage was void and the Princess Mary illegitimate.

Anne Boleyn's coronation was a lavish affair, involving a journey in the royal barge from Greenwich to the Tower on Thursday, 29 May, followed by her formal entry to London two days later with a half-mile long procession of nobility, judges, ambassadors, bishops and gentry. The ceremony itself was held in Westminster Abbey on Sunday, 1 June, after which there was a grand banquet in Westminster Hall. The streets were packed but what was lacking was much enthusiasm amongst the crowds. According to Eustace Chapuys, admittedly not an unbiased correspondent, it was a 'cold, poor, and most unpleasant sight'.[9] Few cheered, raised their caps or shouted 'God Save the Queen'.

Chapuys had been Charles's ambassador to England since August 1529, specifically appointed because his legal training might help him to defend Catherine's marriage. His anti-French attitude also meant that he would use any influence that he might have to weaken Anglo-French understanding. He did everything that he could to provide emotional and material support for Catherine and, later, for Princess Mary. Although Chapuys kept Charles well informed about events in England and Charles kept his pressure on Pope Clement to declare the marriage valid, the emperor's room for manoeuvre was limited. He had defeated Francis in Italy, successfully defended the Low Countries and been crowned by the Pope, but he was in no position to use his military might to invade England in order to prevent Henry from setting Catherine aside. He had too many other problems that required immediate attention. He was also aware of the damage that any such war would do to trade in the Low Countries and how unpopular that would be. He had more to lose than he could possibly gain.

Charles knew that unless an attack on Henry was a joint venture with Francis, the French king would take advantage of his involvement in England to undo the Treaty of Cambrai. Any chance of Charles and Francis working together had been ended by the Anglo-French treaty of 1532 and Francis's actions since. The treaty had committed Henry and Francis to prepare to defend Christendom against the 'Turk'. They did not do so and left it to Charles. Indeed, Francis's envoys had encouraged Suleiman to invade Italy, and then, when the Ottoman army advanced on Vienna instead, the French king offered to take an army into Italy to help defend it.[10] Charles, not surprisingly, had scornfully rejected the offer.

These exchanges go a long way to explain why Charles, despite his words of support for Catherine, had little intention of taking military action against Henry. This is made clear in a letter from Chapuys to the emperor in May 1533. The ambassador refers to Charles's previous 'orders and instructions ... not to make matters worse than they are, not to threaten war, nor in any way imply that there might be a rupture in the friendship and good intelligence between the two countries.' He also mentions that Charles is keen that 'the Queen remains in England' and reassures the emperor that

Catherine 'has no intention of voluntarily quitting this country ... however ill-treated.'[11]

By September 1533 Henry not only had a new wife but a new child – a daughter, born in Greenwich and christened Elizabeth after Henry's mother. After the king's marriage to Anne the Pope had drawn up a bull of excommunication, though he was persuaded by Francis not to issue it immediately. However, Francis was annoyed that the marriage had made his task of backing Henry in Rome very much more difficult. In October 1533 Pope Clement travelled to Marseilles to meet Francis and witness his niece's marriage to the French king's son, Henri. The English envoys attending the meeting, Stephen Gardiner and Edmund Bonner, asked Clement to approve Henry's divorce and withdraw the threat of excommunication, which Clement refused to do. The French king rejected Henry's offer to pay for a French invasion of northern Italy if Francis supported him in deposing Clement. Francis believed that Gardiner and his associates had done more harm than good by their attitude.[12] This, together with Henry's annoyance that Francis was negotiating with Clement while the Pope was threatening to excommunicate him, marked a deterioration in Anglo-French relations.

In March 1534, almost seven years after Henry had first approached him for a decision, Pope Clement announced his verdict on Henry's marriage to Catherine – it was valid. If Henry did not accept this judgement, then he would be excommunicated and the sentence would be imposed by force. Who was to do this was unclear, but the judgement did encourage those who opposed Henry, whether at home or overseas, to plot to bring about his removal. Henry now needed to ensure that his children with Anne Boleyn were accepted as his heirs. In the same month, Parliament passed the Act of Succession making Elizabeth heir presumptive, though, of course, a son was expected in time, and the people of England were required to take an oath accepting the revised succession. This included a preamble that stated that Henry's marriage to Anne was legal and that the Pope had no right to intervene. By the time the Treasons Act and the Act of Supremacy of 1534 had been passed, a refusal to take the oath was regarded as high treason, punishable by death. In January 1535 Thomas Cromwell was appointed vicegerent in spirituals with extensive powers over the English Church.

Henry's conscience could be clear, but freedom of conscience was now to be denied others. In April 1534 Elizabeth Barton, the 'Nun of Kent', was hanged at Tyburn for challenging Henry's marriage to Anne Boleyn and prophesying that the king would die within months of marrying her.

In June 1535 monks from the London Charterhouse were hanged, drawn and quartered for refusing to take the oath. They were soon followed by more significant figures: John Fisher, Bishop of Rochester, a former vice-Chancellor of the University of Cambridge, was beheaded on 22 June and Sir Thomas More, on 6 July. These were executions for dynastic and political reasons, for defying the king's authority, even though the victims were making a stand on an issue of conscience. As Lord Chancellor, More had been responsible for the suppression of Protestant and evangelical ideas. Heretics had been burnt at the stake. Henry, too, was prepared to execute those with more radical beliefs as well as those who rejected his authority. Later in the reign, on 30 July 1540, three evangelical preachers, Barnes, Garrard and Jerome, were burnt for heresy on the same day as three others, Powell, Fetherstone and Abell, were hanged, drawn and quartered as traitors for speaking in favour of the Pope.

Chapter Thirteen

Unrealistic Fears

In June 1534 Henry expressed his concern about the possibility of 'a sudden invasion in the King's absence'[1] by forces of Charles V if he left England for a meeting with Francis later that year. He claimed that he would need to take measures for the security of his new queen and her daughter, Princess Elizabeth, because friends of Catherine of Aragon and her daughter Mary might intrigue against them. Henry wanted Francis to agree that if such an attack took place, they would together 'be bound to invade the Emperor wherever they could injure him most'.[2] How genuine his worries were on this occasion is open to question, but the perceived danger of an invasion played a part in England's foreign policy for the rest of the decade.

Although Henry wrote about the 'perfect confidence that he has in the King's friendship', relations with Francis had deteriorated since their meeting in October 1532. There was an understandable worry that if Francis and Charles came to an agreement, this could lead to a co-ordinated campaign against England. Backed by the Pope, its aim would be to restore the 'true' Catholic religion and papal authority. With hindsight it is possible to argue that this was most unlikely. It would mean either the removal of Henry or forcing him to put aside Anne Boleyn, return to his first marriage with Catherine of Aragon and accept that his successor would be Princess Mary. This would not be in Francis's interest as Mary would be expected to be closely allied to her cousin, Charles. It might suit Charles to threaten action against Henry but actually carrying it out was a different matter. Even if it could be achieved it would be very costly. It would place his cousin on the throne but at the cost of a weakened England which would then be less useful as a future ally against France. Many in Charles's council believed that Henry's treatment of Catherine was a private issue, not a cause for conflict with England.[3]

How obvious all this was to Henry and Cromwell, now his chief minister, is uncertain. Cromwell probably over-estimated the likelihood of an invasion.[4] As someone who was interested in furthering the cause of religious reform when it was safe to do so, he feared that the European powers might eventually unite in a crusade against England. Henry, though, was probably more aware than his minister that any alliance between Charles and Francis was unlikely to be long-lasting because in the end their political self-interest would trump religious zeal.[5] Nevertheless they both recognised the danger of Charles, and perhaps Francis, taking advantage of any internal opposition to the religious changes that Henry had initiated, by sending troops to assist a rebellion. But the defeat of an uprising in Ireland led by Thomas FitzGerald, Lord Offaly, in 1534 and the executions of 1534 and 1535 had been a warning to those in Henry's lands who sought to frustrate or actively oppose the king's actions. Most of those around Henry acquiesced, the more conservative perhaps even thinking that once the succession issue was settled Henry would eventually come to terms with the papacy. Henry, however, liked the new powers that being head of the Church in England gave him, even though a majority of the population, including Henry, were still orthodox in their religious beliefs.

News of the executions of More, a prominent scholar, and Fisher, an influential churchman, caused a stir in Europe. Many rulers who had hitherto shown little or no interest in Henry's actions condemned him in order to gain the approval of the new Pope, Paul III (Alessandro Farnese), who had been elected in October 1534 after Clement's death. Unknown to Henry, Fisher had secretly encouraged Charles, through Chapuys, to intervene in England's affairs. He had been created a cardinal, while in prison, just weeks before his beheading in June 1535. In August of that year Pope Paul drew up another bull of excommunication, though it was again not issued, this time possibly at the request of Charles. He was concerned about the impact that it could have on Henry's treatment of Catherine and her daughter who both still refused to accept the divorce or the royal supremacy.

Henry's most influential English critic was Reginald Pole. He was related to Henry through his mother, Margaret Plantagenet, Duchess of Salisbury, a niece of Edward IV. He had been educated at Oxford and Padua with generous financial assistance from the king. Pole had held various posts in the Church and, in 1529, was sent to Paris as part of the campaign to seek the opinion of European theologians about the king's marriage to Catherine of Aragon. In 1532, realising that Henry had already made his decision, to which he was strongly opposed, Pole left England for Italy. In 1535 Henry demanded that Pole confidentially send him his views about the divorce and the break with Rome. What he received was *Pro Ecclesiasticae Unitate Defensione* (For the Defence of the Unity of the Church), which was soon afterwards published in Rome. It was a devastating critique of Henry's actions in which he denounced Henry as a tyrant driven by lust and greed, who would always put his own selfish wishes before the interests of either

England or the Church. Henry was furious, the more so when Pole was created a cardinal and papal legate to England by Pope Paul, and sent to the courts of Francis and Charles to argue the case for military action against Henry.

Catherine of Aragon's death on 7 January 1536 at Kimbolton Castle removed one obstacle to better relations with Charles. However, there was still the issue of the status of Princess Mary, who Catherine had requested Charles to do all that he could to protect, and Henry's break with Rome that remained an affront to the emperor. There was little mourning at court for Catherine. Henry and Anne, three months pregnant, dressed in yellow satin not the traditional black. Even so all was not well in their marriage. The relationship had always been intense and stormy. Feisty, flirtatious and with an independence of mind, Anne might have had the qualities to delight Henry in courtship, but in a wife the conventional king expected obedience. He also still wanted a son. Had the pregnancy gone smoothly such problems might have been forgotten. On 24 January Henry had a serious accident while jousting at Greenwich. Unseated, he fell heavily beneath his horse and was unconscious for well over an hour. The accident is often believed to have affected his personality as well as his physical health. A few days later Anne had a second miscarriage and received little comfort from Henry who showed more self-pity than concern for his wife. Doubts about the validity of this marriage now grew in the king's mind.

Anne needed all the allies that she could get, but instead she clashed with Thomas Cromwell over his attempts to restore good relations with the emperor[6] and the uses to which money from the first monastic dissolutions should be put[7]. When it came, her end was swift. In late April, in rash comments made while teasing Henry Norris, Groom of the Stool in Henry's privy chamber, about his failure to marry her cousin, Anne Shelton, the queen suggested that he was waiting for Henry to die so that he could marry her. Rumours of infidelity soon spread. By 2 May Anne was in the Tower. A young court musician, Mark Smeaton, who had announced his love for Anne, was arrested and charged with adultery, soon to be followed by Norris, William Brereton, Francis Weston and even Anne's brother, George, Viscount Rochford, who was charged with incest. The king now seemed willing to believe anything of his wife, including witchcraft and plotting to murder her enemies. All pleaded their innocence, except the naive Smeaton, but were found guilty in what was little more than a show trial. Rochford showed his contempt for the court by reading a statement claiming that Anne had once told his wife about Henry's sexual inadequacies. These verdicts made Anne's conviction on a charge of treasonable adultery a

foregone conclusion. The men were beheaded on 17 May, followed by Anne two days later. Her marriage to Henry had already been annulled by Archbishop Cranmer.

Within two weeks Henry had married Jane Seymour (Plate 7), one of Anne's maids of honour. A second Act of Succession declared that Princess Elizabeth was a bastard and she was removed from the succession, just as Mary had been by the first Act. Henry's heirs were to be the children of his marriage to Jane Seymour and if he were to die without an 'heir from his body', Henry would choose his successor. This perhaps opened the way for Henry's natural son, Henry FitzRoy, Duke of Richmond, but he died of consumption (tuberculosis) in July.

In the mid-1530s, despite the fears of some in England, there was little chance of Charles invading. He was fully occupied by other military ventures. The first was a strike against Ottoman power in the Mediterranean with the intention of protecting some of his subjects from the attacks of Hayreddin Barbarossa, a former corsair, appointed as the Ottoman Grand Admiral in 1533. Within a year Barbarossa captured the important bases of Coron, Patras and Lepanto in Greece, raided the southern and western coasts of Italy, and then took Tunis in North Africa, removing Charle[s] Muslim ally, Muley Hassan.

In 1535 Charles (Plate 17) put together a force of 100 warships and transports for nearly 30,000 soldiers from Spain, Italy, Portugal, the Pa[pal] and the Knights Hospitaller of Malta[8]. Charles personally led the expe[dition] that successfully captured the fortress of La Goletta (Plate 21) an[d] Tunis. Barbarossa, however, was able to escape to Algiers and c[ontinue] his depredations in the western Mediterranean.[9] On his return t[o] Charles travelled through Sicily and on to Italy, wintering in Nap[les] he received the news of the death of Catherine of Aragon. In these he had never before visited he was welcomed enthusiastically, as where there were cries of 'long live our victorious Emperor, c[onqueror of] Africa, peace-maker in Italy'[10] (Plate 13). In the spring he mo[ved on to] Rome and eventually Genoa.

By the time that he had reached Rome in April 1536, h[e was at] war with Francis. If he hoped that his success in Tunis wou[ld deter him] from any aggressive moves he was wrong. Once again the s[ubject was] Milan. In November 1535 Duke Francesco Sforza died, [who had] married Charles's niece, Christina of Denmark, in 1534 v[...] 12. The match had been opposed by Charles's sister Mary [... her] guardian, wrote that although she accepted that it was [... for] the family to make the decision 'it is against nature an[d ...]

off a little girl who cannot yet in any sense be called a woman, and expose her to all the dangers of child-bed'. Charles had replied that an element of sacrifice is necessary for the sake of the dynasty and that the age issue 'will be a much greater problem for the duke than for our niece'. Within 18 months the duke was dead, leaving no heir. Francis I renewed his claim to Milan and invaded Savoy, removing Duke Charles III, the emperor's ally. He then crossed the Alps to take Turin.

While in Rome Charles made a lengthy speech to the College of Cardinals. He asked for their support, emphasising his desire for peace, the work that he had done in defence of Christendom and the treachery of Francis over many years. He was angered by the Pope's reply. He was told that Francis, too, had offered peace and that the Church had to be seen as neutral so as to be able to act as a mediator in the future. The Pope had no wish to be seen as dependent on Charles and feared that Francis might follow Henry VIII's lead in denying his authority if he sided with the emperor.

The level of mistrust between the emperor and Francis is revealed by events surrounding the death of Francis's eldest son in August 1536. The 18-year-old Prince Francis died suddenly shortly after drinking from a cup of water handed to him by his secretary, the Count of Montecuccoli, after a game of tennis. The count was accused of being in the pay of Charles and poisoning the prince on the emperor's orders. This charge became the centre of a vicious propaganda campaign against Charles based on little or no evidence, other than a confession extracted under torture that the count later retracted. This did not prevent his execution by his limbs being attached to four horses and then being torn apart as they galloped in different directions. The real cause of the prince's death is uncertain but it was likely to have been tuberculosis.

Despite the Pope's call for peace, the war continued for well over a year. In the Low Countries it took considerable military and financial resources organised by the regent, Mary of Hungary, to repel the attacks of Francis's allies. After a renewed French offensive in early 1537, a stalemate was reached and, in June, a ten-month local truce was agreed. In northern Italy the French failed to capture Milan and then Charles's commander, Leyva, launched a counter-attack into Provence. Wishing to avoid a pitched battle the French withdrew behind well-defended city walls, especially at Avignon, having devastated the countryside to deny the Imperial army essential supplies. Lacking siege equipment and provisions, Charles's army returned to Italy in September after the death of Leyva from complications caused by gout.

In the Mediterranean the Ottoman fleet under Barbarossa raided the Spanish coast and Ibiza in 1536. The following year with a fleet of

170 galleys he landed in southern Italy near Otranto, causing much destruction and enslaving many inhabitants. He later failed to capture the Venetian-held island of Corfu before returning to Istanbul accompanied by French vessels. Francis's alliance with the Ottomans was a threat to Charles but it was unpopular in Europe and made it easier for Charles to claim that Francis was the real threat to peace.

Henry (Plate 18) played no part in these events, though, of course, war between his two rival monarchs suited him very well as it meant that little attention was paid to England. The king's focus was very much on the succession and his authority in the country that had not gone unchallenged. Various local grievances, concerns about the religious policies, opposition to the dissolution of the smaller monasteries during 1536, and unfounded rumours about the abolition of parish churches together resulted in the greatest internal threat that Henry faced during his reign. Known as the Pilgrimage of Grace, it started in Lincolnshire in October 1536 and soon spread to Yorkshire and the rest of the north. By December upward of 30,000 commoners had joined the movement, which also included gentry, clergy and a few from the lesser nobility. While claiming to be loyal subjects of the king, the demands they made, put together by Robert Aske, included the removal of Cromwell and other 'low-born' councillors, the restoration of papal authority in England and recognition of Mary as heir to the throne.

Henry would never accept such terms, but the Duke of Norfolk, sent to deal with the problem, lacked the forces to take on such numbers. Instead, concessions were offered and attempts made to create divisions amongst the 'pilgrims'. A Parliament to be held in the north, protection of land rights and a free pardon to the protestors were all promised, but no ground was given over the running of the Church or the selection of royal councillors. The plan worked. There were differences of opinion amongst the 'pilgrims' and doubts about their next move if they rejected the concessions as insufficient. Most went home, trusting in the king. Once dispersed they lost any power that they had. Over the following months the ringleaders were rounded up, tried and executed.

Chapuys reported these events to Charles and encouraged the emperor to support the protestors. He suggested that the Pope could send Reginald Pole to England to provide guidance and leadership, together with funds. The ambassador also thought that sending soldiers would be helpful and that Englishmen would flock to join any force that was sent. In all this he was wildly optimistic. In light of Charles's war with Francis he was not going to be able to dispatch troops to England even if he wished to. Henry must have known that he had little to fear from a foreign invasion at that time, and it is doubtful whether the majority of the 'pilgrims' would even have accepted such assistance which would have turned them into traitors. They did not regard themselves as rebels aiming to overthrow the king – they wanted their king to change his policies.

With the Pilgrimage of Grace dealt with and the European powers still at war, Henry's twenty-eight year wait for a legitimate male heir now came to an end. Early in 1537 Jane Seymour became pregnant and in October successfully gave birth to a son. However, she died twelve days after the birth of Prince Edward. Henry's daughter, Mary, with whom Jane had developed a good relationship, was the chief mourner at her funeral. After several years of estrangement from her father, she had been reconciled with him after reluctantly accepting Henry as head of the Church in England. Henry dressed in black for the next three months though, within days, the king's representatives in France and the Low Countries had been briefed to find possible candidates to be his next wife.

Charles sailed back to Spain from Genoa in December 1536, joining his family in Valladolid and seeing for the first time his second daughter, Juana, now 18 months old, born shortly after he had left for Tunis. Ten months later Isabella gave birth to another son, Juan, though he died at only five months. The pregnancy and birth had been difficult. As Charles later wrote: 'The Empress suffered much after her confinement, and since then ... was in very bad health.'[11] In fact she never fully recovered. Another pregnancy resulted in a miscarriage in April 1539 and Isabella died just ten days later. Charles withdrew to the Hieronymite monastery of La Sisla, near Toledo, for several weeks. Soon afterwards he made it clear that he had no intention of marrying again. This was perhaps surprising as he was only 39, and had just one son in a world where life could be precarious, as shown by the death of Francis's son. Charles had affairs, usually short-lived because of his constant travelling, and had another son in the 1540s, but his attachment to his wife seemed to grow stronger after her death. He always carried a miniature portrait of Isabella on his future travels.

Henry, on the other hand, wanted a new wife. Cromwell and many royal councillors were keen for it to be a foreign princess because another bride from an English noble family would add yet another faction vying for power, just as the Boleyns and the Seymours had. There was also another reason. If Francis and Charles ended their war, England would be isolated and a marriage alliance with one or the other might help to avoid this. While they were still at war negotiations could perhaps be used to further divide them, though this assumed that Henry would be regarded as a desirable marriage partner. Several eligible members of the Habsburg and Valois families were immediately suggested, though the process was slow because Henry wished to see his future wife in the flesh or, failing that, to have a recent portrait of her. The first French favourite, Mary of Guise, became unavailable because by the time an envoy arrived in France to fetch a portrait, she had been betrothed to James V of Scotland, thus sustaining the 'auld alliance'. James and Mary of Guise were to become the parents of Mary, Queen of Scots and grandparents of James VI of Scotland, James I of England.

The most likely Imperial candidate was Christina of Denmark, Charles's niece, who had returned to the Low Countries after the death of her first husband, the Duke of Milan. Hans Holbein, who had been working at the English court for a number of years, was sent to Brussels in March 1538 and returned after only six days with a drawing that delighted Henry. Holbein later produced a fine portrait of Christina that is now in the National Gallery. Even if she became his first choice, he still continued talks with the French and eventually there were as many as five French noblewomen who were being considered, and the king wanted their portraits. Holbein was kept busy and Henry was often enthusiastic about what he saw.

However, negotiations were complicated both by Henry trying to link his marriage to finding a husband for his daughter Mary, even though in English law she was illegitimate, and further unrealistic demands. These were not only the usual dowry and rights of inheritance issues, but Henry also wanted Charles or Francis, depending on which family he married into, to insist on including England in any peace treaty that they made and not to support the Pope in any attempts to resolve the religious schism in Europe. Charles in particular was never going to accept those terms. When Henry suggested, possibly tongue-in-cheek, that all the French ladies should be brought to Calais for his inspection, Francis sharply responded that it was not the French custom to view damsels like horses for sale. No bride had been found by the summer of 1538, when the emperor and the French king concluded a truce in Nice.

Chapter Fourteen

Dangerous Isolation

After renewed fighting in Piedmont and a slow Spanish advance into Languedoc in the spring of 1538, both Charles and Francis were short of money and no clear-cut victory was in sight. Pope Paul travelled to Nice to act as peacemaker and invited them to join him. Although the two monarchs refused to meet, Queen Eleanor, who had accompanied her husband Francis, made several visits to her brother. Agreement for a ten-year truce was reached in June. Both sides retained the possessions that they then had but the underlying problems, such as Milan, were still unresolved. Pope Paul, besides wishing to be seen as the arbiter, also had his own family ambitions. He used the talks with Charles to arrange the marriage of his grandson Ottavio Farnese to Charles's natural daughter Margaret, widowed at the age of 14 on the death of Alessandro de' Medici the year before.

The truce changed the international situation for the worse as far as Henry was concerned. If Charles, Francis and Pope Paul ever came to trust each other, their thoughts might turn to England. Over the next year and a half, they seemed to be drawing ever closer. Soon after the truce Francis invited Charles to meet him at Aigues-Mortes on the Rhone delta. Charles arrived on 14 July 1538, and was welcomed by Francis who, in a calculated display of trust, boarded the emperor's vessel. They had a private meeting at which they agreed to remain good friends and delegate any further negotiations to their ministers.[1] At the banquet they went out of their way to display mutual respect. The following day Charles returned the confidence that Francis had shown by visiting the king and his family ashore, where he was met by Prince Henri, his former hostage, now Francis's heir. Charles is said to have greeted him warmly. The emperor was also pleased to be able to spend some more time with his sister. The two rulers promised to arrange marriage alliances between their families, with perhaps Charles's son, Philip, marrying Francis's youngest daughter, Margaret, or Maria, Charles's daughter, marrying Francis's youngest son. They also agreed to support each other against anyone who threatened their lands and to plan for future action against both the Turks and Lutherans.

Whether Henry was the target of any of these agreements is questionable. He was not in a position to attack either of them, nor was he a Lutheran, though if this was loosely interpreted as meaning anyone who split from the Catholic Church then it would indeed include the English king. If anything, Charles's attention was directed towards Ottoman aggression in the Mediterranean. In February 1538 the Papacy, Venice, the Knights Hospitaller and Charles had formed an anti-Ottoman Holy League. That year Barbarossa had captured many of the Venetian-controlled islands in the Aegean before taking Actium opposite Prevesa at the mouth of the gulf of Arta in western Greece. The Holy League fleet, under Andrea Doria, blockaded him there for three weeks in September before Barbarossa took advantage of a favourable wind direction to make a surprise move into the open sea. In the subsequent battle the Holy League lost fifty vessels, mainly Venetian, before withdrawing. Barbarossa suffered lighter losses and made his escape, while the League commanders blamed each other for a lack of co-ordination. The chance of ending Ottoman domination in much of the Mediterranean was lost for over thirty years. These events strengthened Charles's wish to renew his efforts against the Turks, particularly against Barbarossa's base at Algiers, though he had to wait another three years before he could put his plans into action.

By 1539 there was good reason for Henry to be concerned about the outbreak of goodwill, peace and harmony between his fellow monarchs, especially as he had no knowledge of Charles's intentions. England had become increasingly isolated. Nothing had yet come of Henry's marriage plans. Mary of Hungary had no high opinion of him and her niece, the 16-year-old Christina, commented that 'If I had two heads, one of them would be at the King of England's disposal', pointing out that his first wife had been poisoned (repeating an unfounded rumour), his second put to death and his third lost for lack of keeping to her child-bed. Worse was to come. In December Pope Paul finally issued the bull of excommunication that called for Henry's removal. He again sent Cardinal Pole to France and Spain and Cardinal Beaton to Scotland with the express purpose of raising support for a crusade against Henry.

The Treaty of Toledo in January 1539 committed Charles and Francis not to sign any new treaties with England without the approval of the other. Soon after this they threatened to withdraw their ambassadors from Henry's court. The French ambassador left without a replacement and Eustace Chapuys spent much of the year in the Low Countries. Besides the formal diplomatic channels, Cromwell had representatives listening to every hostile comment made about England and its king in courts across

Europe. Since most of these were reported without any context or attempt to evaluate their reliability, it was difficult for those in England to judge just how significant they were.

Later in the year Francis offered Charles the chance to travel through France as his guest while on his way to the Low Countries. The emperor wished to impose his authority on the citizens of Ghent, the city of his birth, for their refusal to contribute their share of the taxes that had been demanded from the Low Countries during the recent war with France. Previously, when travelling between Spain and the Low Countries, Charles had travelled across the Bay of Biscay and along the Channel or via the Mediterranean to Genoa and then overland, through Innsbruck and along the Danube and Rhine valleys. The most direct route, through France, had not been an option until now. Many of his advisers were concerned for his safety but Charles accepted the offer on the understanding that affairs of state would not be discussed because he knew that the monarchs would soon fall out if they were.

With Isabella no longer there to act as regent in Spain, he decided that his son Philip, now 12, would have that role, though with a regency council of trusted ministers to take real responsibility for the governance of his lands. He entered France near Bayonne and travelled through Bordeaux and Poitiers accompanied by the dauphin, Henri, and Charles, now Duke of Orleans, Francis's youngest and favourite son. Francis met the emperor at Loches, south of Orleans. The emphasis was on entertainment and pleasure – hunting, banquets and balls. There is no doubt that Francis knew how to turn on the charm when it was required. Christmas was spent at Fontainebleau and on 1 January 1540 they entered Paris, greeted by vast crowds eager to see the emperor who had been their bitter enemy and the subject of hostile propaganda for so long.[2] Charles was dressed in black with his only adornment the gold chain of the Order of the Golden Fleece. He was probably reminded of a visit he had made over seventeen years before – that time to England with Henry VIII as his host.

Henry's response to his lack of foreign allies was to remove any potential threats to him at home, to strengthen coastal fortifications and to prepare England's defensive forces. Internally his main concern was the group around the Pole family. Cardinal Reginald Pole's actions over the previous five years meant that correspondence with him was regarded as treasonable. His younger brother Geoffrey shared his dislike of Henry's divorce and regularly visited Chapuys, trying to persuade him that many people in England would be supportive of an invasion by the emperor. He did little to hide his views and, in August 1538, he was taken to the Tower where he languished for two months before being interrogated. When put under pressure he revealed information about the letters and messages the family had received and about private conversations between family and friends. His brother Henry, Lord Montague, Henry Courtenay, Marquess of Exeter, and his cousin Edward Neville, were soon arrested. All had been close to Henry since his early years and Courtenay's wife had been a confidante of Catherine of Aragon and Mary. As Henry's first cousin, Courtenay was seen as a particular threat. In December all three were tried and executed. Geoffrey Pole was also found guilty but was pardoned, while his mother Margaret Pole, Countess of Salisbury, was imprisoned in the Tower of London where she remained until her botched beheading in 1541. There had never been a full-blown conspiracy but the group's status meant that they had the potential to have widespread influence and if England ever did face an invasion, they could have been possible replacements for Henry.

A sure sign of the growing concern about a possible invasion came in February 1539 when Cromwell ordered officials in every county near the sea to survey the coastline, identify all those sites that might be used as a landing place for an invasion and give advice on the best way of fortifying them. The information was presented in the form of written descriptions supported by plans, which were then put together into maps of the coastline that emphasised the beach areas ideal for enemy landings. They recorded where previous invasion forces had disembarked and showed the church towers and beacons that would be used to communicate news of any landing. They also marked where defensive forces could be mustered and provisioned. Coastal forts were shown and suggested locations for the construction of up to twenty-five new ones were added. In addition, new maps of the coastline from Ipswich to Sandwich were produced, with particular attention paid to the Thames and Medway estuaries and the sandbanks off the coast.

This was the largest mapping exercise that had ever been carried out in England and was not equalled until the nineteenth century. The whole project would have appealed to Henry, who had a great interest in maps and the practicalities of coastal defence, as well as naval matters. Besides refitting the older ships of the navy and commissioning new vessels, there was an expensive programme of construction and reinforcing defences along the south coast from Cornwall to Kent and then north to the Thames. Many of the designs were submitted to the king for his approval, such as those for three of the new castles to be constructed on the east coast of Kent – Deal, Sandown and Walmer. The designers had previously only worked on palaces, such as Nonsuch Palace in Surrey, one of Henry's most ambitious building projects. Started the previous year, it was intended to match the great French chateaux of the Loire, especially Chambord, which Francis showed off to Charles on his journey through France. Plans for the new coastal fortifications were essentially circular stone bastions where artillery could be mounted. The designs did not include the latest ideas in military technology then being developed in Italy, although in 1545 the *trace italienne* was used in plans for the improved defences at Tynemouth (never constructed) and then on the Isle of Wight at Yarmouth.[3] Henry personally inspected some of the work and was also involved in the planning of a new fortress to protect the harbour entrance at Calais.[4] Such fortifications were expensive and funded mainly from the money that was being raised as a result of the dissolution of the monasteries.

As neither Charles nor Francis was willing to ally themselves to Henry, he looked for an alternative. Talks had been held with the Lutheran Schmalkaldic League in 1531 and 1535 but nothing had come of them. In mid-1538 German representatives again visited England. As opponents of Charles V they were keen for an alliance, but would Henry agree to their terms? The Lutherans saw much that they approved of in England. The dissolution of the monasteries had continued apace. Henry believed that many were hot-beds of support for the Pope and could serve as focal points for opposition to royal supremacy. Abbots who resisted were accused of treason and hanged; those who co-operated were generously pensioned off. Although there was some theft and destruction, the process was generally well organised, with rents of over £40,000 a year going to the crown and £750,000 being generated by the sale of land and property during the last eight years of the reign.[5] Henry's denunciation of the worship of relics and images had also opened the way for the destruction of shrines, the most famous of which was that of Thomas Becket at Canterbury, where Charles had once knelt alongside Henry. When it was destroyed in 1538 it is said that two great chests of jewels carried by six or eight men each, together with twenty-four wagon-loads of varied treasures, were removed. However, despite these actions, it was soon obvious that as far as doctrinal issues were concerned, Henry would make no concessions to the Lutherans.

Religion was important to Henry. He attended short masses daily and took duties such as giving alms to the poor seriously. He believed that as his position as monarch was sanctioned by God he needed to be seen as righteous. He had justified his break from Rome as being the removal of the malign influence of the papacy that had permitted the growth of idolatry, superstition and hypocrisy. When it suited him the Renaissance humanist slant of his education convinced him that the word of God was found in the Bible, not in the decrees of the Pope. After 1534 he was seeking a religion that would unify the people of England, one that cleansed the Church of abuses, gave more people access to the word of God, but was essentially conservative in doctrine, avoiding theological 'novelties' that he accused Lutherans and other more radical thinkers of attempting to introduce.

In some ways it was useful for Henry to build up a widespread fear of invasion. It served to strengthen his position because little gets a ruler more support from the people than the threat of a foreign attack. However, the scare of 1539 may have forced Henry's hand in some respects. In May he asked Parliament to pass the Act of Six Articles, which they did after much heated argument. After stating that it aimed to abolish diversity of opinion and establish a uniform religion in England, it affirmed the use of communion in one kind, the sanctity of monastic vows, compulsory clerical celibacy, and private masses, though accepted that auricular confession, while retained, was not required by divine law. Denial of any of the six articles was made punishable by death or life imprisonment. The act was a blow to those who wanted faster progress towards a more evangelical church. It offered the conservative majority a more traditional form of religion than the reformers wished for. It might have been intended to head off any opposition at home and at the same time undermine those calling for a crusade against him from abroad, though in many ways it was a clear statement of Henry's own beliefs rather than a panic reaction to external pressures.[6] The same year saw the placing of a Bible in English (The Great Bible) in every parish church and the introduction of parish registers of births, marriages and deaths. Henry's religious policies can be seen as an attempt to achieve some kind of balance between traditional Catholic teaching, Renaissance humanist reform and evangelical innovation.[7]

Despite earlier failures, envoys were sent to Lutheran rulers in Germany and to King Christian III of Denmark in early 1539. They were not well received but eventually another delegation of Lutherans arrived in late April, shortly before the passing of the Act of Six Articles. Not surprisingly nothing could be agreed and they departed the following month. However, a new marriage alliance was now under discussion. Duke William of Cleves had inherited Guelderland on the death of Duke Charles of Egmond and was soon in conflict with the emperor. He, like Henry, looked for a religious settlement with many traditional doctrines but without papal control. One of his sisters had married the influential Elector of Saxony and another, Anne, was still available for marriage. Henry showed an interest as England's isolation continued to grow. Cromwell, always rather keener on a German alliance than his king, pushed negotiations forward. The king, as usual, wanted her appearance checked and Holbein was set to work again. The result, a full-face portrait that showed Anne at her best, was perfectly acceptable. She was said to be good-natured and virtuous, though poorly educated, could not speak English and lacked the accomplishments associated with ladies of the French, Burgundian or Spanish courts. An agreement was reached in October and, as Charles was being royally entertained during his journey through France, Anne of Cleves was travelling to England. She arrived in Calais in early December but her crossing was delayed by bad weather until after Christmas.

On 1 January Henry and five companions arrived at Rochester and entered Anne's lodgings unannounced. Henry was doing what he had done in his youth, first pretending to be carrying gifts from the king before eventually revealing his true identity. Anne had initially paid him little attention, seemingly more interested in watching the bear-baiting that was taking place below her window. Then, when Henry introduced himself as the king, she was at a loss, unprepared for such a meeting, with no experience of the conventions of courtly love and with no common language to converse in. Henry found her completely unappealing. He discussed the possibility of getting out of the marriage with Cromwell but to break the contract would have given great offence.

The marriage went ahead at Greenwich on 6 January, Henry bitterly regretting it but behaving with dignity. He told Cromwell that he was only carrying through with it to satisfy the expectations of the world and his realm. Henry claimed that he found her so unattractive that it was impossible for him to consummate the marriage though Anne, who seemed to have been completely innocent of the facts of life, did not at first realise anything was wrong. She learnt English quickly, wore English-style clothes and came to enjoy music, but nothing was to change Henry's mind. By Easter he had already become enamoured with one of Anne's maids of honour, the 17-year-old niece of the Duke of Norfolk, Catherine Howard. She was praised by her relatives for her honesty and purity. This time things moved swiftly. The day after midsummer, Anne was moved to Richmond supposedly for her health and, on 6 July, she was informed 'by certain lords … that the marriage was not lawful … and that she should be taken no longer as Queen, but called Lady Anne of Cleves.'[8] She readily agreed to an annulment, was granted a generous pension and various properties, and remained on good terms with the king, who continued to treat her with respect for the rest of his life. Henry married Catherine Howard on 28 July.

Chapter Fifteen

Renewed Friendship

On the same day as Henry's fifth marriage, Thomas Cromwell, his chief minister for almost nine years, was beheaded. It might have been a foolhardy action for the king to take when many in the country believed that it was in danger of invasion, but by then the scare of 1539, whether real or imagined, had receded. Cardinal Pole, who had been sent by the Pope to promote such an attack had failed to receive much encouragement from either the French or Charles, who he visited in Toledo in 1539. Despite all their protestations of friendship, the fundamental issues that divided those two monarchs remained and by mid-1540, their conflicting interests were once again coming to the fore. Henry was, of course, keen to drive a wedge between them. In February 1540 the Duke of Norfolk was sent to France and returned to inform the king that the alliance between Francis and Charles was unpopular amongst many at the French court. He also told him that relations with Francis could be improved by the removal of Cromwell whose reputation there had been blackened by the Bishop of Winchester, Stephen Gardiner, Henry's ambassador to France between 1535 and 1538. Although Henry's distaste for his marriage to Anne of Cleves did not lead directly to Cromwell's fall, it had undermined his position.[1]

His many rivals and enemies, Norfolk and Gardiner chief amongst them, looked to take advantage. In April, however, Cromwell had been created Earl of Essex, and appointed Great Chamberlain of the Household, hardly signs of Henry's disfavour. Henry might have disliked the fact that Cromwell was unenthusiastic about his new marriage plan, which was being strongly encouraged by Norfolk and Gardiner, but there was no major disagreement over policy. Even if Cromwell had been more inclined than many to support an imperial alliance rather than a French one, there was no noticeable change in foreign policy after his fall. He was not charged with plotting with foreign powers against the interests of his king. Instead, his enemies managed to convince Henry that he was planning to bring about radical religious changes,[2] abhorrent to the king. The Act of Attainder passed by Parliament, which led to his execution, accused him of heresy and treason, of supporting heretics, of permitting the spread of their literature, of releasing them from prison, and of himself being a sacramentarian, one who denies the real presence of Christ in the Eucharist, a belief condemned by both Catholics and Lutherans.

Although Cromwell's guilt would have been difficult to establish in a trial, and despite his protestations of innocence and appeals for mercy, he had lost the confidence of the king. Cromwell's removal delighted his opponents at court as well as many in the country, who held him responsible for the policies of which they disapproved during the previous nine years. For almost three decades Henry had been able to rely on Wolsey and then Cromwell to get things done. They had advised and influenced the king but not determined policy, especially foreign policy, in which Henry was always more 'hands-on' than in some other areas of government. Both had been able, hard-working and ambitious, ready to do the king's bidding once his mind was made up. They had also taken the blame for unpopular policies, thus protecting Henry from criticism. Although both had become wealthy in the royal service, Wolsey more than Cromwell ostentatiously enjoying the trappings of power, both were disliked by the nobility for their lowly origins and by others who were jealous of their status. For the last seven years of his reign Henry had no such minister. At times it seemed as if he was influenced first by one faction and then by another, but Henry was never a puppet controlled by others. Various individuals in the Royal Council, such as Norfolk, Gardiner, Wriothesley, Rich, Seymour and the king's secretary, William Paget, had the ear of the king but in the end, it was Henry who made the decisions.

Similarly, Charles had taken more control over the direction of his policies during the course of his reign. In his early years he had been strongly influenced by the mentors of his youth, especially Chièvres, but after his death in 1521, Charles's own priorities gradually came to the fore. Given the extent of his lands he never attempted to establish unified systems of administration or justice across them all. To have done so would have provoked serious opposition as each area sought to retain or even extend their traditional privileges. No single territory dominated his thinking but he was always assertive of what he believed to be his hereditary rights whether in Spain, the Low Countries or Italy, and of his imperial authority in the Holy Roman Empire. He was served by capable ministers, particularly Mercurino di Gattinara until his death in 1530 and then by Francisco de los Cobos in Spain and Nicholas Perrenot de Granvelle in the Empire.

After his journey through France, Charles spent a short time in Brussels in early 1540 before moving on to Ghent. The citizens there had been warned that he intended to make an example of them for challenging his authority, even though by then most had paid their taxes. He arrived with an imposing display of force, accompanied by the regent, Mary of Hungary, ambassadors, princes, nobles and 4,000 troops, who were billeted around the city. With charges of 'breach of allegiance, disobedience, incitement to riot, mutiny and lese-majesty' (offence against the dignity of the sovereign), about twenty-five executions took place. The city was punished by the loss of privileges, a vast fine, the removal of weapons, and the reform of its administration to rid it of the more radical elements. The old abbey of St Bavo's was demolished to make way for a new fortress to intimidate the citizens, and in a formal humiliation, representatives of the different classes had to appear before the emperor and beg for mercy, with their heads uncovered, barefoot, with nooses around their necks. This submission is still remembered today in an annual procession.[3]

Charles spent the rest of the year in the Low Countries which he had not visited since establishing his sister as regent nine years before. In 1541 he travelled to Germany with two objectives – to try again to end the religious schism and to organise another expedition against the Turks, this time to Algiers. The Diet of Regensburg was formally opened, later than planned, on 5 April. A colloquy was arranged where three Catholic and three Protestant theologians, carefully selected to favour conciliation, would debate twenty-three specific issues in an attempt to agree a set of principles. This was to be the last occasion when there was any chance of achieving such an agreement, and even then, it was a faint hope. Like Henry in England, the emperor wished for a settlement that would bring religious unity across Europe. He wanted to be a mediator but again, like Henry, there were limits to the concessions that his conscience would allow. Since the split after the Diet of Worms twenty years before, every effort at reconciliation had failed and each side had become more entrenched in their views. No agreement was reached and Charles later recorded that at the end of July, 'after various debates … they were still far from a conclusion.'[4]

The emperor's plans to lead an expedition against Algiers had been seriously delayed. He set off through Munich and Innsbruck to Italy. It was not until October that the fleet and troops required were ready. This was very late in the year for such a campaign and he received many warnings about the risks involved. But Charles, not wishing to waste the effort and the cost of all the preparations, decided to rely on fortune and the will of God. This time it was an ignominious failure. Rough seas made disembarkation very difficult and once the troops had been landed, a violent storm scattered the fleet with all the supplies that were needed by the army. After a month the decision was made to withdraw to Spain. There were heavy losses of men, ships and equipment, with nothing achieved.

By then, much to Henry's satisfaction, Charles and Francis were already well on the road to war. Francis was not going to miss the opportunity of taking advantage of Charles's difficulties. Having discussed with the emperor the possibility of Milan being granted to his younger son if the prince married either Charles's or Ferdinand's daughter, he had been angered in October 1540 when the emperor formally declared Milan to be an imperial fief, naming his own son Philip as the duke. In 1541 Francis pushed through the wedding of his 12-year-old niece, Jeanne d'Albret, heir to Navarre, to Duke William of Cleves, the brother of Anne, gaining the duke as an ally against Charles. Jeanne herself protested strongly, signing documents declaring that she did not consent to the marriage. She had to be carried to the altar against her will.

If a *casus belli* was needed it was provided when two envoys representing Francis, Antonio Rincon and Cesare Fregoso, were murdered near Milan in August 1541. Rincon was travelling to the Ottoman court in Istanbul to accept Suleiman's proposals for an alliance. Although Charles had not ordered the murders, they were carried out with the full knowledge of his governor in Lombardy, the Marchese del Vasto. Charles denied any involvement, took no action against the governor, and then played a part in the subsequent cover-up that allowed the murderers to escape justice.[5] Francis made full use of this situation in hostile propaganda and then, in July 1542, declared war. A large French force commanded by the dauphin, Henri, advanced to besiege Perpignan on the Spanish border. There was also a co-ordinated attack on the Low Countries. In the north a Danish fleet blocked trade routes, in the south and west the French invaded Luxembourg and Artois, while William of Cleves' troops under Maarten van Rossem swept through Brabant from the east and besieged Antwerp.[6] Mary of Hungary wrote that 'the Netherlands were never in such danger'. These attacks were successfully resisted but the war had not ended. Charles informed Mary that as soon as he had made arrangements for the government of Spain in his absence, and secured his diplomatic position, he would come to lead his forces.

The renewed war meant that any danger of an attack on England had ended and Henry's situation on the international front improved considerably. However, 1541 had not gone so well for the king on a more personal level. His marriage to Catherine Howard proved to be little short of a disaster. He had been kept ignorant of her earlier life in the household of the Dowager Duchess of Norfolk, especially of her sexual experience with at least two men, including Thomas Culpepper who was now in the king's privy chamber. Although she liked the glamour and status of being queen, and despite being able to arouse Henry's enthusiasm and vigour, the ageing king was not a satisfactory partner for the young queen. Matters were made worse by his periodic poor health, particularly a serious illness caused by his chronic leg ulcer in the spring of 1541. His obvious infirmity did not match the view that he wished her to have of him and, at times, he avoided her altogether.

In June the court set out with great pomp to the north of England for the first time in his reign. The royal progress had two purposes – a display of power to the people of the north and to meet the king of Scotland, James V, his sister Margaret's son, at York. James had married the French king's youngest daughter, Madelaine, in 1537, but she had died soon after arriving in Scotland. He had then married Mary of Guise with whom he had two sons, both of whom died in April 1541. Henry had for some time been encouraging James to weaken the power of the Catholic Church in Scotland, offering to assist in any way that he could, and to end Scotland's alliance with France. If Henry was to become directly involved in the conflict between Charles and Francis, it was wise to secure his northern border. Also, as things stood, James was second in line to the English throne after Prince Edward, not yet 4 years old. Henry could not countenance the possibility of James's accession, given his existing friendship with France and his obedience to the Pope.

Travelling with such a large entourage was always slow, especially when the weather was poor, so it was not until 19 September that they arrived in York. Henry had achieved his first objective and now had high expectations of his meeting with James. Henry waited, and waited, but James never arrived. The strong pro-French faction on the Scottish king's council, led by Cardinal Beaton, was hostile to Henry's plans on both religious and political grounds. There was little trust between the two nations and some in Scotland even suggested that James might be at risk of being kidnapped. Henry regarded this as a personal slight, the more so when James excused himself on the grounds that the meeting had not been agreed to by the king of France. After ten days a furious Henry left York and travelled quickly south.

He was soon to suffer a further humiliation. Information about Catherine's earlier behaviour was used by enemies of the Duke of Norfolk who passed on what they knew to Archbishop Cranmer. He had the uncomfortable task of informing the king of what was being said. At first Henry could not believe it and ordered a secret enquiry with the expectation that there was no truth in the stories. What emerged came as a severe shock. Not only were they true but Catherine had entertained her former lovers, Culpepper and Francis Dereham, during the royal progress to the north as well. When questioned by Cranmer, the queen initially denied everything but later broke down and admitted concealing her pre-marital sexual relations. Culpepper, probably under torture, admitted having intercourse with the queen after her marriage, a claim backed up by Lady Rochford, Catherine's chief lady-in-waiting, who had facilitated his entry to her chamber. As the wife of Anne Boleyn's brother who had been executed in 1536, her involvement seems rash in the extreme. Culpepper and Dereham were executed at Tyburn in December and Catherine, along with Jane Rochford, were beheaded in February 1542.

Henry was left angry and full of self-pity. The actions of the king in that mood were difficult to predict though likely to be aggressive. He had been badly hurt and he wanted to restore his reputation and honour. He was no longer able to joust, his sexual prowess was in doubt so it was to military action that he turned. This could also help to restore greater unity on the Royal Council – little could do that more than a war against the old enemy, France. The international situation at the time suited his purpose. Negotiations had been taking place between England and France throughout 1541 but little had been achieved. By the end of the year, they had all but collapsed. Henry's insistence that his daughter Mary was not legitimate made any marriage alliance with Francis's family very difficult. Francis's refusal to pay the pensions that Henry believed were owed him and his backing of the strong anti-English faction in Scotland angered Henry.

The alternative was to support Charles and revisit the policies of the 1510s and early 1520s. Charles wanted Henry's backing and an English invasion of northern France would suit him well. By the 1540s Henry might have abandoned any thoughts of taking the French crown but the idea of limited territorial gains, taking Boulogne and perhaps Normandy, was very appealing. The negotiations with Charles, however, were not straightforward. Henry demanded recognition of his titles 'Defender of the Faith' and 'Head of the Church of England' and his representatives believed that if that was refused, he would end the talks.[7] Charles would never agree but avoided the issue by answering that as he had not granted such titles, he could not acknowledge or remove them and would continue to refer to Henry as the 'King of England, Ireland and France'. Common interests overcame such difficulties. Their negotiators found a way to fudge the wording and, in June 1542, initial plans were made for a joint invasion of France the following year.

However, Henry wished to ensure that the Scots would not invade northern England as soon as he committed a large number of troops in France. He also had several grievances against James. Frequent cross-border raids caused tension between the nations, as did the refuge provided in Scotland for Henry's enemies, all made worse by James's failure to meet Henry. When English and Scottish negotiators met at York in September 1542, the English made extensive demands. Most were accepted but then Henry insisted on the immediate release of some prisoners and an agreement that James should come to London or York by Christmas. Not trusting Henry's motives, the Scots hesitated so the Duke of Norfolk carried out a violent, week-long attack along the River Tweed. James neither wished for nor was ready for war, but Norfolk's destructive raid provoked him to prepare a counter-attack. Over 15,000 poorly-organised men crossed the River Esk near Carlisle but on 23 November at Solway Moss, they were put to flight by a much smaller English force of 3,000, in what was little more than a skirmish. Unlike at Flodden almost thirty years earlier, casualties were not high but many Scottish nobles were taken prisoner. James, who was not present at the battle, died three weeks later, only six days after the birth of a daughter, Mary, who now became queen. Although his death was a result of a fever, the shock of the defeat may well have weakened his constitution.

If Henry was aiming to unite the two countries under his rule, then now might have been the time to do so, but he decided not to launch a full-scale invasion of Scotland – his military ambitions lay elsewhere. Instead, he would attempt to control the country by building up the pro-English party there. He hoped that they would remove Cardinal Beaton, establish military strongholds on Henry's behalf and send the infant queen, Mary, to England, where she would eventually marry Henry's son, Edward. The plans showed a poor grasp of Scottish affairs. None of this happened. James's death resulted in a vicious struggle for power between various noblemen with close links to the crown. The leading participants were the old rivals James Hamilton, 2nd Earl of Arran, who was made regent; and Archibald Douglas, Earl of Angus, who had married Henry's sister, Margaret Tudor, after the death of James IV, although she later obtained a divorce. The French faction led by James V's widow Mary of Guise and Cardinal Beaton also sought to take advantage of the situation. Henry failed to realise that no-one could successfully control Scotland while supporting what looked like English domination.

Nevertheless, by the spring of 1543, Henry seemed to have recovered from the setbacks of the previous 18 months. On 12 July he married the widowed Lady Latimer, Katherine Parr, not for diplomatic gain or for another son but for domestic comfort. In the same month the Treaty of Greenwich with Scotland supposedly brought peace and arranged for the future marriage of Prince Edward to Mary, Queen of Scots, even though the Scots refused to renounce their agreements with France. Most Scots disliked the treaty and, in December, the Scottish Parliament rejected it and confirmed their treaties with the French. This led to the start of what became known as the 'War of Rough Wooing'. Henry sent forces under Edward Seymour, Earl of Hertford, which in May 1544 landed near the port of Leith, entered and destroyed much of Edinburgh, though not the castle,[8] and then withdrew to Berwick. Even this did not settle matters and although Henry's aggression deterred an attack from the north while he was in France, Scotland remained a hostile neighbour with the pro-English party having little support.

All this had much delayed Henry and Charles's plans for a joint invasion of France. In February 1543 Stephen Gardiner and Thomas Wriothesley for Henry, and Eustace Chapuys representing the emperor, had negotiated a treaty by which there should be peace and free movement between their subjects. More significantly 'the princes shall, within two years, by themselves or by lieutenants, make a joint invasion of France, each with 20,000 foot and 5,000 horse, the invasion to last at least four months'.[9] The treaty also stated that if any state attacked England, Ireland, Calais, Spain or the Low Countries, the aggressor would be regarded as a 'common enemy' of both Henry and Charles, and that if in the case of England, Calais or the Low Countries the attack was made by more than 10,000 troops, assistance in the form of men or money would be sent. Francis was called upon to end his alliance with the Turks, end his war against Charles and pay the arrears of the pensions owed to Henry. A part of the agreement that was to be of importance in the future relations between Charles and Henry stated that 'the princes shall treat with him [Francis] separately but communicate to each other his proposals and their answers, and that no agreement shall be made until the claims of both are satisfied.'[10]

A letter from Chapuys to Mary of Hungary in February 1543 mentions that Henry wished the treaty to remain secret until its formal ratification in order to give English subjects time to remove their goods from France. It also shows how important Chapuys believed it was to conclude this alliance with Henry when he refers to 'her instructions to advance the treaty, considering the state of the Emperor's affairs, and fearing the rupture of this treaty and danger of the King's [Henry's] indignation combined with the French practices.'[11] Equally, the importance of communicating the terms to Charles, still in Spain, quickly and safely, was shown by his explaining that two copies of the treaty were dispatched by Henry to Spain, one by sea and another overland through Germany and Italy and then across the Mediterranean, and that Chapuys would do the same, but using different ships and couriers. On ratifying the treaty Charles reluctantly recognised that the joint invasion would not take place in 1543. Francis, soon alert to the situation, offered to meet some of Henry's demands, but it was too late. On 22 June England declared war on France. Although a small English force of 5,000 under Sir John Wallop, the captain of Guînes, immediately raided lands in northern France, destroying several villages and eventually joining Charles's army in the late summer, it was not until 1544 that the major joint campaign took place. Henry and Charles were once again allies in a war against France, just as they had been in the early 1520s.

Chapter Sixteen

Conflicting Aims

While Henry was struggling to control events in Scotland, Charles appointed his son Philip, soon to be 15 years old, as his regent when he left Spain in May 1543. Having finalised the alliance with Henry he was fulfilling his promise to Mary of Hungary to take personal charge of the war against Francis. Shortly before his departure he gave his son three documents which together provide a fascinating insight into Charles's ideas about the role of a monarch. The first outlines Philip's powers and responsibilities. The second is more personal, from father to son. It advises Philip on how he should conduct himself in public, how he should go about the business of government, how to behave in his private life, and his need to listen to the advice of those appointed to help him. Charles emphasises devotion to God, the importance of justice, and that decisions must be made dispassionately, not as the result of anger or prejudice. Although in politics there are more exceptions than rules, Philip should follow a straight path, have good judgement and do good works. As Philip was soon to marry his Portuguese cousin, Maria Manuela, Charles advised him not to overindulge in the pleasures of marriage which he had been told caused the premature death of Charles's uncle, Juan, over forty years earlier. The third document is a confidential assessment of the strengths and weaknesses of his advisers, revealing exactly what Charles thought of them. It shows the emperor to be a shrewd judge of character.[1] Philip was to be grateful for this advice as he gradually took the reins of power in Spain. Charles did not return to Spain for thirteen years.

His fleet of 140 vessels crossed the Mediterranean to Genoa. In Italy he held unsuccessful talks with Pope Paul who disliked his alliance with Henry VIII and refused to believe Charles's claim that Francis was working with the Ottoman fleet in the Mediterranean. The Pope soon learnt his mistake. In August, Nice, though not the citadel, was captured by a joint French-Ottoman force. They left as an Imperial relief army approached. Francis then ordered the evacuation of Toulon so that Barbarossa's fleet of 110 vessels and 30,000 men could winter there, with churches converted to mosques. As news of this spread across Europe, the alliance became an embarrassment to Francis and, in the spring of 1544, he had to pay Barbarossa to leave.

In the summer of 1543 Charles could do little about this so he went north to join his army in the Rhineland. His first target was Francis's ally, Duke William of Cleves, and in August he took the heavily defended city of Duren after it refused to surrender. Its garrison was punished as an example to others with hundreds killed in the onslaught and then prisoners found to be the emperor's subjects were hanged. This treatment led to the rapid surrender of other towns including Julich and then Roermond in Guelderland. Duke William received no assistance from Francis, and in September he submitted to Charles at Venlo. As he often did, Charles at first gave the impression that he would impose a severe punishment but eventually pardoned the duke, who had to accept Charles's sovereignty of Guelderland, swear allegiance to the emperor, return to the Catholic faith and agree to the annulment of his marriage to Jeanne d'Albret. He later married Maria, a daughter of Charles's brother Ferdinand.

After his victory over Duke William, Charles turned his attention to Francis whose armies had captured Landrecies, east of Cambrai, and then Luxembourg. He marched south to besiege Landrecies. Francis moved to relieve the town but when Charles's army, which included Wallop's English soldiers, began to advance in battle order on 3 November, Francis, perhaps remembering Pavia, ordered a withdrawal to avoid a pitched battle. Charles was furious but it was so late in the season that he decided pursuit was impracticable, though he was determined to continue the war in 1544, this time with his English ally. In November he rejected a papal peace mission and, on 31 December, the allies' ambassadors agreed another treaty which was short and to the point. 'Each of the two Princes in person (unless ill) shall assail France, with separate armies, before 20 June next at the latest.'[2] They would each be at the head of an army of '35,000 foot and 7,000 horse', though Charles would provide 2,000 of each for Henry. The plan was made explicit. Charles 'shall invade by Champagne, and the King by the passages of the river Somme, and both shall march with diligence towards Paris, as strategy, victuals and the enemy shall permit'. Once this had been confirmed Charles held an Imperial Diet at Speyer in early 1544 that refused to give a hearing to Francis's ambassadors and agreed to provide Charles with military support.

For Henry the plan represented a large-scale commitment that would require substantial taxes and a greater logistical effort than any that had been attempted since 1523. The army, led by the Dukes of Norfolk and Suffolk, crossed to Calais in late May 1544 and entered French lands, besieging

Boulogne and Montreuil. Before Henry joined them two months later, he appointed Queen Katherine Parr as governor of the realm for the duration of his absence, and gave royal assent to the Third Act of Succession (1543) which reinstated his daughters Mary and Elizabeth to the line of succession after Prince Edward. If all were to die childless, then the heirs of Henry's younger sister, Mary, would be next in line, thus excluding the heirs of his older sister, Margaret – the Scottish line.

On his arrival in France Henry decided that the main objective would be the capture of the besieged cities, especially Boulogne, and not an immediate march south to the Somme and then towards Paris as originally planned. He might have had in mind Suffolk's campaign of 1523 when the capture of Boulogne had been his preferred strategy, but he had been persuaded to allow Suffolk's army to go for the bigger objective despite what turned out to be Henry's realistic concerns about becoming isolated in French territory. Charles was angry when he realised that the English were not advancing south, though Henry argued that without taking Boulogne he would not be able to supply his army.[3]

Battles in northern Italy earlier in 1544 had resulted in a stalemate, the French being unable to end Charles's control of Milan. The decisive events of 1544, therefore, took place further north. Charles's army under his long-serving general, Ferrante Gonzaga, recaptured Luxembourg as planned in May and then moved south to join the emperor at Metz. Their army of over 40,000 men then moved rapidly west to St Dizier on the River Marne, where they were delayed by a siege of over a month. By late August, having at last taken the town, Charles continued west along the north bank of the Marne. On hearing that Francis's army was on the south side of the river between Chalons and Épernay, he undertook a forced march past Chalons, planning to cross the river at Épernay and launch a surprise attack on Francis from the west. He was too late. Épernay had just been occupied by the French so no crossing could be made.[4]

In the 1540s monarchs still wished to be seen leading their troops. Although Charles had been discouraged by his advisers from being directly involved in war in his early years, from the time of the expedition to Tunis in 1535 he was frequently on campaign. He expressed his desire to carry out 'great deeds' and had been brought up to believe that these could be achieved on the battlefield. The risks were high as shown by the capture of Francis at Pavia and the deaths of several of Charles's commanders, such as Bourbon in 1527 at Rome and Philibert, Prince of Orange in 1530 outside Florence. The emperor became involved in strategic planning and in more detailed discussions about tactics and battlefield manoeuvres, often having detailed maps drawn up showing rivers and other physical features that might influence troop movements. However, he always listened carefully to the advice of his generals before making decisions, recognising that they had greater military experience. He had proved his bravery in the face of enemy fire on a number of occasions. He was frequently to be found talking to his soldiers, often at the front line of a siege, encouraging them by his presence. He liked to be in the vanguard of his army so that he could reconnoitre enemy positions and troops dispositions. It was often commented that he was probably at his happiest when on campaign with his army (Plate 22). As he grew older and was increasingly handicapped by the effects of gout, he still wished to be seen as a warrior.

Henry had not taken to the battlefield since his French campaign of 1513, though by the 1540s he was enthusiastically preparing to do so again. He dismissed Charles's concerns that his ill-health and lack of fitness might hinder the campaign – concerns shared by members of Henry's council, though they feared to express them. If Charles was going to be at the head of his army, then so was Henry. He had always maintained an interest in military affairs and had a good knowledge of strategy and military technology. He was in his element supervising details of the artillery bombardment of Boulogne. There had never been any doubt as to his personal bravery, but he was a different man to the one who had regularly been the victor at tournaments. His enormous bulk meant that his armour was now of a great girth and he needed a crane to be hoisted onto his mount. He might well have been troubled by a more mobile campaign (Plates 15 and 16).

After the setback at Épernay, Charles reverted to his original plan of marching along the Marne towards Paris. By 12 September the vanguard, accompanied by the emperor, reached La Ferte-sous-Jouarre, less than 50 miles from the French capital. Despite Francis's efforts to reassure them, the citizens of the capital were starting to panic[5] with some leaving rather than waiting for the chaos that would ensue if enemy troops arrived at the gates. But then Charles swung north, capturing Soissons, thereby facilitating the junction of his forces with those of Henry, should the English king eventually move south. Charles was all the while frustrated by Henry's insistence on taking Boulogne before carrying out the plan that they had agreed. It was dawning on the emperor that Henry's aims were far more limited and that the capture of Boulogne and some surrounding land might satisfy the English king. If Henry had been used by Charles to divert Francis's troops in 1523, then Henry had perhaps now reversed the situation.

Francis had put forward tentative proposals for talks with the emperor's representatives as early as July. Charles himself was aware that he could not afford to keep his large army in the field beyond the end of September. In his memoirs he wrote 'the Emperor, in want of provisions … could not remain long enough to attack those places which would have defended themselves … the more so as the soldiers' pay was in arrears'.[6] Nevertheless, he sought to use his march towards Paris and the threat of Henry attacking from the north to exert more pressure on Francis. He claimed that he could not make peace without Henry's agreement and that he had no way of communicating with the English king. Charles had to decide whether to accept the terms then on offer or, if Henry was willing to join forces, to try to get even more concessions from the French. On 7 September the French provided a safe-conduct pass for Charles's envoy to travel for talks with Henry outside Boulogne. The king was informed of the state of the negotiations and then asked whether he wished to continue the war, and if so, when would he be marching south? He was also told that if he did not do so immediately then Charles would make peace with Francis.

On 14 September Henry formally requested the defenders of Boulogne to surrender and, as it was obvious that no relief was coming, they eventually agreed. Henry entered the city in triumph four days later, reliving his entry to Tournai over thirty years before. With this reverse Francis was now even keener for a settlement with Charles, and on the same day, 18 September, they agreed terms at Crépy. There was both an open and a secret treaty, which together reveal the nature of many such agreements at the time – a statement of laudable aims, followed by duplicitous deals, many of which were then disregarded.

In the public treaty Francis and his sons promised to give up claims to Naples and the Low Countries, return all gains made since the truce of Nice in 1538, end the alliance with the Turks and supply 10,000 soldiers and 600 heavy cavalry for a crusade against them. Charles agreed to hand back land recently taken in France and give up his claim to Burgundy. There was also a plan for the marriage of Charles, Duke of Orleans, Francis's youngest son. He would marry either Charles's daughter Maria or his niece, Ferdinand's daughter Anna, and inherit the Low Countries if he married Maria or Milan if he married Anna. Charles would decide which within a year. This was strongly objected to by Francis's older son, Henri, who believed that the provision of an independent territory for his younger brother would simply divide Valois strength in the future. As it happened this never came about because the Duke of Orleans died almost exactly a year later, so Charles never had to make good on the agreement that he was by then regretting.

It seemed to be a generous offer on Charles's part. It was one of several such marriage ideas that he hoped would result in a permanent settlement between the Habsburgs and the Valois. Charles had wished to offer Francis something substantial that would encourage him to agree to the terms of the secret treaty. This contained a promise from Francis that he would back Charles's call for a general church council intended to settle the religious schism in Germany and to provide troops to fight the heretics if that failed, not to make any agreement with Henry that was against the interests of the emperor and to support Charles if he was ever at war against England. Although Charles had no immediate expectation of a war against Henry, this final clause exemplifies how quickly an ally might become an enemy.

Henry's celebrations were short-lived. Although he had an idea that Charles would make peace, and according to Charles he had agreed to it[7], the Treaty of Crépy meant that he was now left to defend his new possessions in France alone. After spending less than two weeks in the newly captured Boulogne, Henry returned to England but not before the impact of Charles making peace with Francis was felt. The French could now concentrate all their forces against him. The English troops besieging Montreuil commanded by the Duke of Norfolk were forced to withdraw to Boulogne. After Henry's departure Norfolk and Suffolk also left Boulogne for Calais, taking many of their troops with them. When ordered to return by a furious king they were prevented from doing so by the French army, now numbering more than 50,000. They returned to England to face a displeased Henry. The remaining garrison at Boulogne was put under considerable pressure but held out. The approaching winter prevented a more sustained French effort to retake the city and it was then possible for the English to send reinforcements and supplies by sea over the next few months.

There was little chance of peace. For the French there could be no settlement without the return of Boulogne, which Henry had no intention of doing, and Henry insisted that Francis abandon his alliance with Scotland. Neither would give way in talks during October. When Charles offered to mediate, suggesting that Henry should hand Boulogne over to a third party during the talks, any effort to hide the bad feeling between Henry and the emperor ended. Henry complained about Charles's defection, arguing that while he had agreed to independent talks, he had not agreed to any separate peace treaty. Charles replied that the English king had shown bad faith by the prolonged siege of Boulogne and had broken their agreement to march on Paris. He claimed that he had made peace for the good of Christendom and that Henry should support this. The row continued well into 1545 with Henry raising other grievances – English merchants in Spain being mistreated by the Inquisition, Spanish soldiers being used by the French – matched by Charles's protests that Henry was negotiating with the

Lutherans in Germany, and English vessels were illegally seizing ships and cargoes in the Channel.[8]

Francis now took the initiative. He understood that control of the Channel was vital to winning back Boulogne. In the spring his fleet, commanded by Admiral Claude d'Annebault, gathered in the Seine estuary, with ships arriving from around the French coast, including twenty-five galleys from the Mediterranean. Their plan was to attack and destroy the naval base at Portsmouth and capture an English port that could then be exchanged for Boulogne. To make matters worse for Henry, Scotland had not been subdued. An English force was defeated at Ancram Moor in February 1545 and three months later, 2,000 French troops arrived to help the Scots against further English border raids and to encourage an invasion of northern England. There was also the fear that the meeting of a general council of the Church agreed by Charles and Francis, planned for 1545, might bring the European powers together for the crusade against England called for by Pope Paul.

Henry, though, was determined to fight on. The English navy under the Lord Admiral, (John Dudley, Lord Lisle) captured many French trading vessels in the Channel, but its attempt to disrupt the preparation of the French fleet failed. Henry travelled to Portsmouth to command a rapidly mustered army prepared to meet French troops if they were able to land. D'Annebault's fleet crossed the Channel, entered the Solent, left 5,000 soldiers on the Isle of Wight and approached Portsmouth. Although the French had more vessels than the English, many of them were not warships but troop carriers with nearly 30,000 soldiers aboard.[9] The English fleet in harbour was composed almost entirely of warships, though some were small. All seemed set for a major sea battle but wind, or the lack of it, and a reluctance to risk all, meant that it never took place.

The most famous incident in the skirmishing was the sinking of the *Mary Rose*, witnessed by Henry on 19 July. Although first built in 1510, she had been reconstructed in 1536 and, by 1545, was heavily armed with cannons and culverins. These developments had reduced her seaworthiness, though it was still regarded as one of the great ships of the navy, along with the even larger *Henry, Grace à Dieu*, sometimes known as the *Great Harry*. The French galleys were advancing to fire upon the English fleet becalmed in Portsmouth harbour when the wind picked up and enabled the English to leave harbour and engage the French. Leading the way was the *Mary Rose*. It fired a broadside at a galley and while turning sharply to fire from the other side, a strong gust of wind caused her to list to starboard. Water poured into the still open gun-ports and within minutes the ship had sunk.[10] The netting that had been spread across the deck to make boarding by the enemy more difficult prevented most of the crew of 500 escaping and the majority drowned.

Avoiding a decisive battle, the French collected their troops from the Isle of Wight on 23 July and withdrew. They then raided coastal settlements in Sussex but when approached by the Lord Admiral, they returned to Normandy after landing several thousand soldiers near Boulogne to strengthen the besieging French army. Their departure had been precipitated by an outbreak of the plague amongst the soldiers on the crowded vessels, which then spread rapidly through the forces besieging Boulogne. The city remained in English hands. Meanwhile French hopes for an invasion of England from Scotland had come to nothing and it seemed unlikely that Charles would join in any attempt to restore the Catholic faith in England by use of force. Henry had come through another crisis but as Stephen Gardiner was to write: 'We are at war with France and Scotland, we have enmity with the Bishop of Rome; we have no assured friendship with the Emperor.'[11]

There followed a series of diplomatic manoeuvres by three monarchs who, after decades of experience, were fully aware that they could never take offers of friendship or promises of concessions at face value. Each wished to be in a position to take advantage of another's weakness and not to be caught out by any sudden change of allegiance. Henry's main concern was to retain Boulogne and he wished to prevent an alliance between Charles and Francis that would strengthen the French king's hand. He wanted Charles to return to their alliance and sent Stephen Gardiner to persuade the emperor. Offers of marriages between Henry's children and Habsburg princes and princesses achieved nothing. Henry proposed that they should meet again, perhaps in Calais, but Charles's response was that Henry should first agree a truce with Francis. Charles's priority now was to defeat the Lutheran princes in Germany and to do that, he needed peace with France. Henry again held talks with representatives of the Schmalkaldic League who, like Charles, offered to mediate between England and France, but these failed. They recognised that Henry was far more concerned about retaining his gains in France than in helping them against Charles. Henry could see little to be gained from antagonising the emperor by openly supporting the Lutherans, who, in turn, had no wish to lose the possibility of assistance from France if, or as was looking more likely when, Charles turned his armies against them.

Despite the concerns of his council, many of whom advocated handing back Boulogne in return for concessions from Francis, Henry at first planned to take the offensive in 1546. He relieved the Earl of Surrey of his command in Boulogne, sending in his place Edward Seymour, the Earl of Hertford, after his successes in Scotland. However, Henry was now without allies. The cost of capturing Boulogne, strengthening its defences and paying for its garrison had by now reached £1 million and almost bankrupted him.[12] He had resorted to high taxes, forced loans, an increased pace in the sale of monastic lands and even debasement of the coinage. The economic damage was made worse by food shortages across England after the poor harvest of 1545. Paying for and supplying a large army of invasion would be very difficult.

In April 1546 Henry opted for peace talks and sent instructions to Lord Lisle and William Paget 'to treat and conclude upon a peace with certain commissioners sent by the French king.'[13] Francis, too, was ready to negotiate, having also reached the limits of what he could spend. The Treaty of Ardres (also known as the Treaty of Camp) was agreed in May and signed during the summer. England would keep Boulogne for eight years after which it would be returned to France for the payment of 2 million crowns (Henry initially wanted 3 million) and France would pay the pensions that were owed to England. Henry promised not to attack Scotland again unless provoked. It was signed because neither side could afford to keep fighting but relations had not been repaired. No more pensions were ever paid, the English destroyed French fortifications near Boulogne, the French still sent help to the Scots and since minor raids on the English-Scottish border were endemic, Henry's promise meant little.[14] He might have retained Boulogne for a few years but in international terms, Henry was not the major figure that he once had been. By the end of 1546 England was at peace with France and Scotland, though relations with both were fragile and war soon broke out again. By then, though, Henry was dead.

Chapter Seventeen

The End of an Era

After over thirty-seven years on the throne and now aged 55, Henry's health had been deteriorating for a number of years. He had always been quick to move away from any outbreak of plague or sweating sickness and he had avoided catching tuberculosis which had killed his father, his son Henry FitzRoy, and, later, his heir, Edward. But he did catch other common diseases of the time. In 1514 he had smallpox and after 1521, experienced several attacks of what was referred to as ague fever, probably malaria. From the late 1520s he suffered from varicose ulcers on his legs caused by injuries sustained while hunting and jousting. These were seriously aggravated by his fall in 1536. On a number of occasions blood clots spread to his lungs, as in May 1538 and again in March 1541 when it was so serious that he was unable to speak and there were fears for his life. After another such episode in March 1544, he was in almost constant pain until the end of his life.

Henry's injuries made him increasingly sedentary so his tendency to over-eat and drink meant that the athletic young man he had once been became grossly overweight. His diet consisted of large quantities of meat, often up to a dozen helpings twice a day, fine white bread, red wine and ale, with very little fruit or vegetables.[1] One only has to look at the armour made for him in 1544 and compare it with that of 1527 to appreciate the problem. In his last years, specially constructed mobile chairs enabled him to negotiate the corridors of Whitehall Palace and complex lifting contraptions were designed to move him between floors as he could not manage the stairs. The strain on his heart must have been considerable, his diet frequently caused painful constipation and it is likely that he experienced the debilitating effects of type-2 diabetes (Plate 19).

Although he was always prone to rapid mood swings, perhaps made worse by his head injury in 1536 and the frequent pain he suffered, he nevertheless still had the mental capacity and desire to make decisions. What worried him most as he approached death was the very issue that had concerned him so much over the previous twenty-five years – the succession. His son Edward (Plate 20) was still only 9 years old and it was likely that there would be a considerable period before he could take full responsibility for ruling the country. Although Henry did not expect to die quite yet, he knew that the accession of a minor was potentially a difficult time for any dynasty.

In the last few months of Henry's reign, several men who might have expected to be dominant forces in Edward's regency council were removed and others came to the fore. The Duke of Suffolk, who along with Norfolk had commanded Henry's armies for decades, had died in 1545. The wars against France and Scotland had given an opportunity for new men to win the confidence of the king and the people of England. Edward Seymour, Earl of Hertford, the brother of Jane Seymour and uncle of Prince Edward, and John Dudley, Lord Lisle, proved themselves to be capable military leaders. They had shown their complete loyalty to Henry and as reformists in religion had never questioned the king's supremacy in the Church. With the support of William Paget, the king's secretary, they had become the leading figures in the Royal Council by the autumn of 1546. Eustace Chapuys wrote to Mary of Hungary in January 1547 explaining that 'the King's death would be more inopportune for us now than twenty years ago and the Earl and the Admiral [Hertford and Lisle] are the only nobles of age and ability to undertake affairs'. He condemned them as 'stirrers of heresy' who had infected the queen with their beliefs and who would 'drag the whole country into this damnable error.'[2]

On the other hand, Reginald Gardiner, Bishop of Winchester, was specifically excluded by the king from the list of sixteen councillors named in his will to take the reins of government in the event of his death. A classical scholar, respected lawyer and religious conservative, Gardiner worked first for Cardinal Wolsey and then, from about 1527, for the king. He was a long-time council member and leader of many important overseas missions, but by late 1546 Henry had clearly lost confidence in him, referring to him as a wilful man who should not be around his son. This is sometimes taken as a sign that Henry was moving towards further religious reforms in his last months, influenced by Katherine Parr, Hertford and Lisle. But it is more likely that his fear was that others might not be able to control the able, strong-willed Gardiner, who might then use his influence to challenge the royal supremacy that Henry was determined should be passed on to his son.

The other main losers were the Howards. In December the Duke of Norfolk and his son Henry Howard, Earl of Surrey were arrested. Both had made many enemies and Norfolk's position had been weakened by the failure of Henry's marriage to his niece Catherine Howard. Norfolk had served Henry for almost forty years, as soldier, leading council member, and occasional diplomat, willing to carry out much of his king's 'dirty work'. But he, too, had always been regarded as a religious conservative and it is possible that Henry believed that he might also be opposed to the royal supremacy. Surrey, known as a poet but also as a young man with a fiery temper, was brought down by his arrogance and ambition. He had boasted of his Plantagenet ancestry, through both his father and his mother Elizabeth, the daughter of the Duke of Buckingham, executed in 1521. He was reported to have said that his father should 'rule the prince' on Henry's death (never a good topic of conversation). Rumours, probably originating from Hertford and Paget, were put about that father and son were together planning to dispose of the Royal Council, take control of Prince Edward and thus rule the country. Surrey had foolishly included the heraldic arms of Edward the Confessor in his own, the crime for which he was charged with treason. Found guilty, he was sentenced to be 'led through the city of London to the gallows at Tiborne [Tyburn], hanged, [and] disembowelled' but the king commuted the sentence to beheading at Tower Hill on 19 January. Norfolk confessed to having 'concealed high treason in keeping secret the false acts of my son in using the arms of St. Edward the Confessor, which pertain only to kings of this realm.'[3] He was condemned by statute without a trial and royal assent was given, by proxy, for his execution. Due to go to the scaffold at 9.00 am on 28 January, he was saved only by Henry's own death a few hours earlier.

Henry had collapsed on 10 December 1546 though he was still able to discuss matters of state. His condition fluctuated over the following weeks. On 26 December he had talks with his close councillors about his will and, on 30 December, he handed his final will to Hertford. It has been a matter of some dispute whether this will was genuine, but in all likelihood it was. After another relapse he was well enough on 16 January to receive both the French and Imperial ambassadors at Whitehall Palace. During the evening of 27 January, Sir Anthony Denny, Groom of the Stool and one of Henry's closest courtiers, had the courage to do what the doctors feared to do – tell the king that he was nearing death. Henry requested that Thomas Cranmer be sent for but by the time the archbishop arrived, Henry could no longer speak. Unable to hear his confession, Cranmer asked him to give a sign that he put his trust in God. Cranmer reported that the king squeezed his hand. Henry died soon afterwards in the early hours of 28 January.

Just like his father's, Henry's death was kept secret for three days. Hertford was able to gain the support of the councillors to be named as Lord

Protector but could not win over the majority to go ahead with the execution of Norfolk, who though spared was to remain in the Tower of London for the next six years. There was no challenge to Edward's accession, either internally or from the emperor. Chapuys suggested to Charles that the best way to inconvenience England's rulers would be to impose a trade embargo.[4] Henry VIII had achieved his aim of a continuation of the dynasty and the royal supremacy in the Church. Many of the councillors received new titles supposedly based on Henry's last wishes, with Hertford becoming the Duke of Somerset and John Dudley, Lord Lisle, being created the Earl of Warwick.

Henry was embalmed, encased in lead and laid in state at Whitehall Palace until moved to Windsor Castle. The grand tomb that he had commissioned back in the late 1520s, making use of the sarcophagus that had originally been constructed for Cardinal Wolsey, had never been completed. His will instructed that his coffin should be placed temporarily in the vault containing the body of Jane Seymour in the quire of St George's Chapel at Windsor. Henry's tomb was never finished and his body remained with Jane's in the vault, joined in the seventeenth century by those of King Charles I and an infant of Queen Anne. The marble slab on the floor of the chapel that marks the vault was installed in 1837.

Charles heard the news from England while on campaign against the Lutherans. While Henry had been discussing peace with the French in April 1546, Charles was travelling to Regensburg where an Imperial Diet opened in June. The death of Martin Luther in February 1546 had done nothing to heal the religious divide. Charles assured a meeting of German princes that he wished for peace. However, in a letter to his son he revealed that he had deliberately misled them. In his memoirs he wrote about the offence that he had taken at the 'great arrogance and obstinacy' of the Protestants, especially Philip of Hesse who told Charles that he should study the scriptures. He was planning for war. In Regensburg Charles secured the support of the Duke of Bavaria by arranging the marriage of the duke's son to Anna, Ferdinand's daughter. He also worked hard to divide the Protestants by offering the Protestant Duke Maurice of Saxony the chance to replace his cousin, John Frederick, as elector. While in Regensburg, staying at the Golden Cross Inn in Haidplatz, he also had a brief affair with Barbara Blomberg which resulted in the birth of a son in February 1547, by chance on Charles's forty-seventh birthday.

Charles effectively declared war on the princes of the Schmalkaldic League in July when their leaders, John Frederick of Saxony and Philip of Hesse, were denounced as rebels and traitors. Charles claimed that the war was about their defiance of him as emperor, but most people recognised that a major factor was his wish to stop the spread of heresy. His opponents were not caught unawares. By then they had assembled a sizeable army and employed many of the German mercenary soldiers that had become available as a result of the peace between England and France. The conflict started in Bavaria. There followed months of military manoeuvres with only minor clashes, each side looking to gain the advantage. The nearest it got to a full-scale battle was at the end of August when Charles's camp near Ingolstadt was bombarded. Charles heeded the advice of the Duke of Alva who argued that the emperor had little to gain and much to lose from an ill-considered offensive. The leadership of the Schmalkaldic League was divided, running short of money, and facing growing desertions. They had hoped for support from either England or France but none was forthcoming.

At this point Maurice of Saxony invaded Elector John Frederick's lands further north, eventually resulting in the elector taking his troops out of Bavaria to defend his territory. This meant that the princes and towns of southern Germany had little option but to come to terms with Charles. He refused all negotiations and demanded abject surrender. As Charles recorded in his memoirs, he was in Ulm when 'The news of the death of the King of England reached His Majesty'[5], at about the same time as the inhabitants of Augsburg and Strasbourg admitted 'their error ... and tendered their obedience.'[6] This one line about Henry's death makes it appear to be a minor matter compared with the submission of the cities and Charles's gout. He reports that the recurrence of gout had started late in 1546 and when he arrived in Ulm 'he had not yet recovered his health. As happened in his previous attack, he had continued relapses; so that this may be considered his thirteenth attack of gout. At last he resolved to master it by strict adherence to treatment and diet.'[7]

In March 1547 Charles marched north with his army, joining his brother, Ferdinand, and Maurice of Saxony, to form a combined force of 50,000. John Frederick's smaller army was moving north along the river Elbe towards the safety of Wittenberg, which would be difficult for Charles to capture. The elector had believed that his army was safe on the east side of the river and set up camp at Mühlberg. However, on the morning of 24 April, the emperor's forces surprised him. Charles's scouts had found a nearby ford and many troops crossed the river unnoticed in the morning mist. After limited resistance John Frederick's soldiers fled and the duke was captured. Charles marched to Wittenberg where John Frederick's capitulation was signed. His life was spared in return for his ongoing captivity and the loss of his electorate to Duke Maurice, though he was permitted to retain some territory for his sons. Philip of Hesse also surrendered to Charles, believing that he would be treated leniently but he was imprisoned as well.

Meanwhile, in France, Henry's other rival of over thirty years, Francis, was reported to have been saddened by the news of the death of a 'good and true friend' but on the same day, he was seen to be laughing and enjoying himself with the ladies at a ball.[8] It was reported that Francis's mistress, the Duchess of Étampes, rushed into the queen's bedroom shouting that 'We have lost our chief enemy' and that Eleanor at first thought that she was talking about her brother Charles before later realising that it was Henry who had died.[9] However, Francis's pleasure at outliving Henry was brief. He was soon ill himself and by mid-March was preparing for death which came on 31 March, at the age of 52. It has often been believed that the cause was syphilis, for which he was certainly treated, but it is now thought to have been a serious infection of the urinary tract. Unlike the English king he was not succeeded by a minor, but by his second and only surviving son who became Henri II (Plate 11) on his twenty-eighth birthday. Eleanor was invited to remain in France but preferred to leave for Brussels where she could be in closer contact with her family, especially her younger sister, Mary of Hungary, regent of the Low Countries, and her older brother, Charles.

The emperor's comments on Francis's death were as brief as they had been for Henry's. While marching north into Saxony with his brother 'they received news of the death of the King of France'.[10] There is no sign of either regret or pleasure at the passing of the king, his brother-in-law, with whom he had been at war on many occasions. Perhaps this was because he was aware that Francis's successor, the prince who he had held captive for four years, was not going to change French foreign policy and would continue to seek ways of undermining the emperor's position. The new king was also known to have been unhappy with the peace that his father had signed with England in 1546.

Soon after his victory at Mühlberg Charles moved south to Augsburg where he stayed for almost a year in the house of Anton Fugger, now head of the banking family that had done much to assist Charles whenever he was struggling to raise the funds for his many campaigns. There he was painted by Tiziano Vecellio (Titian), who produced two of the best-known portraits of the emperor. The first shows him on horseback, in full armour holding a spear with a commander's red sash, after the Battle of Mühlberg (Plate 23). This is how he would have wished to be seen – the successful Christian warrior defending his religion. In reality he was beginning to age quite rapidly, with the years of travel and responsibility, and, of course, the pain of gout, taking its toll. A truer representation is the seated portrait which shows him as serious and thoughtful, full of determination and authority, though looking older than his years (see cover image of the emperor).

Charles regarded his victory at Mühlberg as one of the high points of his reign and it is easy to understand why. By mid-1547 he had defeated his religious enemies in Germany and his two rival monarchs had died. However, experience would have told him that his underlying problems – French animosity, religious disunity and the Ottoman threat – had not gone away. In his remaining years new issues arose and together these difficulties brought Charles to a point where he made a very unusual decision.

Chapter Eighteen

After Henry

In England the accession of Edward VI may have been peaceful but his reign became one of controversy over the powers of the Lord Protector as against those of the Council, about the extent to which radical reforms should be adopted by the Church of England, and to some extent over foreign policy. In this there was not a complete change from the policies of the last years of Henry VIII but a significant shift in emphasis. Scotland rather than France became the focus of Lord Protector Somerset's foreign policy. He wished to assert England's power by insisting on the marriage of his nephew, King Edward, to their queen, Mary Stuart, as agreed in the Treaty of Greenwich in 1543. He was keen to avoid or at least delay war with France. Although Emperor Charles V believed that Mary was Henry VIII's only legitimate child and therefore that she should have inherited the throne, Somerset was keen to maintain amicable relations with him. Charles could facilitate the employment of mercenaries from his lands, prevent the French from using ports in the Low Countries, and perhaps even deter a French declaration of war because he might take advantage of French involvement to cause problems elsewhere. This worked for a while and probably did delay a major French initiative, but Somerset was aware that his own wish to see further religious changes in England would make any real friendship unlikely.

Negotiations with the Scots failed to achieve the Lord Protector's aims and the French sent troops to Scotland to bolster the anti-English faction. Therefore, in September 1547, an English army of 18,000 invaded and inflicted a major defeat on the Scots at the Battle of Pinkie. Somerset recognised that such victories in Henry's reign had not achieved obedience so he established a series of garrisons, mainly on the east coast and along the border. They were intended to intimidate the Scots into compliance while reassuring those who supported a pro-English policy. But the majority of Scots still did not agree to his demands.

In June 1548 Henri II, not wishing to see the English dominate France's old ally, sent a larger force of 6,000[1] well-trained soldiers supplied with artillery to use against the garrisons. This shifted the balance of power in Scotland. Encouraged by Mary of Guise, the queen's mother, it was agreed by the Scottish Parliament in the Treaty of Haddington that Mary Stuart would travel to France to be educated there and, in time, marry King Henri's young son and heir, Francis. Somerset's garrison policy was proving to be expensive and unsuccessful, especially when additional troops had to be sent north, and even then, some garrisons were abandoned.

These setbacks came at a time when there was widespread discontent in much of rural England. During the summer of 1549, revolts broke out across the southern counties and soon spread to East Anglia, the Midlands and Yorkshire. They were often against enclosure of the common land, but also involved other social, religious and financial grievances. Somerset's initial response to placate the protestors failed to halt them, but it lost him the support of the gentry and landowning classes. In the south-west, troops were needed to put down rebels who had gathered in Exeter protesting about the new Prayer Book. In the best-known uprising, Kett's Rebellion in Norfolk, over 15,000 protestors camped on Mousehold Heath[2] outside Norwich, the largest city in the country after London, before taking the city at the end of July. After a small royal force was repelled, an army of 14,000 under the Earl of Warwick was sent and the rebels were defeated with considerable loss of life in late August. Tudor rule of England had rarely been so threatened.

Henri II sought to take advantage of England's internal problems. France formally declared war in August 1549 and immediately besieged Boulogne. Charles V gave no sign that he would provide direct assistance to the English, though he did permit recruitment in the Low Countries. The Lord Protector needed to withdraw troops from Scotland to help with its defence. But the campaign had started late in the year and heavy rains in September brought it to an end, though it was certain to be renewed the following year. Somerset's policies had failed badly. The marriage of Edward VI to Mary Stuart had been prevented, France had declared war and Boulogne was at risk. The cost of these campaigns – paid for by further debasement of the coinage, the sale of more former church properties and borrowing – further damaged an already difficult economic situation.

Given all these problems it is hardly surprising that the Council turned against Somerset. In October 1549 he was charged with entering 'rash wars', enriching himself from the 'king's treasure' and 'doing all by his own authority'. He was removed from office.[3] The coup was organised by the Earl of Warwick, soon to become the Duke of Northumberland, and as Lord President of the Council, he remained the leading figure in the government until the end of Edward's reign. He recognised that England needed peace[4] and rapidly instigated talks with the French. These centred on how much

Henri II was willing to pay for Boulogne and, as usual, the issue of French pensions. The Treaty of Boulogne, signed in March 1550, ended the war. Boulogne was returned to France for 400,000 crowns, considerably less than the 2 million crowns that had been agreed between Henry VIII and Francis I four years earlier. The pensions question was dealt with by a face-saving clause and although no pension was ever paid, England did not abandon the right to it. The treaty also effectively halted the war between England and Scotland, though this was formally ended the following year. All the garrisons were abandoned and English troops removed from north of the border. The Treaty of Boulogne is often regarded as humiliating for England. However, Northumberland had little real choice and at least Henri paid more for Boulogne than he had first offered, the English were able to remove much of the equipment that they had put into the city since its capture, and they retained dominance in the Channel. Most importantly it brought peace that was welcomed by most ordinary people and also opened the way for negotiations about the marriage of King Edward to Henri's daughter, Elizabeth, born in 1545.

The end of the war between England and France was bad news for Charles V. He had not been actively involved but the return of Boulogne meant that Henri II could now direct his attention against the figure that he considered his main enemy – Charles. The emperor had been angered by attempts in England to prevent Princess Mary celebrating Mass but was in no position to declare war. By the early 1550s he was beset by problems. His victory at Mühlberg had done little to end the religious schism in Germany. This became obvious at the Imperial Diet held at Augsburg in 1548. The Protestants held to their beliefs and there was no backing for a compromise from the papacy. The final statement, the Augsburg Interim, won little support. Catholic princes refused to accept the compromises that had been made and many Protestants rejected them as not going far enough.

Charles's other main issue concerned who would rule his territories after him. Henry VIII was not the only monarch to have succession problems, though Charles's were of a different nature. His son Philip had always been his heir in Spain (and thus Spanish lands in southern Italy and the New World) and Charles's brother Ferdinand, as elected King of the Romans, would be the next Holy Roman Emperor. Charles had long thought of the Low Countries as a possible means of establishing a more permanent peace with France. During the 1540s he had also given serious consideration to the marriage of his eldest daughter, Maria, to his brother's eldest son, Maximilian, with them inheriting the Low Countries. The issue was of importance to England, given that a hostile regime in the Low Countries could be very damaging to English trade and the ports there could be used to launch an invasion. It was also of significance to Charles – it was his homeland. By 1548 he had decided that the Low Countries should remain linked to Spain; in other words, Philip would inherit the provinces. He instructed Philip to travel from Spain to be introduced as his heir. By means of the 'Pragmatic Sanction', the laws of inheritance in all seventeen provinces were arranged so that they would remain under one ruler, the 'Lord of the Netherlands'.

Charles's nephew Maximilian was less than pleased, though he travelled to Spain, married Maria and they acted as Philip's co-regents in his absence. Habsburg family dissension was unusual at the time as Charles had been loyally and capably served by his relatives. But when Charles also questioned who would become Holy Roman Emperor after Ferdinand, there were considerable problems. It had always been assumed that Maximilian would be elected after his father but now Charles was suggesting that it should be Philip. Between 1549 and 1551, family discussions, sometimes acrimonious, were held in Augsburg and Brussels. It was argued that Ferdinand had worked with the German rulers for decades and Maximilian had been brought up in Austria, whereas Philip had no such experience and would not be welcomed as emperor, even if he was elected.

Mary of Hungary acted as peacemaker and a compromise was eventually reached in 1551. Philip would succeed Ferdinand and Maximilian would follow him. Ferdinand signed up to this but did nothing to make it happen, while Maximilian, who being the same age as Philip was likely to lose out, would not do so, remarking: 'God grant that His Majesty [Ferdinand] will one day stand up to His Imperial Highness [Charles] and not always show himself so chicken-hearted as he has hitherto'. The plan was never implemented, but Philip did inherit the Low Countries. This was to have a major significance for England almost forty years later when English support for Dutch rebels, together with continued attacks on Spanish bullion vessels by English privateers, resulted in Philip's decision to send the Armada, intending to use troops based in the Low Countries to invade England.

These Habsburg family concerns meant that Charles paid too little attention to the situation in Germany, despite warnings from Ferdinand. Charles believed that the German princes were too divided to be much of a threat. But many of them still strongly objected to what they regarded as the injustice of the continued imprisonment of Philip of Hesse. Charles's intransigence over this issue resulted in Philip's son-in-law, Duke Maurice of Saxony, recently made an elector, switching sides. In 1551 the Protestant princes held talks with Henri II who now felt free to move against Charles, having regained Boulogne from England. They agreed terms in October 1551 which were confirmed by the Treaty of Chambord in January 1552. King Henri promised financial assistance in return for their acceptance of his plan to take control of the cities of Metz, Toul and Verdun in Lorraine. This would expand French territory and make Charles's route from southern Germany to the Low Countries hazardous.

The Protestant army, now commanded by Maurice, moved south taking cities in Bavaria, including Augsburg. An unprepared Charles, unable to move north, retreated to Innsbruck. Talks about a truce, in which he was represented by Ferdinand, initially failed. Charles complained that few of his subjects in Germany were prepared to help him. Maurice's army advanced along the Lech valley and entered Innsbruck on 23 May shortly after Charles had made a last-minute escape over the Brenner Pass and then east to Villach. Could Maurice have captured the emperor? Probably, but he was aware of the significance of such an act saying that he had 'no cage big enough to hold so large a bird'.

Charles now called upon the extensive, though scattered, resources available to him. He sent out requests for funds to all his lands and Anton Fugger provided another vast loan. The German princes knew that, in time, Charles would be able to muster superior forces so in August 1552 a truce was signed. Philip of Hesse and John Frederick of Saxony were released; Maurice's troops would help Ferdinand against the Ottoman Turks (though only half of them did so); and religious toleration would be extended until a final settlement could be made. Neither side was really happy with the truce but it did pave the way for a more permanent religious settlement signed by Ferdinand at the Imperial Diet held in Augsburg in 1555.

Charles agreed to the truce because he recognised that his true enemy, one that could threaten his patrimony, was the French king, who was stirring up trouble for Charles in Italy, encouraging Ottoman attacks in Hungary and threatening military action against Flanders. The emperor now had time to move his troops from Italy and the Low Countries to where they were needed. His target was Metz, taken by the French in April 1552. They had improved its defences by building new walls and destroying suburbs that could provide cover for besieging troops. From Austria Charles marched north through Germany to Strasbourg where he reluctantly came to terms with the Protestant Margrave Albert Alcibiades of Brandenburg-Kulmbach, who joined him with 15,000 troops. By mid-November his army of 60,000 had besieged Metz, despite warnings from Mary of Hungary that it was too late in the year. Charles knew that he would never be able to afford to assemble such a large army again in the near future and wrote that 'if we fail now it will be very serious indeed.'

The French had ruthlessly expelled many non-combatants from the city so that food supplies and lodgings could be reserved for their soldiers. The strengthened defences withstood the emperor's artillery and attempts to undermine the walls. The winter cold, snow, lack of proper shelter and dwindling supplies sapped the morale of Charles's army. It is reported that the emperor over-ate, drank large quantities of beer and became downcast. He ended the siege in January 1553 and travelled to Brussels. His health had deteriorated and there is much evidence to suggest that during 1553, he suffered a physical and psychological collapse.

He had long suffered from gout and haemorrhoids. At times depression had made him lethargic and unable to concentrate, but this was more serious. Usually conscientious, he was now unable to attend to his work for weeks at a time and refused to meet his advisers. He wished to be alone, spent much time adjusting his clocks and at times broke into tears. He had lost his confidence, blamed himself for recent setbacks and experienced guilt over the concessions that he had made to the German princes, even preparing a statement renouncing them although he was persuaded not to issue it. He relied on his secretary and his sister Mary, who carried out essential government functions and prevented knowledge of his true condition from becoming widely known. It was during this troubled time that an idea he had considered for some time became a definite plan – retirement to a simpler life, free of the endless troubles of ruling his widespread territories.

But Charles was still to make one more decision that impacted upon England. Once Northumberland had made peace with France in 1550, Charles had become increasingly hostile to the more strongly evangelical nature of the Church of England. However, in July 1553, Edward VI died of a lung disease – tuberculosis or acute bronchopneumonia. Once the severity of his illness became known during the spring, there had been much speculation about the succession. According to Henry VIII's will, if Edward died without an heir he was to be succeeded by Mary. It was not only the French who were concerned about that. King Edward wanted to prevent it as Mary would return the country to the Roman Catholic Church, and the Duke of Northumberland realised that he would be immediately removed from power. Edward produced 'My devise for the succession' in which he clearly indicated that he wished Lady Jane Grey, the granddaughter of Henry VIII's younger sister Mary and her husband Charles Brandon, Duke of Suffolk, to succeed him.[5] In May 1553 the marriage of an unwilling Lady Jane Grey to Northumberland's son Guildford Dudley was rapidly arranged.

On Edward's death Northumberland attempted to implement the king's plan, but he was unprepared for any resistance from Mary. As soon as Mary gathered support at Framlingham, Northumberland's small force, which had advanced as far as Cambridge, melted away and the Council abandoned him. The dismayed French ambassador wrote of this 'most sudden change'[6] as Mary entered London to popular acclaim. Northumberland was placed in the Tower and executed on 22 August, having declared in an attempt to escape his fate that all England's recent problems were because 'we have erred from the faith these sixteen years'. The statement was widely distributed in England and across Europe, especially in the lands of Charles V.

Mary, England's first queen regnant, intended to marry in order to establish a Catholic succession and, as she was now 37 years old, she needed to do so soon. But who should she marry and what powers would her husband have? She does not seem to have seriously considered any English nobleman, indeed there was only one possible candidate with Catholic connections, Edward Courtenay. The 26-year-old son of the executed Marquess of Exeter, he had spent the previous fifteen years in the Tower before his release by Mary, who had remained close to his mother. Courtenay was restored to his titles and lands but Mary showed no inclination to marry him, despite his backing by the new Lord Chancellor, Stephen Gardiner, Bishop of Winchester, who had also been released from the Tower and officiated at Mary's coronation on 1 October.

Mary decided that she would ask for advice in the matter of her marriage from her cousin, Emperor Charles. He had provided at least some moral support for her (even if he took no action that might damage his own interests) during the difficult times when she had been declared illegitimate. Charles ignored one likely candidate, Luis, the brother of the king of Portugal, in favour of his own son, Philip, who had been widowed in 1545 at the age of 18 when his Portuguese wife, Maria Manuela, died after giving birth to their son Carlos. Philip was a devout Catholic and would help Queen Mary return England to the 'true church'. Charles believed that the marriage would help Philip's future role as ruler of Spain and the Low Countries by protecting the Atlantic route between them and also securing trade across the North Sea. Philip recognised the benefits of the Anglo-Spanish-Burgundian alliance that had existed under Henry VII and the early days of Henry VIII. Mary of Hungary took the lead, instructing Simon Renard, Charles's ambassador to England, to negotiate the terms of the marriage alliance. Although the majority of her Council were opposed, Mary was keen for this match and the betrothal took place on 30 October.

The marriage treaty, agreed by the end of 1553 and ratified by Parliament in April 1554, severely restricted Philip's powers. He could not take executive decisions without Mary's agreement, take her out of the country or involve England in his wars against France. Their heirs would rule a future state covering England and the Low Countries, but if Mary died childless, her sister Elizabeth would succeed her and Philip would cease to be king. Nevertheless, there was considerable unease in the country about the 'Spanish match'. Supporters of Somerset and Northumberland who had lost their positions on Mary's accession, along with others who feared a return to Catholicism, sought to take advantage of this situation. In early 1554 Thomas Wyatt led an uprising in Kent and marched on London but he failed to gain entry and was defeated. Princess Elizabeth was suspected of involvement because of the attentions paid to her by the disgruntled Edward Courtenay. Both were taken to the Tower. Elizabeth was released after two months and Courtenay, after a year in the Tower, was exiled and died in Italy in 1556.

Philip appointed his younger sister, Juana, as his regent in Spain, against the wishes of their father, Charles, and used funds from a New World bullion shipment to arrive in England in grand style. On 25 July the couple were married by Bishop Gardiner in Winchester Cathedral. (Plates 24 and 25) Philip wanted a successful political outcome and made efforts to be accepted in England. Mary was given precedence at ceremonies and Philip even dined in public and drank beer, both of which he disliked. Charles expressed his surprise when he heard of this, commenting that his son must have changed a lot since he last met him! Philip took part in tournaments and other 'courtly' activities in an attempt to win over the nobility, but failed to learn the language. He could not prevent continued hostility to him, his courtiers and advisers. Many of them soon left what they regarded as an expensive, uncomfortable and xenophobic country.

In November it was announced that Mary was pregnant and although Philip wished to leave England for the Low Countries, Charles persuaded him to stay at least until Mary gave birth. Philip was to become regent if she died in childbirth. She went into confinement in early April but there was to be no child. The phantom pregnancy was a blow from which the marriage never recovered. Philip left for Brussels soon afterwards. Mary wished him to return but he made it a condition that he was given a full-scale coronation. Mary used the opposition of Parliament as a reason to refuse him. He only came to England once more, in March 1557, when he wished England to join the war against France which had restarted the previous year after a truce that had lasted barely eight months. Mary backed him but most of the

Council did not. It was only a French-financed raid on Scarborough in April led by Thomas Stafford,[7] who had fled to France after the defeat of Wyatt's rebellion, which enabled Philip to prevail.

The war was a disaster for Mary's reputation. After taking part in the Spanish-Imperial victory at St Quentin in August, the English force of about 7,000 returned home. Calais was unprepared for the winter offensive ordered by Henri II. The city fell on 7 January 1558, followed by Guînes two weeks later. Centuries of English control had ended. However much a humiliation it seemed at the time, the loss saved the considerable cost of maintaining Calais and removed an ongoing source of friction with France. It also signalled the start of a long-term shift in England's focus, from Europe to the Atlantic and wider trade links.[8] Mary's death in November 1558 meant that Philip was no longer king of England. He supported Elizabeth's accession, perhaps having thoughts of marrying her, though that was not to be. Peace talks had commenced even before Mary's death – both Philip and Henri had run out of money – and the Peace of Cateau-Cambrésis was signed in April 1559. It consisted of two treaties, one between Henri II and Queen Elizabeth of England and a second between Henri II and Philip II of Spain.

Charles did not live to see the end of the conflict with France that he had been involved in for almost his whole reign. He had made good on his decision to abdicate his thrones and leave the international stage. In 1554 he announced that he was not going to attend the Imperial Diet to be held in Augsburg the next year. He was to be represented by his brother Ferdinand, who became de facto Holy Roman Emperor, though this was not formally ratified by the Diet until 1558. It was Ferdinand who signed the Religious Peace of Augsburg in September 1555 allowing German princes to choose between Catholicism and Lutheranism in their lands – 'cuius regio, eius religio' (whose realm, their religion) – an agreement to which Charles's conscience could never be fully reconciled.

On 22 October 1555 Charles resigned as Grand Master of the Order of the Golden Fleece. Three days later in the Great Hall of the Coudenburg Palace, where his coming-of-age ceremony had been held forty years earlier, he abdicated as ruler of the provinces of the Low Countries in favour of Philip. He declared that he had often erred, out of youth, out of self-will and out of weakness, but that he had never wilfully wronged any man, and asked for forgiveness if he had done so unwittingly. Mary of Hungary, his regent in the Low Countries for twenty-five years, also announced her decision to travel to Spain with Charles and their sister Eleanor. In January 1556 he abdicated his Spanish thrones and Philip was declared king, something that had been made easier by the death of Charles's mother Juana in April 1555 after over thirty-five years of confinement in the convent at Tordesillas.

It was rare for a monarch to willingly give up power in this way and to accept the division of his territories, albeit between his son and his brother. Charles had prepared for this by having a set of modest rooms built onto the side of the church of the monastery of Yuste (Plate 26), founded in 1402 by the Order of St Jerome (Hieronymite) in the la Vera valley in Extremadura. His departure from the Low Countries was delayed until September 1556. He landed in Laredo and travelled through Burgos and Valladolid, where he was greeted by his daughter, Juana, and the Spanish court. He met his grandson, Philip's son Carlos, for the first time, and was not impressed, saying: 'His manner and humour please me very little, and I do not know what he will be capable of in the future'. As so often, his judge of character was to prove accurate. Continuing his journey, Charles crossed the pass of Tornavacas over the Sierra de Gredos, carried in a chair where it was too rough and narrow for his horse-drawn litter, and arrived at Jarandilla de la Vera in November. Here he stayed in the palace of the Duke of Oropesa until the following February when his accommodation in the monastery was ready.[9]

His last nineteen months were spent mainly in the four rooms on the first floor, outside on the shaded terrace and in the garden. He was still informed about Spanish and international affairs and was sometimes asked for advice. Though ready to voice his opinions, he no longer had the responsibility to act upon them. More important to him now was his spiritual welfare. His daily routine consisted of breakfast, prayers, time spent with his books and clocks, Mass in church, dinner with readings from a religious text, followed by a siesta. In the afternoons he sometimes entertained guests and discussed philosophical and theological points. He enjoyed his favourite foods as much as ever. Of his fifty staff, directed by Don Luis Mendez de Quijada, twenty were cooks. De Quijada commented that kings must think that their stomachs are not like those of other men. His day finished with a light supper and more prayers.

Charles's sisters came to stay in Jarandilla in September 1557. Eleanor wished to meet Maria, her daughter from her marriage to King Manuel of Portugal, who she had not seen for over twenty-five years. Maria was reluctant, having felt abandoned by her mother and then further offended by the family when her projected marriage to Philip had been dropped so that he could marry Queen Mary. The two did eventually meet in January 1558 but there was no real reconciliation. Eleanor died on the return journey in February. Charles refused to have his grandson Carlos live with him, but he did arrange for his son born in Regensburg in 1547 to live in nearby Cuacos de Yuste so that he could meet him. Known then as Jeromin, the boy had been brought to Spain in 1551. He obviously pleased Charles, who amended his will to provide for him and expressed a wish that he should meet Philip when he returned to Spain. This happened in 1559 and Philip always referred to the newly named Don John of Austria[10] as 'brother' and gave him a place in public ceremonies ahead of all grandees, but behind the royal family.

Early in August 1558 Charles developed persistent cold-like symptoms and by the end of the month was suffering from headaches, a great thirst and fever. Whether malaria or pneumonia, his doctors were unable to do anything to ease them. As he lay in his bedchamber he was able to look through an opening in the wall to the altar of the church, above which hung Titian's *La Gloria*[11]. This portrays Charles, with Isabella, Philip and other family members, dressed in shrouds, praying. Charles's crown is at his feet representing his withdrawal from earthly matters. On 20 September, while he was fully conscious, surrounded by monks, his confessor and the Archbishop of Toledo, the last rites of penance, extreme unction and Holy Communion were performed and he died at about 2.30 am the next morning, aged 58. He had asked his son to decide his last resting place. His body remained behind the altar at Yuste until 1574 when Philip had it moved to El Escorial, his new palace/monastery, together with Isabella's body from Granada. Charles's final journey was in 1654 when the sarcophagi containing his and Isabella's embalmed remains were placed in the newly completed King's Pantheon built beneath El Escorial where they can be visited to this day.

Epilogue

The ideals to which early sixteenth-century princes were encouraged to aspire were common throughout Europe. As might be expected for those destined to rule, though in Henry's case not until he was 10 years old, their education made use of what was considered to be the best of both old and new. It emphasised the values of medieval chivalry – courage, honour, courtesy, justice and helping the weak – as represented by the Order of the Garter and the Order of the Golden Fleece, and the more recent ideas of Renaissance humanism.[1] Initially based upon the study of the classical 'humanities', scholars such as John Colet (1467–1519) and Desiderius Erasmus (1466–1536) studied the original religious sources with the aim of purifying and renewing Christianity, and were influential in the education of both Henry and Charles.

The conflict between the peace and Christian unity expounded by these writers and the desire to win fame and glory on the battlefield is apparent in the actions of both Henry and Charles. They came to power in late adolescence and wished to gain honour and enhance their reputations through their actions, whether as victorious warriors or more subtly by acting as peacemakers in Christian Europe. Despite his pugnacious reputation and considerable ambition, Henry was only at war with England's traditional enemy, France, three times – in 1512–13, 1522–24 and 1542–46. He personally led expeditions to northern France twice – in 1513 and 1544. He declared war on Charles only once, in 1528, and even then, there was no direct military conflict. His wars achieved little at great cost. The capture of Tournai in 1513 and of Boulogne in 1544 provided him with much desired victories and strengthened his negotiating position, but they were the limits of his success. Both were sold back to the French within a few years.

Charles was at war more frequently, though not against England. His ongoing rivalry with Francis I and his son Henri II resulted in wars in each decade from the 1520s to the 1550s. He, too, wished to carry out 'great deeds' and from the early 1530s he played an active part in campaigns against the French in the Pyrenees, eastern France and the Low Countries, while against the Turks he led his forces in defence of Vienna, and attacked

Tunis and Algiers. He gained considerable kudos from his victories but also experienced setbacks which he put down to God's will. The cost of war rose rapidly during the sixteenth century. The size of armies increased and the new equipment that was needed for an effective army was expensive. Both Charles and Henry, as well as Francis I, frequently struggled to pay for their conflicts. Truces and peace settlements were more the result of financial necessity than any real agreement.

There is no doubt that when humanist principles came into conflict with the monarchs' personal and political interests, the latter won out. Nevertheless, both recognised the importance of being able to claim that they were fighting a just war, which included the defence of their honour and the security of Christendom. Both were devout men. Charles was proud of his forebears, the Holy Roman Emperors, the Catholic Monarchs in Spain, the Archdukes of Austria and the Dukes of Burgundy, 'defenders at all times of the Catholic faith', as he made clear in his response to Martin Luther in 1521. He held traditional beliefs and was never going to challenge the basic tenets of his faith. However, he was frequently on bad terms with the various Popes elected during his reign, bemoaning their focus on political manoeuvring and family gain rather than on preventing a permanent schism of the Church.

Henry was for many years a staunch defender of the Catholic Church and the papacy. Although his use of the Pope's conflict with France to justify his invasions of 1513 and 1523 was opportunistic, he was genuinely appalled by Luther's challenge to the papacy. His book attacking Luther gained him the title 'Defender of the Faith'. However, the failure of Pope Clement to grant him an annulment of his marriage to Catherine of Aragon resulted in him leading England away from the Roman Catholic Church and being declared a schismatic and a heretic. For a short time, he might have believed that Charles and other European leaders would take up the Pope's challenge to restore England to the 'true church', but he was well aware that Charles and Francis were unlikely to work together. The royal supremacy gave Henry the final say over doctrine in England and he seems to have enjoyed the role, coming to believe that as head of the English Church, he was God's representative on earth. He did support some doctrinal innovation but never accepted many of the ideas advocated by Lutherans and other reformers.

The two monarchs had different approaches to their work. Henry usually had little desire to be burdened with the minutiae of government. He generally disliked reading or writing policy documents. He promoted men of talent and frequently allowed his chief ministers, Wolsey and Cromwell, to take the lead in policy and to sort out the bureaucratic details. However, he never completely handed over power and there was no doubt that his ministers were working for him. Often well rewarded, they were removed without mercy once they had outlived their usefulness, as were those who the king suspected of disloyalty, even if there was no proof. When his personal interests were at stake – his marriages, religion and foreign policy – Henry became very involved in the direction and detail of policy. These affected his honour, reputation and standing amongst the rulers of Europe.

Charles was more diligent, but therefore more likely to get overwhelmed with the details of one aspect of policy at the expense of attention to others. He had several able ministers, such as Gattinara, Cobos and Granvelle, who served him for decades. When policies failed, he was more likely than Henry to recognise his own responsibility and not immediately cast around for a scapegoat. He could be ruthless towards his enemies and remembered those who gave offence, but ministers or commanders who disappointed him were usually retired or moved to where they could do no harm, not executed.

The very extent and scattered nature of his lands meant that Charles's life was one of travel. He was the most powerful man in Europe but the problems that he faced matched the scale of his territories. Henry's England, with its population of only 3 million, was really the leading second-tier European power after Charles's lands and France, but Henry and his ministers often, though not always, managed to negotiate on equal terms. Henry travelled frequently in southern England between his palaces and hunting lodges, many of them built for him. He left the country a handful of times during his reign and then only to northern France. Charles commissioned just one palace during his reign, in Granada, and he never had the chance to visit it. He not only travelled regularly within each of his widespread lands but also across the continent and beyond, from Valladolid to Vienna, from Algiers to Antwerp.

With France the regular enemy, England's natural ally had been Spain which counter-balanced the 'auld alliance' between France and Scotland. It was also in England's interests to be on good terms with the rulers of the Low Countries which, by the fifteenth century, were dominated by the Dukes of Burgundy. Even though Henry felt let down by Charles's predecessors, when Charles inherited both Spain and the Low Countries, and then became emperor, it was no surprise that Henry regarded him as a potential ally. Charles's rivalry with Francis I meant that for much of his reign he wished to keep England and France apart. Even when Henry divorced his aunt, disinherited his cousin, Mary, and took England out of the Roman Catholic Church, Charles made threatening noises but did not declare war.

Charles wished to defend the entirety of his inheritance so that he could pass it on undiminished, to protect Christian Europe against Ottoman incursions and to support the Catholic Church against heretics. But he recognised that it was impossible for him to tackle all these aims simultaneously. As he explained to his brother in 1542 'the urgency of some public affairs means that I must do what is possible, not what I want'.[2] He was constantly torn between his considerable long-term ambitions and the need to respond to the immediate crises caused, in his view, by his rivals and opponents. Henry's ambitions were more limited. Besides defending his country, he wished to gain territory in France. To do this he sought to take advantage of any opportunity as it arose, particularly when Charles and Francis were at war. In sixteenth-century Europe new friendships and alliances could be forged but they were often just as quickly discarded.

Henry and Charles both ruled for nearly forty years at a time when Europe was undergoing profound changes. They came of age in the early decades of the sixteenth century, influenced both by the new ideas of the Renaissance and by traditional notions of kingship. By the time they were 20 years old, despite relative inexperience, they wielded great power both within their lands and in the conduct of foreign policy, impacting upon the wellbeing of their subjects, making choices about war and peace, and determining matters of life and death. The momentous decisions that they made, whether about their dynasties, religion or international alliances, shaped English and European affairs not just in their lifetimes but for centuries afterwards. Both died before the age of 60, Henry while still controlling his kingdom and Charles in retirement, having abdicated his many titles.

They were always rivals in the quest for honour and reputation. But despite the frequent harsh words and disagreements over Henry's marriage and religious issues, they had been officially at war just once and then only for a few months. They had signed numerous alliances and fought France together in the early 1520s and again in the early 1540s. However, on both occasions, they had rapidly become disillusioned, each believing themselves let down by the other. Despite the festivities and mutual compliments that they enjoyed together when Charles spent over a month in England in 1522, they could never rely on each other for long and lacking real trust, they were indeed uneasy allies.

List of Principal Characters

Henry VIII and his immediate family

Henry VIII (1491–1547), second son of Henry VII and Elizabeth of York, and King of England from 1509.

Arthur (1486–1502), elder brother of Henry VIII and first husband of Catherine of Aragon. His death after just six months of marriage meant that Henry became heir to the throne.

Margaret (1489–1541), elder sister of Henry VIII who married James IV of Scotland, mother of King James V and grandmother of Mary Stuart, Queen of Scots.

Mary (1496–1533), younger sister of Henry VIII, who married King Louis XII of France in 1514 and then Charles Brandon, Duke of Suffolk.

Catherine of Aragon (1485–1536), youngest daughter of Ferdinand and Isabella of Spain, first wife of Henry VIII and Charles V's aunt (his mother's sister).

Mary (1516–1558), daughter of Henry VIII and Catherine of Aragon. Queen of England 1553–1558, who reversed many of the changes to the church made under Henry VIII and Edward VI. In 1554 she married Philip of Spain, Charles V's son.

Anne Boleyn (c.1501–1536), second wife of Henry VIII, the daughter of Thomas Boleyn, an English diplomat. Married in 1533, she was executed three years later.

Elizabeth I (1533–1603), daughter of Henry VIII and Anne Boleyn, Queen of England from 1558.

Jane Seymour (c.1508–1537), third wife of Henry VIII and mother of Henry's son, Edward.

Edward VI (1537–1553), son of Henry VIII and Jane Seymour. Succeeded Henry VIII as King of England in 1547. Many Protestant reforms were introduced during his reign.

Anne of Cleves (1515–1557), fourth wife of Henry VIII. Their marriage in January 1540 was annulled after just six months.

Catherine Howard (c.1524–1542), fifth wife of Henry VIII, the niece of Thomas Howard, Duke of Norfolk. Married in July 1540, she was executed nineteen months later.

Katherine Parr (1512–1548), sixth wife of Henry VIII. Married in July 1543, she outlived him.

Lady Jane Grey (1537–1554), the daughter of Henry Grey and Frances Brandon (the daughter of Charles Brandon and Henry VIII's sister Mary) who was named in Edward VI's will as his successor.

English noblemen and clerics

Charles Brandon (1484–1545), Henry's youthful companion, created Duke of Suffolk in 1514. Married Henry's sister, Mary, and commanded the English army in France in 1523.

Thomas Cranmer (1489–1556), Cambridge academic who helped to make the case for the annulment of Henry's marriage to Catherine of Aragon. Appointed Archbishop of Canterbury in 1532, he was burnt at the stake in 1556 during the reign of Queen Mary.

Thomas Cromwell (1485–1540). Of humble origins, he became Henry's chief minister from 1534 until his execution in 1540. He masterminded the break with Rome and supported further religious changes.

John Dudley (1504–1553), Lord Lisle, Earl of Warwick, Duke of Northumberland, son of Edmund Dudley (executed in 1510). A successful general and admiral, he became Lord President of the Council under Edward VI. Beheaded after his failed attempt to establish Lady Jane Grey as queen instead of Mary in 1553.

Stephen Gardiner (1483–1555), lawyer and diplomat, appointed Bishop of Winchester in 1531. A religious conservative, he was imprisoned during the reign of Edward VI but became Lord Chancellor under Queen Mary.

Thomas Howard, 3rd Duke of Norfolk (1473–1554), long-time military commander and adviser to Henry VIII, saved from execution by Henry's own death in January 1547.

Edward Seymour (1500–1552), Earl of Hertford, Duke of Somerset. Brother of Jane Seymour and uncle of Edward VI, he became Lord Protector during the minority of Edward VI until he was overthrown in 1549 and later executed.

Thomas Wolsey (1473–1530), Archbishop of York (from 1514) and Cardinal (from 1515), Henry's chief minister for fifteen years until his downfall after failing to secure an annulment of Henry's marriage to Catherine of Aragon from the Pope.

Charles V and his immediate family

Charles V (1500–1558), Duke of Burgundy, King of Spain and Holy Roman Emperor.

Ferdinand (1503–1564), Charles's brother, elected 'King of the Romans' in 1531, and succeeded Charles as Emperor.

Eleanor (1498–1558), Charles's older sister, Queen of Portugal by marriage to Manuel I, and Queen of France (1530–1547) by marriage to Francis I.

Isabella (1501–1526), Charles's sister, Queen of Denmark by her marriage to Christian II. Mother of Christina of Denmark.

Mary of Hungary (1505–1558), Charles's sister, Queen of Hungary by her marriage to Louis II, and Charles's regent in the Low Countries from 1531.

Catherine (1507–1578), Charles's youngest sister, Queen of Portugal by her marriage to John III in 1525.

Isabella of Portugal (1503–1539), wife of Charles from 1526, sister of John III, King of Portugal.

Philip II (1527–1598), only surviving son of Charles and Isabella, succeeded Charles as King of Spain and ruler of the Low Countries.

Maria (1528–1603), eldest daughter of Charles and Isabella, married Maximilian, son of Charles's brother, Ferdinand.

Juana (1535–1573), daughter of Charles and Isabella, mother of King Sebastian of Portugal, and regent in Spain (1554–1559).

Margaret of Austria (1480–1530) (sometimes known as Margaret of Savoy because of her marriage to Philibert II of Savoy), Charles's aunt (his father's sister), a major influence on his early life and later his regent in the Low Countries until her death.

Charles's ancestors

Burgundian/Habsburg

Mary of Burgundy (the Rich) (1457–1482), daughter of Duke Charles of Burgundy, married Maximilian I, mother of Philip the Handsome and Charles's grandmother.

Maximilian I (1459–1519) Holy Roman Emperor (1486–1519), father of Philip the Handsome of Burgundy and Margaret of Austria, Charles's grandfather.

Philip the Handsome (1478–1506), Charles's father, Duke of Burgundy and King of Castile (as Philip I) by his marriage to Juana.

Spanish

Isabella (1451–1504), Queen of Castile, wife of Ferdinand of Aragon and Charles's grandmother.

Ferdinand (1452–1516), King of Aragon, wife of Isabella and Charles's grandfather. Together, Ferdinand and Isabella were known as the 'Catholic Monarchs'.

Juana (1479–1555), Charles's mother, daughter of Isabella and Ferdinand, and heir to Castile after her mother's death. Spent over forty-five years in a convent at Tordesillas 'for her own safety'. Often referred to as Juana 'la loca' (Juana 'the mad').

Charles's advisers and commanders

William of Croy, Lord of Chievres (1458–1521), leading nobleman of the Low Countries, chief tutor and then adviser to Charles from 1509 until his death in 1521.

Charles de Lannoy (1487–1527), soldier and statesman, became a knight in the Order of the Golden Fleece in 1516, viceroy of Naples in 1522 and commander-in-chief of Charles's forces in Italy in 1523.

Mercurino di Gattinara (1465–1530), worked for Margaret of Austria in Savoy and then in the Low Countries. He became Charles's chancellor and chief adviser in the early 1520s.

Nicholas Perrenot de Granvelle (1486–1550), lawyer, Burgundian politician, one of Charles's chief advisers in the Holy Roman Empire after 1530.

Francisco de los Cobos (1477–1547), Spanish administrator, became secretary to Charles and then the leading figure in the government of Spain under Charles.

Philibert of Chalon, Prince of Orange (1502–1530), a general in Charles's army in Italy, involved in the 'Sack of Rome' and killed in the latter stages of the Siege of Florence in 1530.

Andrea Doria (1466–1560), major figure in sixteenth-century Genoa. He first served France but, dissatisfied with his treatment by Francis I, switched sides in 1528 to become Charles's admiral for over two decades.

France

Louis XII (1462–1515), King of France during Charles's youth. Married Henry's sister Mary in 1514, three months before his death.

Francis I (1494–1547), King of France from 1515. Charles and Henry's greatest rival on the European stage. Married Charles's sister Eleanor in 1530.

Louise of Savoy (1476–1531), Francis's mother and sister-in-law of Margaret of Austria.

Francis, Duke of Brittany (1518–1536), Francis I's eldest son, who predeceased his father.

Henri II (1519–1559), Francis I's second son and his successor; held as hostage in Spain, along with his older brother, by Charles V between 1526 and 1530. Married Catherine de Medici in 1533.

Charles, Duke of Orleans (1522–1545), Francis I's third son.

Charles, Duc de Bourbon (1490–1527), leading French nobleman, who became Charles's commander after a major dispute with Francis and Louise of Savoy. Died in the attack on Rome in May 1527.

Scotland

James IV (1473–1513), King of Scotland from 1488 and husband of Henry VIII's sister, Margaret. A patron of the arts and sciences, James was regarded as a successful ruler until his decision to invade England in 1513 and his death at the Battle of Flodden.

James V (1512–1542), King of Scotland from 1513 beginning his personal rule in 1528. Married Mary of Guise in 1538 after the death of his first wife, further increasing French influence in Scotland.

Mary Stuart, Queen of Scots (1542–1587). Born six days before her father's death, Mary was betrothed to Francis, eldest son of Henri II and sent to France in 1548, thus frustrating English plans for her to marry Edward VI. Later deposed as Queen of Scotland, she fled to England in 1568 where she was eventually executed.

Ottoman Empire

Suleiman (1494–1566), Ottoman sultan from 1520, known as 'the Magnificent' or 'the Lawgiver', whose advances into central Europe and in the Mediterranean caused Charles great concern.

Hayreddin Barbarossa (1478–1546), the commander of Suleiman's Mediterranean fleet.

Acknowledgements

I would like to thank all those who encouraged my love of history from an early age – my parents, my teachers and the authors whose books I enjoyed and learnt so much from. I have appreciated the resources available at Cambridge University Library and the many museums and galleries that I have visited in Britain and Europe, together with the assistance of the always helpful staff. Many thanks to Sarah-Beth Watkins for suggesting that I write this book, and to Stephen and Robert who read and commented upon parts of the original text. I am indebted to my editor, Michelle Higgs, and to the staff at Pen and Sword, especially Laura Hirst, Claire Hopkins and Lucy May, for all the guidance they have given me.

Most of all I am grateful to Deborah for giving her time so generously, sharing the visits that we have made and for her valuable comments on all aspects of this book.

Cambridge, March 2022

List of Plates

1. Kaiser Maximilian I. A seventeenth-century copy of a portrait by Bernhard Strigel (c.1507). Bayerische Staatsgemaldesammlungen – Alte Pinakothek, Munich. (CC-BY-SA)
2. Margaret of Austria at the age of about 10. Jean Hay (the Master of Moulins). Oil on oak panel. Metropolitan Museum of Art, N.Y. – Robert Lehman Collection. (OA – Public Domain)
3. The Palace of Placentia, usually known as Greenwich Palace, as it appeared in the reign of Henry VIII. *Cassell's Illustrated History of England*, Vol. 2 (1865).
4. The courtyard of Margaret of Austria's palace in Mechelen. Personal photograph.
5. Erasmus of Rotterdam. Frans Huys (1522–1562) after Hans Holbein. National Gallery of Art, Washington – Rosenwald Collection. (CC0)
6. Charles V (c.1520) – Netherlandish painter. Metropolitan Museum of Art, N.Y. – Friedsam Collection, bequest of Michael Friedsam, 1931. (OA – Public Domain)
7. A copy of the 'Whitehall Mural' by George Vertue (1684–1756) after Hans Holbein the Younger (1497–1543). National Gallery of Art, Washington – Gift of Hermann Wunderlich. (CC0)
8. The Tournament on Horseback. Albrecht Dürer c.1517/18. Metropolitan Museum of Art, N.Y. – Rogers Fund, 1921. (OA – Public Domain)
9. The plaque on the wall of the Palazzo Comunale, Bologna, commemorating the meeting of Charles V and Pope Clement VII in 1529–1530 and the emperor's coronation in the Basilica of San Petronius on 24 February 1530. Personal photograph.
10. Francis I. Titian. Bayerische Staatsgemaldesammlungen – Alte Pinakothek, Munich. (CC-BY-SA)
11. Henri II, King of France. Jean Morin (1600–1650) after Francois Clouet. Metropolitan Museum of Art, N. Y. – Ailsa Mellon Bruce Fund (OA – Public Domain)

12. Emperors Charles V and Ferdinand I c.1531. Etching by Christoph Bockstorfer (1490–1553). Metropolitan Museum of Art, N.Y. – Ailsa Mellon Bruce Fund. (OA – Public Domain)

13. Emperor Charles V. Woodcut by Lucas Cranach. Metropolitan Museum of Art, N.Y. – Rogers Fund, 1918. (OA – Public Domain)

14. Mary of Hungary. Engraving by Karel van Sichem after Christoffel van Sichem. National Gallery of Art, Washington – Rosenwald Collection. (CC0)

15. Armour of Henry VIII produced in the Royal Workshops at Greenwich in 1527. Metropolitan Museum of Art, N.Y. – William H. Riggs Gift and Rogers Fund, 1919. (OA – Public Domain)

16. The Field Armour of Henry VIII in 1544. Metropolitan Museum of Art, N.Y. – Harris Brisbane Dick Fund, 1932. (OA – Public Domain)

17. Charles V. Engraving by Lucas Vorsterman (1595–1675), after Titian, after Rubens, (c.1620–1630). Metropolitan Museum of Art, N.Y. – Gift of Georgiana W. Sargent, in memory of John Osbourne Sargent, 1924. (OA – Public domain)

18. Henry VIII. Etching by Wenceslaus Hollar (1607–1677) after Holbein. 1647. Metropolitan Museum of Art, N.Y. – The Elisha Whittelsey Collection, The Elisha Whittelsey Fund, 1951. (OA – Public domain)

19. Henry VIII in 1547. Engraving by Cornelis Massys, Antwerp. Metropolitan Museum of Art, N.Y. – Rogers Fund, 1922. (OA – Public Domain)

20. The future Edward VI. From the workshop of Hans Holbein. Metropolitan Museum of Art, N.Y. – The Jules Bache Collection, 1949. (OA – Public Domain)

21. The victory of Goleta, near Tunis (in 1535), from the Triumphs of Charles V. Etching and engraving by Jacques de Gheyn (1614) after Antonio Tempesta. Metropolitan Museum of Art, N.Y. – Rogers Fund, 1962. (OA – Public Domain)

22. Double-barrelled wheel-lock pistol made for Emperor Charles V by Peter Peck, Munich c.1540–45. Metropolitan Museum of Art, N.Y. – Gift of William H. Riggs, 1913. (OA – Public Domain)

23. Emperor Charles V at Mühlberg. Franz von Lembach after Titian. Bayerische Staatsgemaldesammlungen – Alte Pinakothek, Munich. (CC-BY-SA)

24. The future Philip II of Spain as King Consort of England, 1555. Medal in bronze by Jacopo Nizzola da Trezzo, Milan. Metropolitan Museum of Art, N.Y. – Gift of Lisa Ungar Baskin. (OA – Public Domain)

25. Queen Mary of England. The obverse of a bronze medal by Jacopo Nizzola da Trezzo, Milan. Metropolitan Museum of Art, N.Y. – Robert Lehman Collection, 1975. (OA – Public Domain)
26. A view of Charles V's rooms at Yuste from his gardens. Personal photograph.

Cover images

Emperor Charles V, seated. Portrait by Titian, 1548, Augsburg. Bayerische Staatsgemaldesammlungen – Alte Pinakothek, Munich. (CC-BY-SA)

Henry VIII, after Holbein.

Emperor Charles V's Coat of Arms. The first and fourth quarters of the shield represent his Spanish lands, while the second and third quarters represent his Austrian (Habsburg) and Burgundian territories, with the Granada Pomegranate beneath. (This was also the emblem of Catherine of Aragon.) Other elements are the two-headed eagle, an Imperial Crown and two columns, one with the Imperial Crown and the other with the Royal Crown of Spain. Wrapped around the columns are the motto Plus Ultra. (CC-BY-SA)

The crowned Tudor Rose. (CC-BY-SA)

Bibliography

Anglo, Sydney, *Spectacle, Pageantry and Early Tudor Policy* (Clarendon Press, Oxford, 1997)

Bernard, G.W., 'The Making of Religious Policy 1533–1546: Henry VIII and the Search for the Middle Way' (*The Historical Journal*, Vol. 41, No.2, C.U.P., June 1998)

Bernard, G.W., *War, Taxation and Rebellion in Early Tudor England* (Palgrave Macmillan, 1986)

Blockmans, Wim, *Emperor Charles V (1500–1558)*, trans. Isola van den Hoven-Vardon (Arnold, London, 2002)

Blockmans, Wim and Mout, Nicolette (eds.), *The World of Emperor Charles V* (Proceedings of the Colloquium, Amsterdam, 4–6 October 2000) (Royal Netherlands Academy of Arts and Sciences, Amsterdam, 2004)

Brandi, Karl, *The Emperor Charles V, The Growth and Destiny of a Man and of a World-Empire*, trans. C.V. Wedgwood (Humanities Press, N.J., 1980; first published, 1939)

Charles V, *The Autobiography of the Emperor Charles V*, trans. L.F. Simpson (Longman, London, 1862)

Crowley, Roger, *Empires of the Sea: The Final Battle for the Mediterranean 1521–1580* (Faber and Faber, London, 2008)

Crowson, Paul, *Tudor Foreign Policy* (Adam & Black, London, 1973)

Davies, C.S.L., 'Tournai and the English Crown 1513–1519' (*The Historical Journal*, Vol. 41, No. 1, C.U.P., March 1998)

Dixon, C. Scott and Fuchs, Martina (eds.), *The Histories of Charles V* (Aschendorff, Munster, 2005)

Doran, Susan, *England and Europe 1485–1603* (Routledge, 1996; first published, Pearson, 1986)

Doran, Susan, *England and Europe in the Sixteenth Century* (Palgrave MacMillan, 1996)

Dürer, Albrecht, *Records of Journeys to Venice and the Low Countries: Part 2: Diary of a Journey to the Netherlands 1520-1521* (Project Gutenberg)

Elton, Geoffrey, *England under the Tudors* (Methuen, London, 1955)

Frieda, Leonie, *Francis I* (Weidenfeld & Nicolson, London, 2018)

Frieder, Braden, *Chivalry and the Prefect Prince: Tournaments, Art and Armor at the Spanish Habsburg Court* (Truman State University Press, 2008)

Grant, Neil, *Charles V: Holy Roman Emperor* (Franklin Watts, London, 1970)

Guicciardini, Francisco, *The History of Italy (Storia d'Italia)* trans. and ed. by Alexander Sidney (Collier, New York, 1972)

Guicciardini, Luigi, *The Sack of Rome* trans. and ed. from the 1867 Italian edition by James MacGregor (Italica Press, N.Y. 1993)

Gunn, Steven, *The English People at War in the Age of Henry VIII* (O.U.P., Oxford, 2018)

Gunn, Steven, 'The French Wars of Henry VIII' in Black, Jeremy, *The Origin of War in Early Modern Europe* (John Donald, Edinburgh. 1987)

Gunn, Steven, 'The Structures of Politics in Early Tudor England' (*Transactions of the Royal Historical Society*, Vol. 5, C.U.P., Cambridge, 1995)

Guy, John, *Henry VIII* (Penguin, 2018)

Guy, John, *Tudor England* (O.U.P., Oxford, 1988)

Gwyn, Peter, *The King's Cardinal: The Rise and Fall of Thomas Wolsey* (Pimlico, London, 1992)

Headley, John, *The Emperor and his Chancellor. A Study of the Imperial Chancellery under Gattinara* (C.U.P., 1982)

Heath, Richard, *Charles V: Duty and Dynasty: The Emperor and his Changing World 1500–1558* (Milford Publ., 2018)

Hook, Judith, *The Sack of Rome 1527* (Macmillan, London, 1972)

Iongh, Jane de, *Margaret of Austria, Regent of the Netherlands*, trans. from the Dutch by M.D. Herter Norton (Jonathan Cape, London, 1954; first published in Holland, 1941)

Iongh, Jane de, *Mary of Hungary, Second Regent of the Netherlands*, trans. from the Dutch by M.D. Herter Norton (Faber &Faber, London, 1958)

Jardine, Lisa, *Worldly Goods: A New History of the Renaissance* (Macmillan, London, 1996)

Kamen, Henry, *Spain 1469–1714: A Society of Conflict* (Longman, 1983, 2nd edition, 1991)

Knecht, R.J., *Francis I* (C.U.P., Cambridge, 1982)

Knecht, R.J., *French Renaissance Monarchy: Francis I and Henry II* (2nd edition, Longman, 1996)

Koenigsberger, H., *The Habsburgs and Europe 1516–1660* (Cornell Univ. Press, Ithica, N.Y., 1971)

Koenigsberger, H., *Monarchs, States-general and Parliaments: The Netherlands in the Fifteenth and Sixteenth Centuries* (C.U.P., Cambridge, 2001)

Loades, David, *The Fighting Tudors* (National Archives, 2009)

Loades, David, *Henry VIII* (Amberley, Stroud, 2013)

Loades, David, *Henry VIII: Court, Church and Conflict* (National Archives, 2007)

MacCulloch, Diarmaid, 'Henry VIII and the Reform of the Church' in MacCulloch, Diarmaid (ed.), *The Reign of Henry VIII* (Macmillan, Basingstoke, 1995)

MacCulloch, Diarmaid, *Thomas Cromwell: A Life* (Allen Lane, London, 2018)

MacDonald, Steward, *Charles V: Ruler, Dynast and Defender of the Faith, 1500–1558* (Hodder & Stoughton, 1992)

MacGregor, Neil, *Germany: Memories of a Nation* (Penguin, London, 2014)

Mackie, J.D., *The Earlier Tudors 1485–1558* (Clarendon Press, Oxford, 1952)

Maltby, William, *The Reign of Charles V* (Palgrave, Basingstoke, 2002)

Matusiak, John, *The Tudors and Europe* (The History Press, Cheltenham, 2020)

Murphy, Neil, 'Henry VIII's First Invasion of France: The Gascon Expedition of 1512' (*English Historical Review*, Vol. 130, No. 542, Feb. 2015, O.U.P.)

Norwich, John Julius, *The Popes* (Chatto & Windus, London, 2011)

Parker, Geoffrey, *Emperor: A New Life of Charles V* (Yale University Press, 2019)

Parker, Geoffrey, 'The Political World of Charles V' in Soly, Hugo (ed.), *Charles V 1500–1558 and his Time* (Mercatorfonds, Antwerp, 1999)

Parker, Geoffrey, *Imprudent King: A New Life of Philip II* (Yale University Press, 2014)

Penn, Thomas, *Winter King: The Dawn of Tudor England* (Allen Lane, London, 2011)

Pollard, A.F., *Wolsey* (Longman, London. 1929)

Potter, David, Foreign Policy – in MacCulloch, D. (ed.), *The Reign of Henry VIII* (Macmillan, Basingstoke, 1998)

Prieto, Maria Teresa Rodriguez, *Yuste: Monastery of St Jerome* (Patrimonio Nacional, 2008)

Rady, Martin, *The Emperor Charles V* (Longman, London, 1988)

Rex, Richard, 'The Religion of Henry VIII' (*The Historical Journal*, Vol. 57 No. 1, C.U.P., March 2014)

Richardson, Glenn, *The Field of Cloth of Gold* (Yale University Press, 2013)

Richardson, Glenn, *Renaissance Monarchy* (Arnold, London, 2002)

Rodriguez-Salgado, Mia J., 'Charles V and his Dynasty', in Soly, Hugo (ed.), *Charles V 1500–1558 and his Time* (Mercatorfonds, Antwerp, 1999)

Rodriguez-Salgado, Mia J., *The Changing Face of Empire: Charles V, Philip II and Habsburg Authority 1551–1559* (C.U.P., Cambridge, 1988)

Sansom, C.J., *Tombland* (Mantle, 2018)

Scarisbrick, J.J., *Henry VIII* (Methuen, London, 1990; first published by Eyre & Methuen, 1968)

Soly, Hugo (ed.), *Charles V 1500–1558 and his Time*, (Mercatorfonds, Antwerp, 1999)

Starkey, David, *Henry, Virtuous Prince* (Harper Perennial, London, 2009)

Starkey, David, *Henry VIII: Personalities and Politics* (Vintage, London, 2002; first published, 1985)

Stedall, Robert, *Elizabeth I's Secret Lover: Robert Dudley, Earl of Leicester* (Pen and Sword History, 2020)

Strong, Roy, *Splendour at Court* (Weidenfeld and Nicolson, London, 1973)

Thomas, Hugh, *The Golden Age: The Spanish Empire of Charles V* (Allen Lane, London, 2010)

Tracy, James D., *Emperor Charles V, Impresario of War: Campaign Strategy, International Finance and Domestic Politics* (C.U.P., Cambridge, 2002)

Tremlett, Giles, *Catherine of Aragon: Henry's Spanish Queen* (Faber & Faber, London, 2010)

Weightman, Christine, *Margaret of York, Duchess of Burgundy 1446–1503* (Alan Sutton, Gloucester, 1989)

Weir, Alison, *Henry VIII: King and Court* (Vintage, London, 2008; first published by, Jonathan Cape, 2001)

Wooding, Lucy, 'Henry VIII and Religion' (*History Review*, 62, December 2008)

Notes and References

Abbreviations used

CSP Milan   Calendar of State Papers, Milan

CSP Spain   Calendar of State Papers, Spain

Hall   *Edward Hall's Chronicle containing the history of England, during the reign of Henry IV and succeeding monarchs to the end of the reign of Henry VIII*

L&P Henry VIII   Letters and Papers, Foreign and Domestic, Henry VIII

Memoirs   *The Autobiography of the Emperor Charles V. Recently discovered in the Portuguese Language by Baron Kervyn de Lettenhove* – English translation by Leonard Francis Simpson (Longman, London, 1862)

Chapter One: Dynastic Marriages and The Anglo-Spanish Alliance

1. Pollard A.F., *The Reign of Henry VII from Contemporary Sources, used in Doran, Susan, England and Europe 1485–1603*, 99–100
2. Tremlett, Giles, *Catherine of Aragon*, 74
3. Ibid. 83
4. CSP Spain June 1500
5. Tremlett, Giles, *Catherine of Aragon*, 87
6. Penn, Thomas, *Winter King*, 205
7. CSP Spain June 1500
8. CSP Spain April 1509
9. Ibid. May 1509
10. Ibid. May1509

11. Hall, quoted in Tremlett, Giles, *Catherine of Aragon*, 152
12. CSP Spain July 1509
13. Loades, David, *Henry VIII: Court, Church and Conflict*, 60
14. The fact that Henry VIII's older sister Margaret had married James IV of Scotland did not prevent his invasion of England in 1513. The marriage of King Francis I to Eleanor, sister of Charles V, in 1530, did not stop the frequent wars between the two monarchs.

Chapter Two: The Education of Princes

1. Starkey, David, *Henry: Virtuous Prince*, 87–92
2. Ibid. 118
3. Ibid. 240
4. Loades, David, *Henry VIII: Court, Church and Conflict*, 31–32
5. The original tournaments consisted of two teams of horsemen who charged each other in formation with their lances levelled. Having done so, those remaining on horseback would quickly turn to charge again. The name tournament, sometimes called a tourney, comes from the Latin *tornare*, to turn. The initial charge was often followed by a mêlée, general fighting between the two teams. A joust involved two horsemen armed with lances, usually separated by a barrier or tilt, riding towards one another with the aim of breaking the lance against the opponent's shield or unhorsing him. Running the ring was where a horseman had to catch a suspended ring on the tip of his lance while riding at speed. It was often used to demonstrate horsemanship skills. Other activities at a tournament could involve a sword fight between horsemen, and fighting on foot with swords or axes, either in single combat or in groups.
6. Stedall, Robert, *Elizabeth's Secret Lover: Robert Dudley*, 6
7. Parker, Geoffrey, in Soly, Hugo, *Charles V 1500–1558 and his Time*
8. Parker, Geoffrey, *Emperor*, 9
9. Dürer, Albrecht, *Diary of his Journey to the Netherlands 1520–21*
10. Parker, Geoffrey, *Emperor*, 21
11. Guy, John, *Henry VIII*, 6
12. Thomas, Hugh, *The Golden Age: The Spanish Empires of Charles V*, 16
13. Koenigsberger, Helmut, *Monarchs, States-general and Parliaments: The Netherlands in the Fifteenth and Sixteenth Centuries*, 93–95. Many people in the province of Brabant, especially in Antwerp, regarded the

English as very important trading partners, though in Flanders they were often considered as commercial rivals.

14. Richardson, Glenn, *Renaissance Monarchs*, 25

Chapter Three: Overseas Adventures

1. Elton refers to Surrey as 'resenting the priest ridden peace policy' (*England under the Tudors*, 72) though Gwyn argues that he was more cautious in his attitude to war with France (*The King's Cardinal*, 10).
2. Murphy, N., 'Henry VIII's First Invasion of France: The Gascon Expedition of 1512', *English Historical Review*, Vol 130, No. 542 (Feb. 2015), 25–56. The article has provided much of the detail here about the 1512 campaign.
3. Ibid. 38
4. Accounts vary as to whether he was captured and then stabbed or whether he was forced off his vessel in the fighting and drowned because of the weight of his armour.
5. CSP Milan 4 Sept 1513 Ambassador de Laude to Massimiliano Sforza
6. Ibid.
7. Davies, C.S.L., 'Tournai and the English Crown 1513–1519', *The Historical Journal*, Vol 41, No. 1 March 1998
8. CSP Milan 22 September 1513
9. CSP Milan 13 September 1513
10. CSP Milan 13 September 1513
11. Brandi, Karl, *The Emperor Charles V*, 52
12. Memoirs, 4
13. Brandi, Karl, *The Emperor Charles V*, 52
14. Gwyn, Peter, *The King's Cardinal*, 23
15. L & P Henry VIII March 1514
16. Ibid. May 1514
17. Ibid. April 1514
18. Ibid. May 1514
19. Doran, Susan, *England and Europe 1485–1603*, 31
20. L & P Henry VIII August 1514
21. Ibid.
22. Ibid.
23. Pollard, A.F., *Wolsey*, 16
24. Scarisbrick, J.J., *Henry VIII*, 48

Chapter Four: New Rivalries

1. Frieda, Leonie, *Francis I*, 45
2. Parker, Geoffrey, *Emperor*, 43
3. Gwyn, Peter, *The King's Cardinal*, 82
4. CSP Spain February 1516
5. Ibid. March 1516
6. L & P Henry VIII Feb 1517
7. Crowson, P.S., *Tudor Foreign Policy*, 78
8. L & P Henry VIII February 1517
9. Gwyn, Peter, *The King's Cardinal*, 81
10. L & P Henry VIII July 1517
11. Matusiak, John, *The Tudors and Europe*, 18
12. CSP Spain October 1518
13. Crowson, P.S., *Tudor Foreign Policy*, 79
14. Gwyn, Peter, *The King's Cardinal*, 95
15. Davies, C.S.L., 'Tournai and the English Crown 1513–1519'

Chapter Five: The Imperial Election and Royal Meetings

1. Scarisbrick, J.J., *Henry VIII*, 100
2. Potter, David, 'Foreign Policy', in MacCulloch, D. (ed.) *The Reign of Henry VIII*
3. CSP Spain April 1520
4. Richardson, Glenn, *The Field of Cloth of Gold*, Appendices A and B
5. Ibid. 177
6. Anglo, Sydney, *Spectacle, Pageantry and Early Tudor Policy*, 142
7. Richardson, Glenn, *The Field of Cloth of Gold*, 8
8. CSP Spain July 1520

Chapter Six: Taking Sides

1. Dürer, Albrecht, *Diary of his Journey to the Netherlands 1520–21*. None of these articles are known to exist today, many having been melted down and others lost. Some similar objects sent later have been preserved.
2. Ibid
3. CSP Spain November 1520

4. Leo X (1513–1521), Adrian VI (1522–1523), Clement VII (1523–1534), Paul III (1534–1549) and Julius III (1549–1555).
5. Gwyn, Peter, *The King's Cardinal*, 150
6. Ibid. 151–152
7. In later propaganda it is usually reported as being the memorable and resounding 'Here I stand; I can do no other. God help me. Amen.'
8. Brandi, Karl, *The Emperor Charles V*, 131
9. CSP Spain August 1521

Chapter Seven: Charles in England

1. Anglo, Sydney, *Spectacle, Pageantry and Early Tudor Policy*, 176
2. Ibid. 179
3. Hall, 634
4. Much of the following detail is taken from *Edward Hall's Chronicle*, 634–642
5. Anglo, Sydney, *Spectacle, Pageantry and Early Tudor Policy*, 184
6. Hall, 635
7. Ibid.
8. Ibid. 636
9. CSP Spain June 1522
10. Anglo, Sydney, *Spectacle, Pageantry and Early Tudor Policy*, 185
11. Ibid. 187–202 provides a detailed description of all the pageants.
12. Hall, 638–640
13. CSP Spain June 1522
14. Ibid.
15. Hall, 640
16. Ibid. 641
17. CSP Spain June 1522
18. Hall, 641

Chapter Eight: The 'Great Enterprise'

1. Gwyn, Peter, *The King's Cardinal*, 356
2. Bernard, G.W., *War, Taxation and Rebellion in Early Tudor England*, 53–55
3. Gwyn, Peter, *The King's Cardinal*, 370
4. They were also known as the Knights of St John.

5. CSP Spain January 1523
6. Ibid. March 1523
7. Ibid. April 1523
8. Ibid. July 1523
9. Bernard, G.W., *War, Taxation and Rebellion in Early Tudor England*, 14
10. Hall, 671
11. Bernard, G.W., *War, Taxation and Rebellion in Early Tudor England*, 5
12. CSP Spain February 1524
13. Ibid.
14. Bernard G.W., *War, Taxation and Rebellion in Early Tudor England*, 22
15. Hall, 685
16. Charles V to Louis de Praet, 12 August 1524
17. CSP Spain March 1524
18. Ibid. January 1525
19. These notes, found in the Vienna Archives, are quoted in Karl Brandi's biography, *The Emperor Charles V*, 219–221
20. CSP Spain February 1525
21. Ibid.

Chapter Nine: Rapidly Changing Alliances

1. Descriptions of the battle and a consideration of why the French lost can be found in Heath, Richard, *Charles V: Duty and Dynasty*, 108–111 and Knecht, R. J,, *Francis I*, 165–172
2. Scarisbrick, J.J., *Henry VIII*, 136
3. By the old Julian calendar
4. CSP Spain March 1525
5. L & P Henry VIII March 1525
6. Ibid.
7. Gunn, Steven, *The English People at War in the Age of Henry VIII*, 6
8. L & P Henry VIII April 1525
9. Ibid.
10. See Bernard, G.W., *War, Taxation and Rebellion in Early Tudor England* (Henry VIII, Wolsey and the Amicable Grant of 1525) for a detailed account and analysis.
11. L & P Henry VIII March 1525
12. Ibid. June 1525
13. Ibid. March 1525
14. Ibid. January 1526

15. Ibid. January 1526
16. Ibid. February 1526

Chapter Ten: Personal Matters

1. Three known daughters are mentioned here. It has often been claimed that Charles had another daughter, born to Germaine de Foix, widow of King Ferdinand of Aragon, said to be Charles's lover during his first visit to Spain. Geoffrey Parker has convincingly rejected this suggestion. Parker, Geoffrey, *Emperor, A New Life of Charles V*, Appendix IV, 545–546
2. L & P Henry VIII June 1525
3. L & P Henry VIII May 1525
4. Bernard, G.W., *The King's Reformation: Henry VIII and the Remaking of the English Church*
5. Rex, Richard, 'The Religion of Henry VIII', *The Historical Journal*, March 2014, CUP

Chapter Eleven: Hopes Destroyed

1. L & P Henry VIII February 1526
2. Ibid.
3. Ibid. March 1526
4. Knecht, R.J., *Francis I*, 209
5. Ibid. 211
6. L & P Henry VIII September 1526
7. Ibid. March 1526
8. Ibid.
9. Ibid. October 1526
10. Ibid.
11. Mackie, J. D., *The Early Tudors 1485–1558*, 317
12. L & P Henry VIII May 1527
13. Ibid. April 1527
14. Hook, Judith, *The Sack of Rome 1527*.
15. Memoirs, 14
16. L & P Henry VIII August 1527
17. Gwyn, Peter, *The King's Cardinal*, 514
18. Doran, Susan, *England and Europe in the Sixteenth Century*, 104

19. L & P Henry VIII October 1528
20. Quoted in Brandi, K., *The Emperor Charles V*, 276

Chapter Twelve: Coronation and Divorce

1. Knecht, R.J., *Francis I*, 222
2. Ibid. 237
3. Memoirs, 16
4. First used by Ferdinand of Aragon after the discovery of the New World, the motto was used by Charles, in its French form 'Plus Oultre' as he left the Low Countries for Spain in 1517. Meaning 'Further beyond', it was intended as an encouragement for him to take risks, strive for greater achievements and ignore the ancient myth of the Pillars of Hercules near the Straits of Gibraltar which had the warning 'Non plus Ultra' – 'nothing further beyond'. Charles also used the two columns or pillars as his emblem.
5. Pollard, A.F., *Henry VIII*, 169
6. MacCulloch, Diarmaid, 'Henry VIII and the Reform of the Church' in MacCulloch (ed.), *The Reign of Henry VIII*, 168. Tyndale had produced an English version of the Bible and already fled to the Low Countries. He later denounced Henry's divorce from Catherine of Aragon and was executed for heresy in 1536 near Brussels.
7. Charles V to Isabella July 1531
8. Jardine, Lisa, *Worldly Goods*, 383
9. CSP Spain June 1533
10. Richardson, Glenn, *Renaissance Monarchy*, 84
11. CSP Spain May 1533
12. Knecht, R.J., *Francis I*, 231

Chapter Thirteen: Unrealistic Fears

1. L & P Henry VIII June 1534
2. Ibid.
3. Loades, David, *Henry VIII*, 263
4. Elton, G.R., *England under the Tudors*, 151
5. Crowson, P.S., *Tudor Foreign Policy*, 112
6. Loades, David, *Henry VIII, Court, Church and Conflict*, 91
7. Guy, John, *Henry VIII*, 58

8. The Knights Hospitaller (The Knights of St. John), driven out of Rhodes in 1522, had been granted possession of Malta by Charles in 1530
9. Heath, Richard, *Charles V: Duty and Dynasty*, 212–215
10. Brandi, Karl, *The Emperor Charles V*, 368
11. Memoirs, 32

Chapter Fourteen: Dangerous Isolation

1. Parker, Geoffrey, *Emperor*, 259
2. Heath, Richard, *Charles V: Duty and Dynasty*, 236
3. Doran, Susan (ed.), *Henry VIII:Man and Monarch*. (Catalogue of the exhibition at the British Library, 2009). 235
4. Ibid. 214–220
5. Mackie, J.D., *The Earlier Tudors 1485–1558*, 400
6. Wooding, Lucy, *Henry VIII and Religion*
7. MacCulloch, Diarmaid, 'Henry VIII and the Reform of the Church' in MacCulloch (ed.), *The Reign of Henry VIII*
8. Hall, 839

Chapter Fifteen: Renewed Friendship

1. Loades, David, *Henry VIII*, 289
2. Ibid. 290
3. Heath, Richard, *Charles V: Duty and Dynasty*, 239
4. Memoirs, 43
5. Parker, Geoffrey, *Emperor*, 279
6. Heath, Richard, *Charles V: Duty and Dynasty*, 275
7. L & P Henry VIII February 1543
8. Loades, David, *Henry VIII*, 305
9. L & P Henry VIII February 1543
10. Ibid.
11. Ibid.

Chapter Sixteen: Conflicting Aims

1. Heath, Richard, *Charles V: Duty and Dynasty*, 260–263; and Parker, Geoffrey, *Emperor*, 288–293

2. L & P Henry VIII December 1543
3. Knecht, R.J., *Francis I*, 368
4. Parker, Geoffrey, *Emperor*, 303
5. Knecht, R.J., *Francis I*, 369
6. Memoirs, 70–71
7. Ibid. 71
8. Scarisbrick, J.J., *Henry VIII*, 451
9. Loades, David, *The Fighting Tudors*, 93
10. The French claimed that their guns had damaged the *Mary Rose* just above the waterline and that it was this that caused the sinking of the ship as it turned. Other explanations include the suggestion that the combined weight of the cannons and very large crew destabilised the vessel or that the crew failed to follow instructions either because of ill-discipline or language problems.
11. Muller, J.A., *The Letters of Stephen Gardiner* (1933), 185 quoted in Loades, David, *Henry VIII*, 310
12. Loades, David, *The Fighting Tudors*, 90
13. L&P Henry VIII April 1546
14. Doran, Susan, *England and Europe 1485–1603*, 53

Chapter Seventeen: The End of an Era

1. Guy, John, *Henry VIII*, 100
2. L&P Henry VIII January 1547
3. Ibid.
4. Ibid.
5. Memoirs, 136
6. Ibid.
7. Ibid.
8. Knecht, R.J., *Francis I*, 416
9. Ibid.
10. Memoirs, 139

Chapter Eighteen: After Henry

1. Loades, David, *The Fighting Tudors*, 104 and Guy, John, *Tudor England*, 202. Susan Doran gives the size of the French force as 10,000 in *England and Europe 1485–1603*, 54

2. Sansom, C.J., *Tombland*. An excellent historical novel set during Kett's Rebellion around Norwich in 1549.
3. Somerset was held in the Tower until released early in 1550 when he was restored to the Council. However, in late 1551, he was arrested and executed in January 1552.
4. Doran, Susan, *England and Europe 1485–1603*, 56. Somerset was probably about to open negotiations but was replaced before he could do so.
5. Originally the document identified Lady Jane Grey's future male heirs but as it became likely that Edward would die soon, he changed it to include Lady Jane herself.
6. Loades, David, *John Dudley, Duke of Northumberland*, 265
7. The grandson of the Duke of Buckingham executed by Henry VIII in 1521.
8. Loades, David, *The Fighting Tudors*, 135
9. Heath, Richard, *Charles V: Duty and Dynasty*, 349–350
10. Don John was thereafter educated at the royal court and went on to be the victorious commander of the Spanish-Papal-Italian fleet at the Battle of Lepanto in 1571.
11. Also known as 'The Final Judgement', it was commissioned by Charles in 1550. After its completion in 1554 he had taken it with him to Yuste. It is now in the Prado Museum, Madrid.

Epilogue

1. The term 'Christian humanism' is often used in this context. It is now regarded as controversial because the modern humanist movement is specifically non-religious.
2. Quoted in Parker, G., *Emperor*, 516

Index

211